IT'S HERE!

PRENTICE HALL
SCIENCE

FINALLY, THE PERFECT FIT.

NOW YOU CAN CHOOSE THE PERFECT FIT FOR ALL YOUR CURRICULUM NEEDS.

The new Prentice Hall Science program consists of 19 hardcover books, each of which covers a particular area of science. All of the sciences are represented in the program so you can choose the perfect fit to *your* particular curriculum needs.

The flexibility of this program will allow you to teach those topics you want to teach, and to teach them *in-depth*. Virtually any approach to science—general, integrated, coordinated, thematic, etc.—is possible with Prentice Hall Science.

Above all, the program is designed to make your teaching experience easier and more fun.

ELECTRICITY AND MAGNETISM
Ch. 1. Electric Charges and Currents
Ch. 2. Magnetism
Ch. 3. Electromagnetism
Ch. 4. Electronics and Computers

HEREDITY: THE CODE OF LIFE
Ch. 1. What is Genetics?
Ch. 2. How Chromosomes Work
Ch. 3. Human Genetics
Ch. 4. Applied Genetics

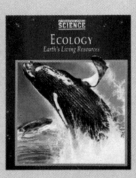

ECOLOGY: EARTH'S LIVING RESOURCES
Ch. 1. Interactions Among Living Things
Ch. 2. Cycles in Nature
Ch. 3. Exploring Earth's Biomes
Ch. 4. Wildlife Conservation

PARADE OF LIFE: MONERANS, PROTISTS, FUNGI, AND PLANTS
Ch. 1. Classification of Living Things
Ch. 2. Viruses and Monerans
Ch. 3. Protists
Ch. 4. Fungi
Ch. 5. Plants Without Seeds
Ch. 6. Plants With Seeds

EXPLORING THE UNIVERSE
Ch. 1. Stars and Galaxies
Ch. 2. The Solar System
Ch. 3. Earth and Its Moon

EVOLUTION: CHANGE OVER TIME
Ch. 1. Earth's History in Fossils
Ch. 2. Changes in Living Things Over Time
Ch. 3. The Path to Modern Humans

EXPLORING EARTH'S WEATHER
Ch. 1. What Is Weather?
Ch. 2. What Is Climate?
Ch. 3. Climate in the United States

THE NATURE OF SCIENCE
Ch. 1. What is Science?
Ch. 2. Measurement and the Sciences
Ch. 3. Tools and the Sciences

ECOLOGY: EARTH'S NATURAL RESOURCES

Ch. 1. Energy Resources
Ch. 2. Earth's Nonliving Resources
Ch. 3. Pollution
Ch. 4. Conserving Earth's Resources

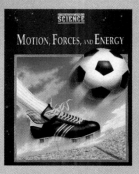

MOTION, FORCES, AND ENERGY

Ch. 1. What Is Motion?
Ch. 2. The Nature of Forces
Ch. 3. Forces in Fluids
Ch. 4. Work, Power, and Simple Machines
Ch. 5. Energy: Forms and Changes

PARADE OF LIFE: ANIMALS

Ch. 1. Sponges, Cnidarians, Worms, and Mollusks
Ch. 2. Arthropods and Echinoderms
Ch. 3. Fish and Amphibians
Ch. 4. Reptiles and Birds
Ch. 5. Mammals

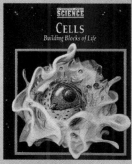

CELLS: BUILDING BLOCKS OF LIFE

Ch. 1. The Nature of LIfe
Ch. 2. Cell Structure and Function
Ch. 3. Cell Processes
Ch. 4. Cell Energy

DYNAMIC EARTH

Ch. 1. Movement of the Earth's Crust
Ch. 2. Earthquakes and Volcanoes
Ch. 3. Plate Tectonics
Ch. 4. Rocks and Minerals
Ch. 5. Weathering and Soil Formation
Ch. 6. Erosion and Deposition

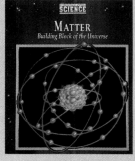

MATTER: BUILDING BLOCK OF THE UNIVERSE

Ch. 1. General Properties of Matter
Ch. 2. Physical and Chemical Changes
Ch. 3. Mixtures, Elements, and Compounds
Ch. 4. Atoms: Building Blocks of Matter
Ch. 5. Classification of Elements: The Periodic Table

CHEMISTRY OF MATTER

Ch. 1. Atoms and Bonding
Ch. 2. Chemical Reactions
Ch. 3. Families of Chemical Compounds
Ch. 4. Chemical Technology
Ch. 5. Radioactive Elements

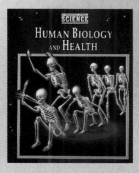

HUMAN BIOLOGY AND HEALTH

Ch. 1. The Human Body
Ch. 2. Skeletal and Muscular Systems
Ch. 3. Digestive System
Ch. 4. Circulatory System
Ch. 5. Respiratory and Excretory Systems
Ch. 6. Nervous and Endocrine Systems
Ch. 7. Reproduction and Development
Ch. 8. Immune System
Ch. 9. Alcohol, Tobacco, and Drugs

EXPLORING PLANET EARTH

Ch. 1. Earth's Atmosphere
Ch. 2. Earth's Oceans
Ch. 3. Earth's Fresh Water
Ch. 4. Earth's Landmasses
Ch. 5. Earth's Interior

HEAT ENERGY

Ch. 1. What Is Heat?
Ch. 2. Uses of Heat

SOUND AND LIGHT

Ch. 1. Characteristics of Waves
Ch. 2. Sound and Its Uses
Ch. 3. Light and the Electromagnetic Spectrum
Ch. 4. Light and Its Uses

A COMPLETELY INTEGRATED LEARNING SYSTEM...

The Prentice Hall Science program is an *integrated* learning system with a variety of print materials and multimedia components. All are designed to meet the needs of diverse learning styles and your technology needs.

THE STUDENT BOOK

Each book is a model of **excellent writing and dynamic visuals**—designed to be exciting and motivating to the student *and* the teacher, with relevant examples integrated throughout, and more opportunities for many different activities which apply to everyday life.

Problem-solving activities emphasize the thinking process, so problems may be more open-ended.

"Discovery Activities" throughout the book foster active learning.

Different sciences, and other disciplines, are integrated throughout the text and reinforced in the "Connections" features (the connections between computers and viruses is one example).

TEACHER'S RESOURCE PACKAGE

In addition to the student book, the complete teaching package contains:

ANNOTATED TEACHER'S EDITION

Designed to provide **"teacher-friendly"** support regardless of instructional approach:

■ **Help is readily available** if you choose to teach thematically, to integrate the sciences, and/or to integrate the sciences with other curriculum areas.

■ **Activity-based learning** is easy to implement through the use of Discovery Strategies, Activity Suggestions, and Teacher Demonstrations.

■ **Integration** of all components is part of the teaching strategies.

■ For instant accessibility, all of the teaching suggestions are wrapped around the student pages to which they refer.

ACTIVITY BOOK

Includes a **discovery activity for each chapter,** plus other activities including problem-solving and cooperative-learning activities.

THE REVIEW AND REINFORCEMENT GUIDE

Addresses **students' different learning styles** in a clear and comprehensive format:

■ Highly visual for visual learners.

TEACHER'S RESOURCE PACKAGE

FOR THE PERFECT FIT TO YOUR TEACHING NEEDS.

■ Can be used in conjunction with the program's audiotapes for auditory and language learners.

■ More than a study guide, it's a guide to comprehension, with activities, key concepts, and vocabulary.

ENGLISH AND SPANISH AUDIOTAPES
Correlate with the Review and Reinforcement Guide to aid auditory learners.

LABORATORY MANUAL ANNOTATED TEACHER'S EDITION
Offers **at least one additional hands-on opportunity per chapter** with answers and teaching suggestions on lab preparation and safety.

TEST BOOK
Contains **traditional and up-to-the-minute strategies for student assessment.** Choose from performance-based tests in addition to traditional chapter tests and computer test bank questions.

STUDENT LABORATORY MANUAL
Each of the 19 books also comes with its own Student Lab Manual.

ALSO INCLUDED IN THE INTEGRATED LEARNING SYSTEM:

■ Teacher's Desk Reference
■ English Guide for Language Learners
■ Spanish Guide for Language Learners
■ Product Testing Activities
■ Transparencies

■ Computer Test Bank (IBM, Apple, or MAC)
■ VHS Videos
■ Videodiscs
■ Interactive Videodiscs (Level III)
■ Interactive Videodiscs/ CD ROM
■ Courseware

All components are integrated in the teaching strategies in the Annotated Teacher's Edition, where they directly relate to the science content.

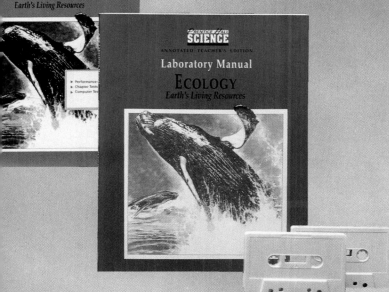

THE PRENTICE HALL SCIENCE
INTEGRATED LEARNING SYSTEM

The following components are integrated in the teaching strategies for
THE NATURE OF SCIENCE.

- Spanish Audiotape
  English Audiotape
- Activity Book
- Review and
  Reinforcement Guide
- Test Book—including
  Performance-Based Tests
- Laboratory Manual,
  Annotated Teacher's Edition

- Product-Testing Activities:
  Testing Bubble Gum
  Testing Shampoo
  Testing Cereals
  Testing Pens
- Laboratory Manual
- English Guide for
  Language Learners
- Spanish Guide for
  Language Learners

- Interactive Videodisc/
  CD ROM:

  Paul ParkRanger and
  the Mystery of the
  Disappearing Ducks

INTEGRATING OTHER SCIENCES

Many of the other 18 Prentice Hall Science books can be integrated into **THE NATURE OF SCIENCE.**
The books you will find suggested most often in the Annotated Teacher's Edition are
EVOLUTION: CHANGE OVER TIME; PARADE OF LIFE: ANIMALS; EXPLORING THE UNIVERSE;
HEAT ENERGY; PARADE OF LIFE: MONERANS, PROTISTS, FUNGI, AND PLANTS; DYNAMIC EARTH;
ECOLOGY: EARTH'S NATURAL RESOURCES; MOTION, FORCES, AND ENERGY; MATTER: BUILDING
BLOCK OF THE UNIVERSE; SOUND AND LIGHT; and EXPLORING EARTH'S WEATHER.

INTEGRATING THEMES

Many themes can be integrated into **THE NATURE OF SCIENCE.**
Following are the ones most commonly suggested in the Annotated Teacher's Edition:
SCALE AND STRUCTURE, SYSTEMS AND INTERACTIONS, and UNITY AND DIVERSITY.

For more detailed information on teaching thematically and integrating
the sciences, see the Teacher's Desk Reference and teaching strategies throughout
the Annotated Teacher's Edition.

For more information, call 1-800-848-9500 or write:

 PRENTICE HALL

Simon & Schuster Education Group
113 Sylvan Avenue Route 9W
Englewood Cliffs, New Jersey 07632
Simon & Schuster A Paramount Communications Company

Annotated Teacher's Edition

Prentice Hall Science
The Nature of Science

Anthea Maton
Former NSTA National Coordinator
Project Scope, Sequence,
    Coordination
Washington, DC

Jean Hopkins
Science Instructor and Department
    Chairperson
John H. Wood Middle School
San Antonio, Texas

Susan Johnson
Professor of Biology
Ball State University
Muncie, Indiana

David LaHart
Senior Instructor
Florida Solar Energy Center
Cape Canaveral, Florida

Charles William McLaughlin
Science Instructor and Department
    Chairperson
Central High School
St. Joseph, Missouri

Maryanna Quon Warner
Science Instructor
Del Dios Middle School
Escondido, California

Jill D. Wright
Professor of Science Education
Director of International Field
    Programs
University of Pittsburgh
Pittsburgh, Pennsylvania

Prentice Hall
A Division of Simon & Schuster
Englewood Cliffs, New Jersey

ISBN 0-13-400417-5

2 3 4 5 6 7 8 9 10   97 96 95 94 93

Contents of Annotated Teacher's Edition

To the Teacher

Welcome to the *Prentice Hall Science* program. *Prentice Hall Science* has been designed as a complete program for use with middle school or junior high school science students. The program covers all relevant areas of science and has been developed with the flexibility to meet virtually all your curriculum needs. In addition, the program has been designed to better enable you—the classroom teacher—to integrate various disciplines of science into your daily lessons, as well as to enhance the thematic teaching of science.

The *Prentice Hall Science* program consists of nineteen books, each of which covers a particular topic area. The nineteen books in the *Prentice Hall Science* program are

The Nature of Science
Parade of Life: Monerans, Protists, Fungi, and Plants
Parade of Life: Animals
Cells: Building Blocks of Life
Heredity: The Code of Life
Evolution: Change Over Time

Ecology: Earth's Living Resources
Human Biology and Health
Exploring Planet Earth
Dynamic Earth
Exploring Earth's Weather
Ecology: Earth's Natural Resources
Exploring the Universe
Matter: Building Block of the Universe
Chemistry of Matter
Electricity and Magnetism
Heat Energy
Sound and Light
Motion, Forces, and Energy

Each of the student editions listed above also comes with a complete set of teaching materials and student ancillary materials. Furthermore, videos, interactive videos and science courseware are available for the *Prentice Hall Science* program. This combination of student texts and ancillaries, teacher materials, and multimedia products makes up your complete *Prentice Hall Science* Learning System.

About the Teacher's Desk Reference

The *Teacher's Desk Reference* provides you, the teacher, with an insight into the workings of the *Prentice Hall Science* program. The *Teacher's Desk Reference* accomplishes this task by including all the standard information you need to know about *Prentice Hall Science*.

The *Teacher's Desk Reference* presents an overview of the program, including a full description of each ancillary available in the program. It gives a brief summary of each of the student textbooks available in the *Prentice Hall Science* Learning System. The *Teacher's Desk Reference* also demonstrates how the seven science themes incorporated into *Prentice Hall Science* are woven throughout the entire program.

In addition, the *Teacher's Desk Reference* presents a detailed discussion of the features of the Student Edition and the features of the Annotated Teacher's Edition, as well as an overview section that summarizes issues in science education and offers a message about teaching special students. Selected instructional essays in the *Teacher's Desk Reference* include English as a Second Language (ESL), Multicultural Teaching, Cooperative-Learning Strategies, and Integrated Science Teaching, in addition to other relevant topics. Further, a discussion of the Multimedia components that are part of *Prentice Hall Science*, as well as how they can be integrated with the textbooks, is included in the *Teacher's Desk Reference*.

The *Teacher's Desk Reference* also contains in blackline master form a booklet on Teaching Graphing Skills, which may be reproduced for student use.

Integrating the Sciences

The *Prentice Hall Science* Learning System has been designed to allow you to teach science from an integrated point of view. Great care has been taken to integrate other science disciplines, where appropriate, into the chapter content and visuals. In addition, the integration of other disciplines such as social studies and literature has been incorporated into each textbook.

On the reduced student pages throughout your Annotated Teacher's Edition you will find numbers within blue bullets beside selected passages and visuals. An Annotation Key in the wraparound margins indicates the particular branch of science or other discipline that has been integrated into the student text. In addition, where appropriate, the name of the textbook and the chapter number in which the particular topic is discussed in greater detail is provided. This enables you to further integrate a particular science topic by using the complete *Prentice Hall Science* Learning System.

Thematic Overview

When teaching any science topic, you may want to focus your lessons around the underlying themes that pertain to all areas of science. These underlying themes are the framework from which all science can be constructed and taught. The seven underlying themes incorporated into *Prentice Hall Science* are

Energy
Evolution
Patterns of Change
Scale and Structure
Systems and Interactions
Unity and Diversity
Stability

The primary themes in this textbook are Scale and Structure, Systems and Interactions, and Unity and Diversity. Primary themes throughout *Prentice Hall Science* are denoted by an asterisk.

A detailed discussion of each of these themes and how they are incorporated into the *Prentice Hall Science* program are included in your *Teacher's Desk Reference*. In addition, the *Teacher's Desk Reference* includes thematic matrices for the *Prentice Hall Science* program.

A thematic matrix for each chapter in this textbook follows. Each thematic matrix is designed with the list of themes along the left-hand column and in the right-hand column a big idea, or overarching concept statement, as to how that particular theme is taught in the chapter.

CHAPTER 1

What Is Science?

ENERGY	• Physics is involved in the study of energy—its forms and transformations.
EVOLUTION	• One of the large mysteries scientists study is how the relatively few and simple organisms of 3 billion years ago gave rise to the many complex organisms that inhabit Earth today.
PATTERNS OF CHANGE	• The freezing or boiling point of a pure substance can change when other substances are added.
*SCALE AND STRUCTURE	• Scientists seek answers to questions about the microscopic world and the macroscopic world, as well as answers to global questions.
*SYSTEMS AND INTERACTIONS	• Scientific experiments should include a control setup and an experimental setup in order to determine if any changes or interactions are due to the variable being tested.
*UNITY AND DIVERSITY	• Although science can be broken down into diverse and specialized branches, most discoveries involve several branches of science working together.
STABILITY	

CHAPTER 2

Measurement and the Sciences

ENERGY	
EVOLUTION	
PATTERNS OF CHANGE	• Although mass is constant, weight changes based on location.
***SCALE AND STRUCTURE**	• The metric system is a decimal system in which units increase by powers of 10.
***SYSTEMS AND INTERACTIONS**	• Gravitational forces between objects are directly proportional to mass and inversely proportional to distance.
***UNITY AND DIVERSITY**	• All objects, no matter how disparate, share the properties of length, mass, volume, density, and temperature.
STABILITY	• The density of any substance is constant.

CHAPTER 3

Tools and the Sciences

ENERGY	• The electromagnetic spectrum is divided into visible light, ultraviolet light, infrared light, X-rays, and radio waves. • Each form of light is characterized by a different amount of energy carried by the light wave.
EVOLUTION	
PATTERNS OF CHANGE	• Our view of the universe changes as we observe it through visible light, infrared and ultraviolet light, radio waves, and X-rays. • Air pressure varies from location to location.
*SCALE AND STRUCTURE	• A microscope provides a magnified view of an object. • Compound-light microscopes can magnify up to 1000 times. • Electron microscopes can magnify more than 1 million times.
*SYSTEMS AND INTERACTIONS	• Because ultraviolet light, infrared light, and X-rays do not easily pass through Earth's atmosphere, telescopes are launched into space or above the atmosphere in order to observe these forms of light emitted by distant objects.
*UNITY AND DIVERSITY	• Although all objects in space are unified because they are made up of matter and energy, the amount and type of energy emitted by such objects vary from object to object.
STABILITY	

Comprehensive List of Laboratory Materials

Item	Quantities per Group	Chapter
Balance, triple-beam	1	2
Beaker, medium	3	2
Bread	2 slices	1
Card holder	1	3
Graduated cylinder, medium	2	2
Index card, white, unlined	1	3
Jar with lid	2	1
Lens holder	2	3
Lens, convex, or magnifying glass	2 of different sizes	3
Medicine dropper	1	1
Meterstick	1	2,3
Metric ruler	1	2
Objects:		
irregular	1	2
regular	1	2
Paper towel	1	2
Pebble, small	1	2
Thermometer, Celsius	1	2

THE NATURE OF SCIENCE

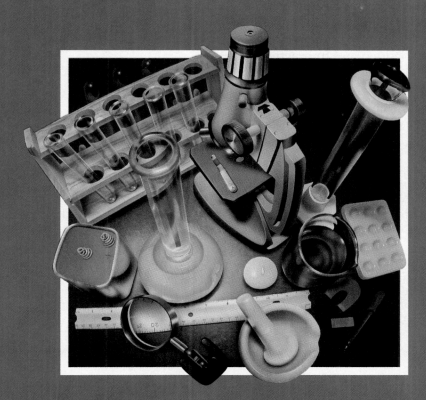

Anthea Maton
Former NSTA National Coordinator
Project Scope, Sequence, Coordination
Washington, DC

Jean Hopkins
Science Instructor and Department Chairperson
John H. Wood Middle School
San Antonio, Texas

Susan Johnson
Professor of Biology
Ball State University
Muncie, Indiana

David LaHart
Senior Instructor
Florida Solar Energy Center
Cape Canaveral, Florida

Charles William McLaughlin
Science Instructor and Department Chairperson
Central High School
St. Joseph, Missouri

Maryanna Quon Warner
Science Instructor
Del Dios Middle School
Escondido, California

Jill D. Wright
Professor of Science Education
Director of International Field Programs
University of Pittsburgh
Pittsburgh, Pennsylvania

Prentice Hall
Englewood Cliffs, New Jersey
Needham, Massachusetts

Prentice Hall Science
The Nature of Science

Student Text and Annotated Teacher's Edition
Laboratory Manual
Teacher's Resource Package
Teacher's Desk Reference
Computer Test Bank
Teaching Transparencies
Product Testing Activities
Computer Courseware
Video and Interactive Video

The illustration on the cover, rendered by Keith Kasnot, depicts some of the variety of tools used in the exploration of the natural world.

Credits begin on page 124.

SECOND EDITION

ISBN 0-13-400409-4

2 3 4 5 6 7 8 9 10   97 96 95 94 93

Prentice Hall
A Division of Simon & Schuster
Englewood Cliffs, New Jersey 07632

STAFF CREDITS

Editorial:	Harry Bakalian, Pamela E. Hirschfeld, Maureen Grassi, Robert P. Letendre, Elisa Mui Eiger, Lorraine Smith-Phelan, Christine A. Caputo
Design:	AnnMarie Roselli, Carmela Pereira, Susan Walrath, Leslie Osher, Art Soares
Production:	Suse F. Bell, Joan McCulley, Elizabeth Torjussen, Christina Burghard
Photo Research:	Libby Forsyth, Emily Rose, Martha Conway
Publishing Technology:	Andrew Grey Bommarito, Deborah Jones, Monduane Harris, Michael Colucci, Gregory Myers, Cleasta Wilburn
Marketing:	Andrew Socha, Victoria Willows
Pre-Press Production:	Laura Sanderson, Kathryn Dix, Denise Herckenrath
Manufacturing:	Rhett Conklin, Gertrude Szyferblatt

Consultants

Kathy French	National Science Consultant
Jeannie Dennard	National Science Consultant
Brenda Underwood	National Science Consultant
Janelle Conarton	National Science Consultant

Contributing Writers

Linda Densman
Science Instructor
Hurst, TX

Linda Grant
Former Science Instructor
Weatherford, TX

Heather Hirschfeld
Science Writer
Durham, NC

Marcia Mungenast
Science Writer
Upper Montclair, NJ

Michael Ross
Science Writer
New York City, NY

Content Reviewers

Dan Anthony
Science Mentor
Rialto, CA

John Barrow
Science Instructor
Pomona, CA

Leslie Bettencourt
Science Instructor
Harrisville, RI

Carol Bishop
Science Instructor
Palm Desert, CA

Dan Bohan
Science Instructor
Palm Desert, CA

Steve M. Carlson
Science Instructor
Milwaukie, OR

Larry Flammer
Science Instructor
San Jose, CA

Steve Ferguson
Science Instructor
Lee's Summit, MO

Robin Lee Harris Freedman
Science Instructor
Fort Bragg, CA

Edith H. Gladden
Former Science Instructor
Philadelphia, PA

Vernita Marie Graves
Science Instructor
Tenafly, NJ

Jack Grube
Science Instructor
San Jose, CA

Emiel Hamberlin
Science Instructor
Chicago, IL

Dwight Kertzman
Science Instructor
Tulsa, OK

Judy Kirschbaum
Science/Computer Instructor
Tenafly, NJ

Kenneth L. Krause
Science Instructor
Milwaukie, OR

Ernest W. Kuehl, Jr.
Science Instructor
Bayside, NY

Mary Grace Lopez
Science Instructor
Corpus Christi, TX

Warren Maggard
Science Instructor
PeWee Valley, KY

Della M. McCaughan
Science Instructor
Biloxi, MS

Stanley J. Mulak
Former Science Instructor
Jensen Beach, FL

Richard Myers
Science Instructor
Portland, OR

Carol Nathanson
Science Mentor
Riverside, CA

Sylvia Neivert
Former Science Instructor
San Diego, CA

Jarvis VNC Pahl
Science Instructor
Rialto, CA

Arlene Sackman
Science Instructor
Tulare, CA

Christine Schumacher
Science Instructor
Pikesville, MD

Suzanne Steinke
Science Instructor
Towson, MD

Len Svinth
Science Instructor/
Chairperson
Petaluma, CA

Elaine M. Tadros
Science Instructor
Palm Desert, CA

Joyce K. Walsh
Science Instructor
Midlothian, VA

Steve Weinberg
Science Instructor
West Hartford, CT

Charlene West, PhD
Director of Curriculum
Rialto, CA

John Westwater
Science Instructor
Medford, MA

Glenna Wilkoff
Science Instructor
Chesterfield, OH

Edee Norman Wiziecki
Science Instructor
Urbana, IL

Teacher Advisory Panel

Beverly Brown
Science Instructor
Livonia, MI

James Burg
Science Instructor
Cincinnati, OH

Karen M. Cannon
Science Instructor
San Diego, CA

John Eby
Science Instructor
Richmond, CA

Elsie M. Jones
Science Instructor
Marietta, GA

Michael Pierre McKereghan
Science Instructor
Denver, CO

Donald C. Pace, Sr.
Science Instructor
Reisterstown, MD

Carlos Francisco Sainz
Science Instructor
National City, CA

William Reed
Science Instructor
Indianapolis, IN

Multicultural Consultant

Steven J. Rakow
Associate Professor
University of Houston—
Clear Lake
Houston, TX

English as a Second Language (ESL) Consultants

Jaime Morales
Bilingual Coordinator
Huntington Park, CA

Pat Hollis Smith
Former ESL Instructor
Beaumont, TX

Reading Consultant

Larry Swinburne
Director
Swinburne Readability
Laboratory

CONTENTS

THE NATURE OF SCIENCE

Activity Bank/Reference Section

Features

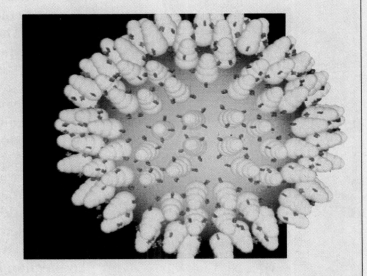

CONCEPT MAPPING

Throughout your study of science, you will learn a variety of terms, facts, figures, and concepts. Each new topic you encounter will provide its own collection of words and ideas—which, at times, you may think seem endless. But each of the ideas within a particular topic is related in some way to the others. No concept in science is isolated. Thus it will help you to understand the topic if you see the whole picture; that is, the interconnectedness of all the individual terms and ideas. This is a much more effective and satisfying way of learning than memorizing separate facts.

Actually, this should be a rather familiar process for you. Although you may not think about it in this way, you analyze many of the elements in your daily life by looking for relationships or connections. For example, when you look at a collection of flowers, you may divide them into groups: roses, carnations, and daisies. You may then associate colors with these flowers: red, pink, and white. The general topic is flowers. The subtopic is types of flowers. And the colors are specific terms that describe flowers. A topic makes more sense and is more easily understood if you understand how it is broken down into individual ideas and how these ideas are related to one another and to the entire topic.

It is often helpful to organize information visually so that you can see how it all fits together. One technique for describing related ideas is called a **concept map**. In a concept map, an idea is represented by a word or phrase enclosed in a box. There are several ideas in any concept map. A connection between two ideas is made with a line. A word or two that describes the connection is written on or near the line. The general topic is located at the top of the map. That topic is then broken down into subtopics, or more specific ideas, by branching lines. The most specific topics are located at the bottom of the map.

To construct a concept map, first identify the important ideas or key terms in the chapter or section. Do not try to include too much information. Use your judgment as to what is really important. Write the general topic at the top of your map. Let's use an example to help illustrate this process. Suppose you decide that the key terms in a section you are reading are School, Living Things, Language Arts, Subtraction, Grammar, Mathematics, Experiments, Papers, Science, Addition, Novels. The general topic is School. Write and enclose this word in a box at the top of your map.

SCHOOL

Now choose the subtopics—Language Arts, Science, Mathematics. Figure out how they are related to the topic. Add these words to your map. Continue this procedure until you have included all the important ideas and terms. Then use lines to make the appropriate connections between ideas and terms. Don't forget to write a word or two on or near the connecting line to describe the nature of the connection.

Do not be concerned if you have to redraw your map (perhaps several times!) before you show all the important connections clearly. If, for example, you write papers for Science as well as for Language Arts, you may want to place these two subjects next to each other so that the lines do not overlap.

One more thing you should know about concept mapping: Concepts can be correctly mapped in many different ways. In fact, it is unlikely that any two people will draw identical concept maps for a complex topic. Thus there is no one correct concept map for any topic! Even though your concept map may not match those of your classmates, it will be correct as long as it shows the most important concepts and the clear relationships among them. Your concept map will also be correct if it has meaning to you and if it helps you understand the material you are reading. A concept map should be so clear that if some of the terms are erased, the missing terms could easily be filled in by following the logic of the concept map.

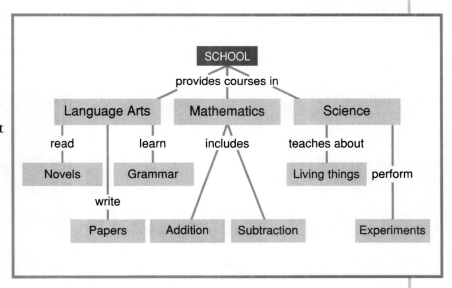

The Nature of Science

TEXT OVERVIEW

In this textbook students will learn about the nature of science. They will discover how scientists use the scientific method to investigate a problem. They will become familiar with the basic rules of laboratory safety.

Next, students will learn how to make measurements using the metric system. They are introduced to the metric units for measuring length, mass, volume, weight, density, and temperature, and to the tools used to make those measurements, including the metric ruler, the triple-beam balance, and the Celsius thermometer.

Finally, students will learn that scientists use many kinds of tools in their investigations inside and outside the laboratory. They are introduced to different kinds of microscopes and telescopes and to other scientific instruments used to study our world and the universe.

TEXT OBJECTIVES

1. Explain the goal of science and describe the steps in the scientific method.
2. List important safety precautions to follow in a science laboratory.
3. Identify and compare the metric units used to measure length, mass, volume, density, weight, and temperature.
4. Explain the role of tools such as microscopes and telescopes in scientific studies.

THE NATURE OF SCIENCE

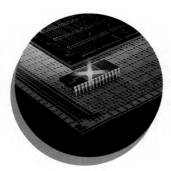

▲ Science has provided us with computer chips and circuits, which are used in modern electronic equipment.

Do you read the newspaper or watch the news on television? Perhaps you prefer the radio or even science magazines. Whatever your preference, you know that it's hard to escape hearing about advances in science.

Computers, CD players, microwave ovens, and even hand-held video games all became possible through discoveries in science. Science, for better or for worse, is all around us. It is through science that we have developed new sources of energy—and have found ways to make traditional sources more efficient and less polluting. Science has given us television, telephones, and other forms of communication. A list of scientific advances that have improved our lives could fill this textbook alone!

What exactly is science? How do scientists go about making discoveries? If you think that science is a job for white-coated laboratory workers who never look up from their microscope or get involved in the world around

Not all the effects of science are positive. Here you see two well-protected scientists carrying hazardous wastes from a chemical spill. ▶

INTRODUCING THE NATURE OF SCIENCE

USING THE TEXTBOOK

Begin your introduction of the textbook by having students examine the textbook-opening photographs and captions. Before they read the textbook introduction, ask them the following questions:

• **What do the two photographs on page A8 show?** (Computer circuits and hazardous wastes.)

• **How do those photos demonstrate the positive and negative effects of science?** (Science created both the chips and circuits in electronic equipment and the chemicals in the hazardous wastes. But whereas the chips and circuits are generally seen as a positive result, the chemicals are sometimes considered a negative result.)

Now have students read the textbook introduction.

• **Besides the things mentioned in the**

textbook, think of other ways that science has contributed to our lives. (Accept all logical answers. Encourage students to think beyond the category of modern conveniences.)

• **How do you think scientists think of making or doing these things?** (Accept all logical answers. Suggest that often scientists see a need or a problem and work to find an answer, but sometimes they discover something by accident or luck.)

• **Why is it important to think of scien-**

CHAPTERS

them, you're in for a surprise. In this textbook you will find out about the nature of science and the ways in which scientists investigate the world. You will have an opportunity to explore and discover a few things yourself. We hope you discover something that few people really understand: Science is fun. Now go to it—and enjoy!

It has been through the work of environmental scientists that people have begun to take seriously the threat to many of Earth's greatest creatures, among them the African elephant.

CHAPTER DESCRIPTIONS

1 What Is Science? Chapter 1 begins with a discussion of the nature of science and its branches. The question of how scientists work is treated next, with the steps of the scientific method described in detail. The chapter closes with a discussion of important laboratory safety procedures.

2 Measurement and the Sciences In Chapter 2 the metric system of measurement used by scientists all over the world is explained in detail. The units used to measure length, volume, weight, mass, density, and temperature, as well as the tools used to make the measurements, are described.

3 Tools and the Sciences Chapter 3 deals with various tools scientists use in their work. The different kinds of microscopes and telescopes are explained and compared. X-rays, CT scans, MRI, seismographs, submersibles, and barometers are also described.

Discovery Activity

What Is It?

1. Examine carefully a leaf (or another part of a plant), a magnifying glass, and a rock.

2. Write down a list of characteristics you would use to describe each of these objects. Your list should include size, color, texture, shape, and any other feature you feel is important.

3. Provide your description of each object to a parent or guardian without showing the actual object. See if the parent or guardian can determine what the object is by your description alone.

   ■ How helpful was your description? What sort of tools or instruments would have allowed you to describe each object better?

A ■ 9

---

tists as more than people in white coats in laboratories? (Accept all logical answers. Scientists do a lot of their work out in the world, and their discoveries can have a major impact on the world.)

DISCOVERY ACTIVITY
What Is It?

Begin your introduction to the textbook by having students perform the Discovery Activity. Suggest that students record their observations in list or chart form, creating a separate list or chart for each of the three objects. They may want to give their descriptions to others outside class, besides their parent or guardian, and collect additional responses.

Remind students to ask each person how the description was helpful. Have them bring their descriptions and responses to class and discuss their findings. Encourage them to think of tools or instruments, practical or fanciful, that would help them better describe the objects.

SECTION	HANDS-ON ACTIVITIES
1–1 Science—Not Just for Scientists pages A10–A18 Multicultural Opportunity 1–1, p. A10 ESL Strategy 1–1, p. A10	**Student Edition** ACTIVITY (Discovering): Reading a Food Label, p. A13 ACTIVITY (Discovering): Homestyle Classification, p. A16 ACTIVITY BANK: Observing a Fish, p. A100 **Activity Book** CHAPTER DISCOVERY: Discovering Science, p. A9 **Teacher Edition** What Is Science? p. A10d
1–2 The Scientific Method—A Way of Problem Solving pages A18–A29 Multicultural Opportunity 1–2, p. A18 ESL Strategy 1–2, p. A18	**Student Edition** ACTIVITY (Discovering): To Grow Or Not To Grow, p. A21 ACTIVITY (Discovering): Graphing Temperatures, p. A23 ACTIVITY (Doing): Expanding Water, p. A24 ACTIVITY (Discovering): A Rocky Observation, p. A28 LABORATORY INVESTIGATION: A Moldy Question, p. A34 ACTIVITY BANK: What Do Seeds Need to Grow? p. A102 **Activity Book** ACTIVITY : Testing a Hypothesis, p. A21 ACTIVITY BANK: A Small World, p. A115 **Product Testing Activity** Testing Bubble Gum **Laboratory Manual** Testing a Hypothesis, p. A17
1–3 Science and Discovery pages A30–A31 Multicultural Opportunity 1–3, p. A30 ESL Strategy 1–3, p. A30	**Product Testing Activity** Testing Shampoo
1–4 Safety in the Science Laboratory pages A31–A33 Multicultural Opportunity 1–4, p. A31 ESL Strategy 1–4, p. A31	**Teacher Edition** Great Expectations, p. A10d
Chapter Review pages A34–A37	

OUTSIDE TEACHER RESOURCES

Books

Brinkworth, B. J. *An Introduction to Experimentation*, Elsevier.
Dixon, B. *What Is Science For?*, Collins.
Haines, Gail Kay. *Test-Tube Mysteries*, Dodd, Mead.

Harre, R., and D. G. Eastwood. *The Method of Science*, Crane, Russak.
Penny, R. K. *The Experimental Method*, Longman.

Smith, Norma. *How Fast Do Your Oysters Grow? Investigate and Discover Through Science Projects*, Julian Messner.

OTHER ACTIVITIES	MEDIA AND TECHNOLOGY
Activity Book ACTIVITY: Scientific Notation, p. A27 ACTIVITY: Practice With Exponents, p. A29 **Review and Reinforcement Guide** Section 1–1, p. A5	**Video/Videodisc** The Eagle's Story (Supplemental) **Video** The Greenhouse Effect (Supplemental) **English/Spanish Audiotapes** Section 1–1
Student Edition ACTIVITY (Writing): Changing Theories, p. A19 ACTIVITY (Thinking): What's the Word? p. A27 **Activity Book** ACTIVITY: The Case of the Sleeping Frog, p. A15 ACTIVITY: Just a Spoonful of Sugar, p. A17 ACTIVITY: Explain Why, p. A19 **Review and Reinforcement Guide** Section 1–2, p. A7	**Interactive Videodisc/CD ROM** Paul ParkRanger and the Mystery of the Disappearing Ducks **English/Spanish Audiotapes** Section 1–2
Student Edition ACTIVITY (Reading): An Unexpected World, p. A31 **Review and Reinforcement Guide** Section 1–3, p. A11	**Video/Videodisc** The Mystery of a Million Seals (Supplemental) **English/Spanish Audiotapes** Section 1–3
Activity Book ACTIVITY: Organizing Data, p. A27 **Review and Reinforcement Guide** Section 1–4, p. A13	**English/Spanish Audiotapes** Section 1–4
Test Book Chapter Test, p. A9 Performance-Based Tests, p. A75	**Test Book** Computer Test Bank Test, p. A17

*All materials in the Chapter Planning Guide Grid are available as part of the Prentice Hall Science Learning System.

Audiovisuals

Doing Better in Science, two filmstrips with cassettes, LA

Organizing a Science Project, filmstrips,

Encyclopaedia Britannica

The Scientific Method, film, Encyclopaedia Britannica

What Is Science?, 16-mm film, Coronet

CHAPTER OVERVIEW

Understanding and exploring the world around us is one of the greatest human desires. Humans want to know about the mysteries that make up their world. This wanting to know leads to inquiry and discovery. Science is often thought of as cold facts born out of mental geniuses. Science, however, is more than a simple list of facts. Science involves a constant search for information and understanding of the universe.

Scientists deal with problems in an orderly and systematic manner. This is known as the scientific method. First, the problem must be stated in a clear, concise manner. Second, information that relates to the problem must be gathered, and accurate records must be kept. After the facts or clues of the investigation are known, a hypothesis can be made.

In the testing of the hypothesis, experiments will help to prove or disprove the suggested hypothesis. Data and measurements must be recorded accurately. Experimentation is a purposeful activity and should be designed to include safety procedures for the participants.

1-1 SCIENCE—NOT JUST FOR SCIENTISTS
THEMATIC FOCUS

The purpose of this section is to introduce students to the study of science. They will learn that scientists uncover truths about nature called facts. Then scientists use facts to solve larger mysteries of nature. In the last part of the section, students will be introduced to the three main branches of science—life science, earth science, and physical science. They will learn that within each branch are many smaller branches.

The themes that can be focused on in this section are evolution and scale and structure.

Evolution: The patterns that occur when organisms or their environments change or when physical objects are affected by forces are among the most significant of the patterns that scientists analyze. One of the large mysteries that scientists study is how the relatively few and simple organisms of 3 billion years ago gave rise to the many complex organisms that inhabit Earth today.

*Scale and structure: The questions that interest scientists occur at a wide variety of levels—from microscopic organisms that can only be studied with the aid of scientific instruments to problems concerned with the behavior of matter in the entire universe.

PERFORMANCE OBJECTIVES 1-1

1. Explain what is meant by a fact.
2. Explain the difference between a theory and a law.
3. Identify the main branches of science.

SCIENCE TERMS 1-1

theory p. A14
law p. A15

1-2 THE SCIENTIFIC METHOD—A WAY OF PROBLEM SOLVING
THEMATIC FOCUS

The purpose of this section is to explain the scientific method to students. They will learn that the seven steps of the scientific method are stating the problem, gathering information, forming a hypothesis, experimenting, recording and analyzing data, stating a conclusion, repeating the work. Students will learn that a hypothesis is a proposed solution to the problem and that experiments are carried out to test the hypothesis. Students will be introduced to some important methods of recording and analyzing data. These include making data tables and graphs. Students will learn the importance of reaching a conclusion. They will discover that scientists state a conclusion only after an experiment has been run many times with the same results.

The themes that can be focused on in this section are systems and interactions and energy.

*Systems and interactions: The scientific method is a systematic procedure for exploring questions about our environment. A key part of the method is experimentation—setting up an experimental and a control apparatus that differ by just one variable. The scientific method can help to explore complex and interrelated phenomena by focusing on just one question or hypothesis at a time.

Energy: Most of the interactions in scientific experiments involve some sort of energy exchange. The life processes of living organisms, the principles that explain the movement of stars and galaxies, the chemical and physical factors that change our environment—all these involve changes in energy.

PERFORMANCE OBJECTIVES 1-2

1. Describe the steps in the scientific method.
2. Explain how a hypothesis is developed.
3. Discuss the importance of a variable and a control in a scientific experiment.

SCIENCE TERMS 1-2

scientific method p A18
hypothesis p. A20
variable p. A21
control p. A21
data p. A22

1-3 SCIENCE AND DISCOVERY
THEMATIC FOCUS

The purpose of this section is to help students understand the role that luck plays in scientific discovery. Although there are many well-known stories of inventions or scientific discoveries being uncovered through "luck," students should realize that recognizing what to do with an unexpected event requires a great deal of prior experience. And after the "lucky" event has occurred, the orderly procedures of the scientific method are then customarily used.

The themes that can be focused on in this section are unity and diversity and patterns of change.

*Unity and diversity: The progress of scientific research and applications is advanced not only by careful and thorough procedures, but sometimes also through unexpected events. All aspects of scientific work involve some types of luck. And scientists who are curious and courageous enough to explore unexpected occurrences are often those who make significant contributions.

Patterns of change: Often the history of scientific progress has been changed by someone who identified an event that did not match the expected pattern. In looking for ways to explain the unexpected, completely new theories have been formulated.

PERFORMANCE OBJECTIVES 1–3

1. Explain how luck can play a role in scientific discoveries.

2. Discuss how luck must be supported by scientific expertise.

1-4 SAFETY IN THE SCIENCE LABORATORY

THEMATIC FOCUS

The purpose of this section is to explain to students the importance of observing proper safety procedures in a science laboratory. First, students must learn to follow the teacher's directions or the directions given in the textbook exactly as stated. They must learn the meanings of the safety symbols and all the important safety precautions. It is important that students take as many precautions as possible to protect themselves and their fellow workers.

The scientific laboratory is a place of adventure and discovery, a place to satisfy our curiosity, a place to better understand the facts and main concepts of science. When we work in a laboratory, we must use scientific tools. As with any

tools, a certain amount of care and precaution is necessary.

The themes that can be focused on in this section are systems and interactions and scale and structure.

*Systems and interactions: Students who are beginning the study of science have many adventures in store when they work in science laboratories. Because they are not equipped to predict the results of many experiments, it is very important that safety procedures be learned until they are automatic.

*Scale and structure: Dangerous materials and equipment in a science laboratory come in all sizes. It is not just large pieces of equipment or strong forces that require safety precautions. Very small quantities of some chemicals can be hazardous.

PERFORMANCE OBJECTIVES 1–4

1. List the important safety rules you must follow in the classroom laboratory.

2. Explain the reasons for each laboratory safety rule.

3. Describe how to respond to possible laboratory emergencies.

Discovery *Learning*

TEACHER DEMONSTRATIONS MODELING

What Is Science?

Write the letters S, C, I, E, N, C, E in a vertical column on the chalkboard.
• **What does science mean to you?** (Responses might include the following: It's a class in school, it's a subject, it's studying about how things are made.)

Write the words Simple, Casual, Ideas, Excites, Natural, Curious, and Exploration next to the letters on the chalkboard.
• **What are simple, casual ideas?** (Students probably will say that they are normal things we think about.)
• **What do you predict natural curious exploration means?** (Most students will

say that natural curiosity will lead to trying to find out how something is made or what it is made of.)

Point out that science is simple, casual ideas that were excited by natural curiosity that leads to exploration. Have students look around the classroom.
• **Do you think that most of the things you see in this room were developed by a genius?** (No.)
• **Who do you think thought of making a drinking glass?** (Responses might include someone who needed a glass; it probably started with a gourd, and after glass was developed, they made a container of glass.)

Point out that the needs of people and what they think about are the prime movers of new inventions.

Great Expectations

Pour 125 mL of water into a 500-mL beaker. Point out that water is a common substance. Add 50 mL of white vinegar. Remark that vinegar and water are both common everyday substances. Place the beaker on a ring stand and heat over a Bunsen burner until boiling. Show students a box of baking soda.
• **What is baking soda used for?** (Accept all logical answers.)

Point out that almost every kitchen has a box of baking soda. Measure 15 mL of baking soda. Pour the baking soda into the heated mixture and stir—the mixture will bubble rapidly. Explain to students that in a laboratory, we must always expect the unexpected.

CHAPTER 1
What Is Science?

INTEGRATING SCIENCE

This chapter provides you with numerous opportunities to integrate various areas of science, as well as other disciplines, into your curriculum. Blue numbered annotations on the student page and integration notes on the teacher wraparound pages alert you to areas of possible integration.

In this chapter you can integrate language arts (pp. 12, 19, 27, 31), life science and evolution (pp. 13, 27, 30), life science and zoology (pp. 14, 25), physical science and heat (p. 15), life science and microbiology (p. 16), earth science and geology (pp. 17, 28), earth science and ecology (p. 17), mathematics (pp. 21, 23), and earth science and astronomy (p. 29).

SCIENCE, TECHNOLOGY, AND SOCIETY/COOPERATIVE LEARNING

Our society is dependent on science and technology, but the percentage of scientifically literate members of society is alarmingly small. Many well-educated people think of pseudoscience—UFOs, ESP, astrology, and crystals—as science. Our ability to help shape national policy by voting is threatened if we do not understand the science underlying issues of local, national, and global concern.

The great power of science and technology also includes great responsibilities: attention to long-term consequences of technology; the necessity of a global, not a local, perspective; and the

INTRODUCING CHAPTER 1

DISCOVERY LEARNING

▶ *Activity Book*

Begin your teaching of the chapter by using the Chapter 1 Discovery Activity from your *Activity Book.* Using this activity, students will perform simple experiments investigating gravity, the water displaced by a submerged object, and an inclined plane. The emphasis is on making accurate observations and drawing inferences from those observations.

USING THE TEXTBOOK

Begin by having students observe the chapter-opener illustration.
• **What do you see in this picture?** (Do not expect scientific answers. Most students will reply with descriptions of the *Megalosaurus* and its environment.)

Direct students' attention to the chapter-opener text.

• **What was strange about the rocks at the Connecticut State Dinosaur Park?** (Unusual scratches.)
• **What did Dr. Coombs know about the scratches right away?** (That they were dinosaur footprints.)

Point out to students that these scratches represent a type of fossil. A fossil is the remains or evidence of a living thing. Fossils that are formed from the footprints or other imprint of an organism—without the actual organism being

What Is Science?

Scientists, like most people, love a mystery. Recently, Dr. W. P. Coombs Jr., of Western New England College, was called upon to solve a most interesting puzzle. Strange scratches had been found on some rocks unearthed at the Connecticut State Dinosaur Park. Dr. Coombs is a dinosaur expert. He took one look at the scratches on the exposed rocks and immediately knew what they were—dinosaur footprints. The scratches appeared in groups of three, leading Dr. Coombs to conclude that the scratches were made by an animal having three toes with sharp claws. They were clearly the work of the meat-eating dinosaur called *Megalosaurus*.

There was something peculiar about the footprints. Only the tips of the dinosaur's toes seemed to have touched the rocks. But *Megalosaurus* did not run on its toes, at least not on land. Dr. Coombs quickly realized that the prints had been made under water, where most of the animal's weight would have been kept off the rocks. From scratches on rocks, Dr. Coombs had discovered the first evidence of a swimming, meat-eating dinosaur. Unearthed rocks, a sharp eye, and some smart detective work had led to an important scientific discovery.

Journal *Activity*

You and Your World Is this your first science course? Or are you an old hand at science? In either case, in your journal jot down your feelings about taking a science course. It might be interesting to go back to your entry at the end of the year and see if you still feel the same.

An artist's interpretation of the first swimming, meat-eating dinosaur

A ■ 11

---

embedded in the rock—are called trace fossils.

Have students assist you in listing Dr. Coombs's observations on the chalkboard.

1. The scratches were in groups of three.
2. Only the tips of the dinosaur's toes touched the rock.

For each observation, have students note the conclusions drawn.

Observation 1: The dinosaur had three toes and sharp claws. Therefore, the dinosaur must have been a meat-eating dinosaur, probably a *Megalosaurus*.

Observation 2: The animal could have walked on its toes, but the *Megalosaurus* did not do this on land. Therefore, the footprints must have been made under water.

• **Based on his observations and conclusions, what did Dr. Coombs finally conclude about the origin of the footprints?** (They were made by a swimming, meat-eating dinosaur—the first evidence of any such animal to be discovered.)

---

importance of considering the impact on future generations.

Cooperative learning: Using preassigned lab groups or randomly selected teams, have groups complete one of the following assignments.

• After discussing some of the major topics that will be covered during the year in science class, brainstorm problems and/or issues that are related to topics students will be studying. The problems and/or issues they list must also be related to technology and must have an impact on society.

• Prepare a chart by dividing a sheet of paper vertically into three columns. Label each column with one of the following: science, technology, society. Play the song "We Didn't Start the Fire" (from Billy Joel's *Stormfront*) for the class. As the song plays, have group members classify entries in the song into the appropriate column on their chart.

Be sure to tell students that not all the entries in the song can be classified into one of the three columns. For song entries that students are unfamiliar with, these entries can be randomly divided among groups and library time provided for brief research. Groups can then report their findings to the class. This activity should help students see the role of science in many facets of their lives.

See Cooperative Learning in the *Teacher's Desk Reference.*

JOURNAL ACTIVITY

You may want to use the Journal Activity as the basis of class discussion. As students discuss their feelings about taking a science course, help them realize all the prior knowledge they will bring to the class. Students may have attended museums, collected items of scientific interest, or seen movies about science. Students should be instructed to keep their Journal Activity in their portfolio.

1-1 Science—Not Just for Scientists

MULTICULTURAL OPPORTUNITY 1-1

Scientists from the community can provide students with first-hand knowledge about careers in science. Identify some local people with careers related to science. As much as possible, mention individuals of different ethnic backgrounds, especially women, with whom students can relate. These neighbors will help students see that they too can enter careers in science.

Keep in mind that some findings of modern science as well as some types of scientific experiments may be incompatible with the beliefs of certain ethnic groups and may violate taboos of students' cultures. The support of respected members of the community of different cultural backgrounds may help you alleviate concerns and promote understanding.

ESL STRATEGY 1-1

Pair LEP students with English-speaking students and ask them to prepare brief reports on a specific scientific theory that became a law. Ask English-speaking students to assist the LEP students in selecting the topic and conducting research. Have volunteers share their findings with the class.

TEACHING STRATEGY 1-1

FOCUS/MOTIVATION

Ask students if they have ever been to a science museum or have ever watched a science or nature program on television. Have volunteers share their experiences with the class.

• **What is the first thing you think of when you hear the word** *science?* (Answers will vary.)

Use student responses to gain an understanding of how students perceive the field of science. For example, some may think of science as something that takes place primarily in a laboratory. Others may associate science with exciting fields of study, such as outer space. Still others

Figure 1–1 *Whenever you observe and question natural occurrences, such as a lightning storm, you are acting as a scientist does.*

may think of science as carrying out experiments or discovering new things.

CONTENT DEVELOPMENT

Continue the Motivation discussion by pointing out that science involves a constant search for information about the universe. Emphasize that science involves analyzing and relating information, as well as making discoveries. Also, stress that science is concerned with explaining why things happen the way they do.

1-1 Science—Not Just for Scientists

You are a scientist! Does that statement surprise you? If it does, it is probably because you do not understand exactly what a scientist is. But if you have ever observed the colors formed in a drop of oil in a puddle or watched a fire burn, you were acting like a scientist. You are also a scientist when you watch waves breaking on the shore or lightning bolts darting through the night sky. Or perhaps you have walked through the grass in the morning and noticed drops of dew or have screamed with delight as you watched a roller coaster dipping up and down the track. Whenever you observe the world around you, you are acting like a scientist. Does that give you a clue to the nature of science and scientists?

Scientists observe the world around them—just as you do. For that reason, whenever you make an observation you are acting like a scientist. But scientists do more than just observe. The word *science* comes from the Latin *scire,* which means "to know." So science is more than just observation. And real scientists do more than just observe. They question what they see. They wonder what makes things the way they are. And they attempt to find answers to their questions.

No doubt you also wonder about and question what you see—at least some of the time. Hopefully, you will be better able to find answers to some of your questions as a result of reading this chapter. That is, you will be better able to approach the world as a scientist does.

GUIDED PRACTICE

Skills Development
Skill: Relating facts

Have students make a list of the things they know about themselves, such as gender, address, phone number, name, age school, friends' names, etc.

• **Are you absolutely sure these are things you know?** (Accept all answers, but lead students to suggest that they are absolutely sure of their knowledge in this area.)

Figure 1–2 *The goal of science is to understand events that occur in the world around us—such as this rare desert snowstorm in Arizona.*

The Nature of Science

The universe around you and inside of you is really a collection of countless mysteries. It is the job of scientists to solve those mysteries. **The goal of science is to understand the world around us.**

How do scientists go about understanding the world? Like all good detectives, scientists use special methods to determine truths about nature. Such truths are called facts. Here is an example of a fact: The sun is a source of light and heat. But science is more than a list of facts—just as studying science is more than memorizing facts. Jules Henri Poincaré, a famous nineteenth-century French scientist who charted the motions of planets, put it this way: "Science is built up with facts, as a house is with stones. But a collection of facts is no more a science than a heap of stones is a house."

So scientists go further than simply discovering facts. Scientists try to use facts to solve larger mysteries of nature. In this sense, you might think of facts as clues to scientific mysteries. An example of a larger mystery is how the sun produces the heat and light it showers upon the Earth. Another larger mystery is how the relatively few and simple organisms of 3 billion years ago gave rise to the many complex organisms that inhabit the Earth today.

Using facts they have gathered, scientists propose explanations for the events they observe. Then they perform experiments to test their explanations. In the next section of this chapter, you will learn how scientists go about performing experiments and uncovering the mysteries of nature.

ACTIVITY
DISCOVERING

Reading a Food Label

You may wonder why studying science is important in your life. If you have ever read the ingredients on a food label, then you already know one reason. A knowledge of chemistry helps you learn what ingredients are in the foods you eat!

Look at the label on a box of cereal. The ingredients are listed, in order, by the amount present in the food.

Make a list of the ingredients that are present in the food label you are examining. Next to each ingredient indicate with a checkmark whether it is familiar to you.

■ Find out what each ingredient is and how the body uses it.

■ Which ingredients are preservatives?

Report your findings to your class.

Activity Bank

Observing a Fish, p.100

ACTIVITY
DISCOVERING

READING A FOOD LABEL

Discovery Learning
Skills: Making comparisons
Materials: food labels

This activity will provide students with an opportunity to gather data from various food labels and to interpret the data on the labels. Students may be surprised to learn how many additives and preservatives are in common food products. The ingredients they discover and how they are used in the body will vary, depending on the labels chosen.

ENRICHMENT

A scientific problem is often stated in the form of a question. You can illustrate this by posing the following situation: Suppose that you have three gardens in your yard—one on the east side, one on the south side, and one on the west side. The plants are all of the same type, but you notice that the plants on the south side are at least 5 cm taller, on the average, than the plants on the east side or the west side.

• **Can you recognize the scientific problem in this situation?** (The observation that plants on the south side are taller than plants on the east side or the west side.)

• **Can you state this problem in the form of a question?** (Why are plants on the south side taller, on the average, than plants on the west side or the east side?)

• **Would you say these are "facts"?** (Accept all answers.)

Explain that in order "to know," we must question the things we observe and the "facts."

• **Could any of the facts about you change?** (Accept all answers, but lead students to agree that they could move and change addresses, girls marry and change last names, their age changes every year, they could live in a different house, etc.)

• **Which facts about you are not likely to change?** (Accept all answers, but lead students to suggest that during their lifetime, many facts about them will change.)

CONTENT DEVELOPMENT

● ● ● ● **Integration** ● ● ● ●

The derivation of the word *science* may be used to integrate language arts into your science lesson.

The reference to the millions of organisms on the Earth and their origins can lead to a discussion of evolution.

Life science deals with living things and their relationship to one another and their environment. Life science can be divided into a number of specialized branches. Four examples are zoology, the study of animals; botany, the study of plants; ecology, the study of the relationships between living organisms and their environment; and microbiology, the study of microscopic organisms.

Physical science is the study of matter and energy. There are two main branches of physical science—chemistry and physics. Chemistry involves the study of what substances are made of and how they change and combine. Physics is the study of forms of energy and motion.

Earth science deals with the study of the Earth, its history, its changes, and its place in the universe. Some of the specialized branches of earth science are geology, the study of the Earth's origin, history, and structure; meteorology, the study of the Earth's atmosphere, weather and climate; and oceanography, the study of the Earth's oceans, including their physical features, life forms, and natural resources. Another branch of earth science is astronomy, the study of the position, composition, size, and other characteristics of the planets, stars, and other objects in space. Interestingly, astronomy in college courses is considered a part of physics, not earth science.

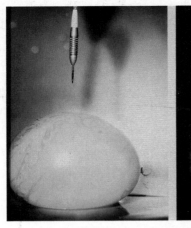

Figure 1–3 *It had long been a theory that a liquid did not retain its shape when removed from its container. However, scientists were forced to change that theory after observing the photographs shown here. The photographs show that the water in the balloon retained its balloon shape for 12 to 13 millionths of a second after the balloon had been burst by a dart.*

After studying facts, making observations, and performing experiments, scientists may develop a **theory.** A theory is the most logical explanation for events that occur in nature. Keep in mind that scientists do not use the word theory as you do. For example, you may have a theory about why your favorite soccer team is not winning. Your theory may or may not make sense. But it is not a scientific theory. A scientific theory is not just a guess or a hunch. A scientific theory is a powerful, time-tested concept that makes useful and dependable predictions about the natural world.

When a scientist proposes a theory, that theory must be tested over and over again. If it survives the

Figure 1–4 *Life science includes the study of animals such as the* ❶ *diamondback rattlesnake.*

14 ■ A

1–1 (continued)

CONTENT DEVELOPMENT

Explain that after making observations, collecting facts, and experimenting, scientists may develop a theory. A theory is the most logical explanation of events that occur in nature. Point out that theories are tested over and over. If a theory proves to be correct every time it is tested, it may be called a law. But even in a science, a law can be changed if further observation and experimentation do not support the law.

• **Why do you think science allows us to come up with new answers for old ideas?** (Accept all logical answers.)

Point out that allowing for questions and new scientific explanations is the heart of science. Scientists are always looking for new and better ways of explaining and understanding the things around us.

FOCUS/MOTIVATION

Ask all the scientists in the class to raise their hand.

• **What did you observe on the way to school today?** (Accept all answers.)

Select one or two students to describe in detail what they observed.

• **Could you have taken another route to school?** (Most students will say that they can take an alternative route to school.)

• **Would you still have ended up at school?** (Yes.)

• **Would you have observed the same things if you had traveled another way?** (Probably not.)

Emphasize that even though they would have arrived at school, they prob-

tests, the theory may be accepted by the scientific community. However, theories can be wrong and may be changed after additional tests and/or observations.

If a theory survives many tests and is generally accepted as true, scientists may call it a **law.** However, as with theories, even scientific laws may change as new information is provided or new experiments are performed. This points out the spirit at the heart of science: Always allow questions to be asked and new scientific explanations to be considered.

Branches of Science

One of the skills you will develop as you continue to study science is the ability to organize things in a logical, orderly way—that is, to classify things. Classification systems are an important part of science. For example, biologists classify all life on Earth into five broad kingdoms of living things. Astronomers classify stars into five main types according to their size. And chemists classify the 109 known elements according to their properties, or characteristics.

Even the study of science can be classified into groups or, in this case, what we call branches of science. There can be many branches of science, each determined by the subject matter being studied. For our purposes, however, we will consider only the three main (overarching) branches of science: life science, earth science, and physical science.

LIFE SCIENCE Life science deals with living things and their parts and actions. Smaller branches of life science include zoology (the study of animals) and botany (the study of plants).

EARTH SCIENCE Earth science is the study of the Earth and its rocks, oceans, volcanoes, earthquakes, atmosphere, and other features. Usually earth science also includes astronomy. Astronomers explore nature beyond the Earth. They study such objects as stars, planets, and moons.

PHYSICAL SCIENCE Physical science is the study of matter and energy. Some physical scientists explore what substances are made of and how they change

Figure 1–5 *What branch of science includes the study of planet Saturn?* ❶

Figure 1–6 *Physics is the branch of physical science that studies the heat and light given off by a campfire. What branch of physical science would study the chemical changes that occur when wood burns?* ❷

A ■ 15

INTEGRATION
SOCIAL STUDIES

Laws change in government as well as in science. For example, certain drugs that were once legally obtainable at drugstores are now illegal drugs that cannot be used under any circumstances. An interesting example is heroin, which at the turn of the century could be bought as tablets in many drugstores. Today, of course, heroin is illegal.

The photograph of the campfire can help to integrate the physical science concept of heat.

REINFORCEMENT/RETEACHING

Emphasize the definition of a fact as a truth about nature. Point out that a fact is something that can be verified by measurement, observation, or some other method.

Challenge students to list as many scientific facts as they can think of in ten minutes. Some possible examples include radius of the Earth, distance to the moon, rising and setting of the sun, rise and fall of ocean tides, relative sizes of the planets, heating of the Earth by the sun, phases of the moon, composition of ocean water, and composition of the atmosphere.

ably would not have observed the very same things. Then point out that the students are all scientists in that they are observing the world around them.

CONTENT DEVELOPMENT

Have students consider the following question.
• **In a city, state, or country, there are laws (often called civil laws) that govern people's behavior. How do these laws differ from scientific laws?** (A civil law dictates behavior; people must obey the law and not break it. Natural events, however, do not obey scientific laws; a scientific law simply describes the way events occur in nature. If observations of natural events prove a scientific law wrong, the law is changed.)

● ● ● ● **Integration** ● ● ● ●
Use the photograph of the diamondback rattlesnake to integrate zoology into your lesson and the photograph of Saturn to generate an astronomy discussion.

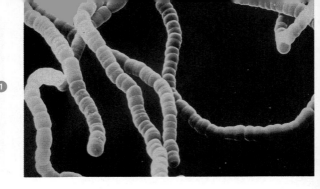

Figure 1-7 Bacteria are among the living things examined by scientists who explore the microscopic world.

and combine. This branch of physical science is called chemistry. Other physical scientists study forms of energy such as heat and light. This is the science of physics.

It is important for you to remember that the branches of science are a handy way to classify the subject matter scientists study. But it would be a mistake to think that any branch works independently of the others. To the contrary, the branches of science actually interweave and overlap most of the time. Science does not happen in a vacuum, and the great discoveries of science do not usually occur unless scientists from many branches work together.

Questions Scientists Ask

Even within a particular branch of science, the subjects studied are often quite specialized. Such specialization is usually based on the types of questions scientists might ask about their world. Let's see how this works.

QUESTIONS AT THE MICROSCOPIC LEVEL Many scientists seek truths about the microscopic world around them. Life scientists, for example, might ask how tiny bacteria invade the body and cause disease. Or they may try to determine how each cell in your body performs all of the functions necessary for life. Physical scientists may question how parts of an atom interact or why some chemical compounds are harmless while others are poisonous (toxic). Earth scientists examine the internal structure of rocks to determine why some rocks last for millions of years while others are worn away by wind and water in a matter of decades.

ACTIVITY
DISCOVERING

Homestyle Classification

Is classification only for scientists? Not at all. Choose a room in your home and take a careful look around. Make a list of the various ways in which objects are classified. (For example, all of your socks are probably grouped together in one drawer.)

■ Does this activity suggest ways in which you might classify objects in order to organize them better?

16 ■ A

Figure 1–8 *Scientists who study volcanoes want to know not only why a volcano erupts but also how such eruptions can be predicted. Why is the ability to predict an eruption of great importance?* ❶

❷

QUESTIONS AT THE MACROSCOPIC LEVEL Other scientists search for answers to questions that involve the macroscopic world, or the world of objects visible to the unaided eye. Macroscopic questions usually involve large groups of objects. Earth scientists, for example, may want to determine the forces that caused a particular volcano to erupt or the causes of an earthquake in a certain area. Physical scientists may question why it takes longer to stop a heavy car than a light one. And life scientists might examine the populations of organisms in an area to determine how each organism interacts with other organisms and with the surrounding environment.

QUESTIONS AT THE GLOBAL LEVEL Some of the questions scientists seek to answer have a more global or world viewpoint. Earth scientists, for example, may study wind patterns throughout the atmosphere in order to determine how weather can be more accurately predicted. Life scientists may seek to determine how pollutants poured into the air or water in one part of the world affect living things far off in another part of the world. And physical scientists may search for the fundamental forces in nature that govern all events in the universe.

As you can see, there are many types of questions to be answered and many areas of science you may wish to pursue in future years. But whether or not you want to become a scientist, you can still ask questions about your world and seek answers to those questions. The study of science is not restricted to scientists! Anyone with the curiosity to ask questions and the energy to seek answers can call a small part of science his or her own. Any takers?

Figure 1–9 *Much of science deals with global issues. One such* ❸ *issue is the worldwide effects of pollution on our environment.*

HISTORICAL NOTE
FAMOUS EXPERIMENTS

Students may enjoy researching some famous experiments in the history of science. Possible experiments include
• Millikan's Oil Drop Experiment to determine the charge on an electron (1910)
• Count Rumford's cannon-drilling experiment to investigate the nature of heat (late 1700s)
• Benjamin Franklin's kite experiment that led to the invention of the lightning rod (mid-1700s)
• Oersted's discovery of electromagnetism (1820)
• Becquerel's discovery of radioactivity (1896)
• Rutherford's experiments to determine atomic structure (early 1900s)

As students research an experiment, have them note the scientific problem being investigated, how the experiment was designed and carried out, and the information yielded by the experiment.

REINFORCEMENT/RETEACHING

Emphasize that scientists do more than uncover facts; they seek to explain why and how things happen as they do. For example, a scientist may wonder why two children in the same family have different-colored hair and eyes, or why a candle goes out in a closed container.
• **Which do you think is harder to discover—facts, or the answers to questions involving "how and why"?** (Answers may vary; many may feel that facts are easier to discover, yet certain facts may be very difficult to discover.)
• **What types of facts might be very hard to discover?** (Facts about things that we cannot see or touch, such as atoms, the interior of the Earth, or heavenly bodies in distant galaxies.)

CONTENT DEVELOPMENT

● ● ● ● **Integration** ● ● ● ●

Use the photographs of volcanoes and pollution to integrate geology and ecology into your lesson.

1-2 The Scientific Method—A Way of Problem Solving

MULTICULTURAL OPPORTUNITY 1-2

Ask students to research prominent women scientists or scientists who represent various ethnic groups. For example: Myra Adele Logan, an African-American physician, was the first woman to perform open-heart surgery; Hilda Geiringer, a Jewish academic who was forced to flee Germany and come to the United States in the 1930s, made significant contributions in the field of probability and statistics; Luis W. Alvarez, a Spanish American, won the Nobel prize for his study of subatomic particles; C. H. Li, a Chinese immigrant, was the first to isolate human growth hormone.

ESL STRATEGY 1-2

To reinforce some of the terms used in this section, have students match the words in Column A with their definitions in Column B.

Column A	Column B
1. theory	**a.** done to see if hypothesis is correct
2. hypothesis	
3. microscopic level	**b.** the world around you
	c. recorded observations
4. macroscopic level	**d.** unable to see with eyes alone
5. data	**e.** factor being tested
6. variable	**f.** proposed solution to a problem
7. experiment	**g.** logical explanation

1-1 Section Review

1. What is the goal of science?
2. Describe the three main branches of science. Give an example of a question that might be asked by scientists in each branch.

Critical Thinking—*Applying Concepts*
3. How might advances in technology affect the kinds of questions scientists ask about the world?

Guide for Reading

Focus on these questions as you read.

▶ *What is the scientific method?*
▶ *How does it help scientists to discover truths about nature?*

1-2 The Scientific Method— A Way of Problem Solving

You have read about the goal of science, the branches of science, and the types of questions scientists ask. By now you may be wondering just what separates science from other subject areas. After all, historians ask questions about the causes of conflicts between nations, philosophers ask questions about the nature of existence, and experts on literature seek the hidden meaning and symbolism in great novels. In fact, just about every area of study asks questions about the world. So what's so special about science?

What distinguishes science from other fields of study is the way in which science seeks answers to questions. In other words, what separates science is an approach called the **scientific method.** The scientific method is a systematic approach to problem solving. **The basic steps in the scientific method are**

> **Stating the problem**
> **Gathering information on the problem**
> **Forming a hypothesis**
> **Performing experiments to test the hypothesis**
> **Recording and analyzing data**
> **Stating a conclusion**
> **Repeating the work**

1-1 continued

ENRICHMENT

▶ *Activity Book*

Because scientists study both very small quantities as well as very large ones, they need convenient ways to record a wide range of numbers.

The symbols called exponents and their use in scientific notation are frequently used in scientific work. Students will gain a better understanding of these important scientific tools in the Chapter 1 activities called Practice With Exponents and Scientific Notation.

INDEPENDENT PRACTICE

Section Review 1-1

1. The goal of science is to understand the world around us.

2. Life science deals with living things and their parts and actions. Earth science is the study of the Earth and its rocks, oceans, volcanoes, earthquakes, atmosphere, and other features. Physical science is the study of matter and energy. Questions will vary.

3. Answers will vary. Technological advances may provide answers to current scientific problems as well as opening up new areas of exploration. For example, a more powerful type of microscope or telescope could extend the boundaries of scientific research.

REINFORCEMENT/RETEACHING

Review students' responses to the Section Review questions. Reteach any material that is still unclear, based on their responses.

The following example shows how the scientific method was used to solve a problem. As you will see, the steps of the scientific method often overlap.

Stating the Problem

Bundled up in warm clothing, heads bent into the wind, two friends walked along the beach. Drifts of snow rose against the slats of a fence that in the summer held back dunes of sand. Beyond the fence, a row of beach houses drew the attention of the friends.

There, from the roofs of the houses, hung glistening strips of ice. Only yesterday these beautiful icicles had been a mass of melting snow. Throughout the night, the melted snow had continued to drip, freezing into lovely shapes.

Near the ocean's edge, the friends spied a small pool of sea water. Surprisingly, it was not frozen as were the icicles on the roofs. What could be the reason for this curious observation, the friends wondered?

Without realizing it, the friends had taken an important step in the scientific method. They had recognized a scientific problem. A scientist might state this problem in another way: What causes fresh water to freeze at a higher temperature than sea water?

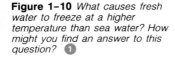

ACTIVITY WRITING

Changing Theories

Albert Einstein once stated that he would consider his work a failure if new and better theories did not replace his own. Using the following words, write an essay describing how new evidence can change an existing theory. ❶

data
variable
hypothesis
scientific method
control
experiment
conclusions

Figure 1–10 *What causes fresh water to freeze at a higher temperature than sea water? How might you find an answer to this question?* ❶

A ■ 19

ACTIVITY WRITING

CHANGING THEORIES

This activity will help to reinforce the concept that a theory may well be accepted for a time and then shown to be false or modified to fit new data.

Integration: Use this Activity to integrate language arts into your science lesson.

an answer to a problem, they usually use the scientific method. Explain that the scientific method is an orderly and systematic approach to solving a problem. Tell students that the scientific method has seven basic steps. Write the steps on the chalkboard as you say them.

CONTENT DEVELOPMENT

Point out that before you can solve a problem, you must understand what the problem is and be able to state the problem. Explain that problems come in all sizes and forms. But to get the right answers to a problem, you must ask the right questions. Explain that stating the problem is sometimes one of the hardest steps in the scientific method.

REINFORCEMENT/RETEACHING
▶ *Activity Book*

Students who are learning about the scientific method for the first time should be provided with the Chapter 1 activity called The Case of the Sleeping Frog.

CLOSURE
▶ *Review and Reinforcement Guide*

Have students complete Section 1–1 in their *Review and Reinforcement Guide*.

TEACHING STRATEGY 1-2

FOCUS/MOTIVATION

Have students imagine that they are to meet a friend at a certain store in the shopping center at two o'clock. They are

ten minutes late, and the friend is not there.

• **What is the problem?** (Where is the friend?)

• **What evidence do you have?** (Accept all logical answers.)

• **How could you collect more evidence?** (Accept all logical answers.)

• **How is this situation similar to a scientific problem?** (Accept all logical answers.)

Explain that when scientists search for

1–2 (continued)

CONTENT DEVELOPMENT

Point out that a suggested solution to a problem is called a hypothesis. A hypothesis involves not only logic but hunches, intuition, and the taking of chances. Tell students that a hypothesis should not only consist of all the known facts but should also predict other things or events that are likely to occur. There are two main parts to a hypothesis: an explanation and a prediction.

Have students state the scientific problem that is suggested by each observation. Then ask them to form at least one hypothesis for each problem. If students feel that more information is needed before a hypothesis can be formed, they should indicate the type of information that is needed and how it might be obtained.

1. Fossils of tropical marine animals have been found in the mountains of northern Canada.
2. A survey of pets in a certain town indicates that 50 percent of all dogs have fleas, whereas only 20 percent of all cats have fleas.

3. Areas at or near the equator have 12 hours of light and 12 hours of darkness all year round.
4. When a bar magnet is suspended horizontally from a string, one end of the magnet always points north.
5. The water in Red Creek is considerably colder than the water in Meadow Lake, even though the two bodies of water are within a few hundred meters of each other.

Gathering Information on the Problem

A scientist might begin to solve the problem by gathering information. The scientist would first find out how the sea water in the pool differs from the fresh water on the roof. This information might include the following facts: The pool of sea water rests on sand, while the fresh water drips along a tar roof. The sea water is exposed to the cold air for less time than the fresh water. The sea water is saltier than the fresh water.

Forming a Hypothesis

Using all of the information that has been gathered, the scientist might be prepared to suggest a possible solution to the problem. A proposed solution to a scientific problem is called a **hypothesis** (high-PAHTH-uh-sihs). A hypothesis almost always follows the gathering of information about a problem. But sometimes a hypothesis is a sudden idea that springs from a new and original way of looking at a problem.

Among the hypotheses that might be suggested as solutions to our problem is this: Because fresh water does not contain salt, it freezes at a higher temperature than sea water.

Performing Experiments to Test the Hypothesis

A scientist does not stop once a hypothesis has been suggested. In science, evidence that either supports a hypothesis or does not support it must be found. This means that a hypothesis must be tested to show whether or not it is correct. Such testing is usually done by performing experiments.

Experiments are performed according to specific rules. By following these rules, scientists can be confident that the evidence they uncover will clearly support or not support a hypothesis. For the problem of the sea water and fresh water, a scientist would have to design an experiment that ruled out every factor but salt as the cause of the different freezing temperatures.

Let's see how a scientist would actually do this. First, the scientist would put equal amounts of fresh water into two identical containers. Then the scientist would add salt to only one of the containers. The salt is the **variable,** or the factor being tested. In any experiment, only one variable should be tested at a time. In this way, the scientist can be fairly certain that the results of the experiment are caused by one and only one factor—in this case the variable of salt. To eliminate the possibility of hidden or unknown variables, the scientist must run a **control** experiment. A control experiment is set up exactly like the one that contains the variable. The only difference is that the control experiment does not contain the variable.

In this experiment, the scientist uses two containers of the same size with equal amounts of water. The water in both containers is at the same starting temperature. The containers are placed side by side in the freezing compartment of a refrigerator and checked every five minutes. *But only one container has salt in it.* In this way, the scientist can be fairly sure that any differences that occur in the two containers are due to the single variable of salt. In such experiments, the part of the experiment with the variable is called the experimental setup. The part of the experiment with the control is called the control setup.

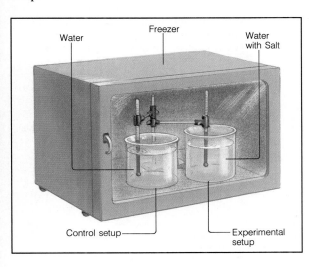

Water   Freezer   Water with Salt

Control setup   Experimental setup

Figure 1–11 *What is the variable in this experiment? Explain your answer.*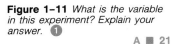

A ■ 21

ACTIVITY
DISCOVERING

To Grow or Not to Grow?

Your friend tells you that plants grow more slowly when salt is added to their soil.

1. Design and conduct an experiment to find out if this is true. Make sure your experiment has both a control and a variable.

2. Record all data and make a graph of your results.

■ What conclusion can you draw from the graph?

INTERPRETING GRAPHS

When interpreting a graph, it is important to note the slope of the line or curve. Slope is defined as the change in y divided by the change in x. This means that slope is equal to the change in the dependent variable with respect to the change in the independent variable.

When the dependent variable is changing very rapidly with regard to the independent variable, the slope is great, and the line or curve is steep. When the dependent variable is changing gradually with regard to the independent variable, the slope is small, and the line or curve rises gently.

1-2 (continued)

FOCUS/MOTIVATION

Collect a number of graphs from newspapers or magazines. Show the graphs to the class.

• **Why do you think graphs are used with newspaper and magazine articles?** (Answers will vary.)

• **How do graphs help us understand?** (Graphs are helpful because they make it easy to interpret data.)

CONTENT DEVELOPMENT

Explain that while an experiment is being conducted, scientists keep accurate data. Because large amounts of data are frequently collected, scientists usually use a data table to record the measures. Have students observe Figure 1–12. Remark that a data table is a simple way to keep records. Read the caption. Explain that time intervals of five minutes are at the top of each table. The temperature for each time interval is recorded just below.

• **What was the temperature of the unsalted water after 20 minutes?** (Accept only the answer in the data table: 5°C.)

• **What was the temperature of the water-salt mixture after 20 minutes?** (Accept only the answer in the data table: 5°C.)

Recording and Analyzing Data

To determine whether salt affects the freezing temperature of water, a scientist must observe the experiment and write down important information. Recorded observations and measurements are called **data.** In this experiment, the data would include the time intervals at which the containers were observed, the temperatures of the water at each interval, and whether the water in either container was frozen or not. In most cases the data would be recorded in data tables such as those shown in Figure 1–12.

Data tables are a simple, organized way of recording information from an experiment. Sometimes, however, it is useful to visually compare the data. To do so, a scientist might construct a graph on which to plot the data. Because the data tables have two different types of measurements (time and temperature), the graph would have two axes. See Figure 1–13.

The horizontal axis of the graph would stand for the time measurements in the data tables. Time measurements were made every 5 minutes. So the horizontal axis would be marked with intervals of 5 minutes. The space between equal intervals would have to be equal. For example, the space between 10 minutes and 15 minutes would be the same as the space between 20 minutes and 25 minutes.

The vertical axis of the graph would stand for the temperature measurements in the data tables. The starting temperature of the water in the experiment was 25°C. The lowest temperature reached in the

Figure 1-12 *Scientists often record their observations in data tables. According to these data tables, at what temperature did the experiment begin? At what time intervals were the temperature measurements taken?* ❶

WATER (Control setup)							
Time (min)	0	5	10	15	20	25	30
Temperature (°C)	25	20	15	10	5	0*	−10
* Asterisk means liquid has frozen.							
WATER WITH SALT (experimental setup)							
Time (min)	0	5	10	15	20	25	30
Temperature (°C)	25	20	15	10	5	0	−10*

• **What was the temperature of the control setup after 30 minutes?** (Accept only the answer in the data table: −10°C.)

• **What was the temperature of the experimental setup after 30 minutes?** (Accept only the answer in the data table: −10°C.)

• **After how many minutes did the water-salt solution freeze?** (Accept only the answer in the data table: 30 minutes.)

GUIDED PRACTICE

Skills Development

Skill: Interpreting graphs

Explain that although a data table allows a scientist to record a large amount of data in a small space, the data are not always easy to interpret in table form. A scientist will frequently use a graph to help understand the data. Have students

experiment was −10°C. So the vertical axis would begin with 25°C and end at −10°C. Each interval of temperature would have to be equal to every other interval of temperature.

After the axes of the graph were set up, the scientist would first graph the data from the experimental setup. Each pair of data points from the data table would be marked on the graph. At 0 minutes, for example, the temperature was 25°C. So the scientist would place a dot where 0 minutes and 25°C intersect—in the lower left corner of the graph. The next pair of data points was for 5 minutes and 20°C. So the scientist would lightly draw a vertical line from the 5-minute interval of the horizontal axis and then a horizontal line from the 20°C interval of the vertical axis. The scientist would then put a dot at the place where the two lines intersected. This dot would represent the data points 5 minutes and 20°C. The scientist would continue to plot all of the data pairs from the data table in this manner.

When all of the data pairs were plotted, the scientist would draw a line through all the dots. This line would represent the graph of the experimental setup data. Then the scientist would follow the same procedure to graph the data pairs from the control setup. Figure 1–13 shows what the two lines would look like.

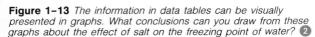

ACTIVITY

DISCOVERING

Graphing Temperatures

1. Over a ten-day period, read the weather section of a newspaper.

2. Each day, record in a chart the day's date and the high and low temperatures for the town nearest where you live.

3. After ten days, plot your data in a graph. Use the vertical axis for temperature and the horizontal axis for day. Use red pencil for daily high temperatures and blue pencil for daily low temperatures. ❶

4. Draw lines connecting the points for both the daily highs and lows.

■ Based on your graph, write a short essay describing the temperature patterns you observed.

Figure 1–13 *The information in data tables can be visually presented in graphs. What conclusions can you draw from these graphs about the effect of salt on the freezing point of water?* ❷

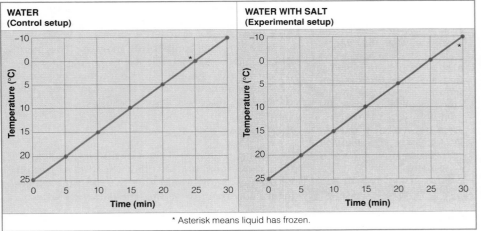
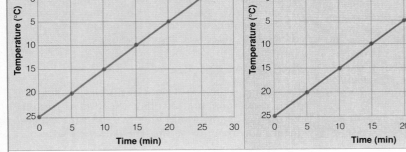

* Asterisk means liquid has frozen.

ACTIVITY

DISCOVERING

GRAPHING TEMPERATURES

Discovery Learning

Skills: Making observations, making comparisons, making calculations, making graphs

This activity will provide students with experience in obtaining data and recording those data. By graphing the high and low temperatures, students will gain experience in graphing skills as well. Students will likely note that temperature ranges vary considerably between high and low temperatures. The amount of variation will be somewhat dependent on the area in which they live and the time of year.

Integration: Use this Activity to integrate mathematics into your science lesson.

observe Figure 1–13. Explain that the data from Figure 1–12 was plotted on a grid to make the graphs.

• **Which axis shows the time elapsed?** (The horizontal axis shows the time elapsed.)

• **Which axis shows the temperature?** (The vertical axis shows the temperature.)

• **Which graph shows the control setup?** (The graph at the left shows the control setup.)

• **Which graph shows the experimental setup?** (The graph at the right shows the experimental setup.)

• **How are the graphs similar?** (Both graphs have the same scales on the axes, and the lines connecting the dots are the same.)

• **How are the graphs different?** (One graph shows the control data, and the other graph shows the experimental data. The freezing point is different on the graphs.)

INDEPENDENT PRACTICE

▶ *Product Testing Activity*

Have students perform the product test on bubble gum from the Product Testing Activity worksheets. In this product test students will use graphing and statistical skills to help them evaluate data and organize their results.

REINFORCEMENT/RETEACHING

▶ *Activity Book*

A simple introduction to the use of the scientific method is provided by the Chapter 1 activity called Explain Why.

ACTIVITY
DOING

EXPANDING WATER?

Skills: Making observations, applying concepts, making inferences

Materials: small pan, water, freezer unit

Through this activity students will discover that unlike most substances, water expands when it freezes. In designing the procedure, students should plan to check on the status of the water at regular intervals and record their observations at each step.

Students will easily be able to see that water expands when it freezes because the frozen water will have risen above the top of the container.

1-2 (continued)

REINFORCEMENT/RETEACHING

Have students research magazines to find graphs. Teams might share and discuss how each graph helps the reader to interpret the data.

CONTENT DEVELOPMENT

Explain that after the results from many experiments have been gathered and recorded, a scientist can sometimes state a conclusion to the problem. In this experiment a scientist might conclude that "salt lowers the temperature at which water freezes." The original hypothesis "Does salt lower the freezing point of water?" would be answered yes. Point out that a scientist might decide to

Figure 1-14 *Based on what you have learned, can you explain why mountain roads are often salted before a snowfall? What evidence do you have that this road was salted?* ①

The results from a single experiment are not enough to reach a conclusion. A scientist must run an experiment over and over again before the data can be considered accurate. From the data in this experiment, the scientist would quickly find that the temperatures in both containers fall at the same rate. But the fresh water freezes at a higher temperature than the salt water.

Stating a Conclusion

If the two friends walking along the beach had followed the same steps as a scientist, they would now be ready to state a conclusion. Their conclusion would be this: When salt is dissolved in water, the freezing temperature of the water goes down. For this reason, fresh water freezes at a higher temperature than does sea water.

Why does this happen, you may ask? This question sounds very much like the beginning of a new puzzle. It often happens in science that the solution of one problem leads to yet another problem. Thus the cycle of discovery goes on and on.

Repeating the Work

Although the two friends might be satisfied with their conclusion, not so with a scientist. As you read before, a scientist would want to repeat the experiment many times to be sure the data were accurate.

ACTIVITY
DOING

Expanding Water?

Most substances on Earth contract, or become smaller in volume, when they freeze. Is water an exception? Using a small pan, water, and a freezing compartment, perform an experiment to discover whether or not water contracts when it freezes. Write down what you did in the form of a procedure and your results in the form of a conclusion.

24 ■ A

go further into the investigation and ask another question, such as, "How does salt lower the freezing point of water?"

REINFORCEMENT/RETEACHING

Have students design an experiment to test the hypothesis "Does salt lower the boiling point of water?" After the experiment has been designed, students might do the experiment.

ENRICHMENT

Have students think about other common substances that might lower or raise the boiling or freezing points of water. Then have teams state their hypothesis as a question, design an experiment, and conduct the experiment.

GUIDED PRACTICE

Skills Development

Skill: Applying concepts

Ask students to find the flaws in the following experiments:

1. Gerard wants to find out if egg yolk causes silver to tarnish. He labels two sil-

So a scientific experiment must be able to be repeated. And before the conclusion of a scientist can be accepted by the scientific community, other scientists must repeat the experiment and check the results. So when a scientist writes a report on his or her experiment, that report must be detailed enough so that scientists throughout the world can repeat the experiment for themselves. In most cases, it is only when an experiment has been repeated by scientists worldwide is it considered to be accurate and worthy of being included in new scientific research.

PROBLEM Solving ? ? ?

Fact or Fiction? ❶

Perhaps one of the most interesting aspects of life science is the amazing variety of plants and animals living on planet Earth. Some of these organisms are so unusual that it is often difficult to determine if a statement is true or a figment of someone's imagination. Read the following hypothesis to see what we mean.

Hypothesis: Turtle eggs develop into male turtles in cold temperatures and into female turtles in warm temperatures.

Predict whether this hypothesis is fact or fiction. Then design a simple experiment to show if the hypothesis is or is not correct. Make sure your experiment has an experimental setup and a control setup.

A ■ 25

PROBLEM SOLVING
FACT OR FICTION?

The Problem Solving feature gives students an opportunity to apply the scientific method to a situation in life science.

Here is one way a biologist might design this experiment. A great quantity of turtle eggs is collected. Batches of 25 eggs are put in containers at different temperatures. After 60 days, the following data are recorded:

26°C: 21 males, 2 females
28°C: 13 males, 11 females
30°C: 1 male, 19 females
32°C: 1 male, 20 females

You might put these data on the chalkboard and ask students what conclusions they could make from the data.

Explain that actual research has confirmed that when green turtle eggs are incubated at low temperatures, mostly males hatch. Higher temperatures produce mostly females. Similar studies have shown that temperature variations affect sex determination in other reptiles, too.

Integration: Use the Problem Solving feature to integrate zoology into your lesson.

GUIDED PRACTICE

Skills Development
Skills: Making observations, recording data, relating cause and effect, making inferences

At this point have students complete the in-text Chapter 1 Laboratory Investigation: A Moldy Question. In the investigation students will use experimental procedures and the scientific method to determine variables that affect the growth of mold on bread.

REINFORCEMENT/RETEACHING

▶ *Activity Book*

Students who need practice with the concepts of this section should be provided with the Chapter 1 activity called Just a Spoonful of Sugar. In the activity they will design and conduct a simple experiment to show the effect of adding sugar to the water used for cut flowers.

ver spoons A and B. He puts egg yolk on both spoons. Then he places spoon A in a closed container and leaves spoon B out in the open air. He checks the spoons over the next few days to see if either has tarnished. (Egg yolk, which is supposed to be the variable, should not be put on both spoons. Other factors, such as exposure to air, should be kept the same for both spoons.)

2. Daria wants to find out if fertilizer causes plants to grow taller. She takes two plant shoots of the same size and type and labels them A and B. She adds fertilizer to plant A but not to plant B. Then she places plant A in a sunny window and waters it every day. She places plant B on a bookshelf away from the sun and waters it every other day. (The experiment has too many variables. Daria has varied the amount of light and water each plant receives. Except for the fertilizer, all other conditions should be kept the same.)

Answers

① It would be almost impossible to choose lions for an experimental group and a control group so that only one variable was different between the two groups. (Making inferences)

② Having a jointed foot. (Interpreting charts)

Integration

① Language Arts

② Life Science: Evolution: See *Evolution*, Chapter 2.

1–2 (continued)

CONTENT DEVELOPMENT

Emphasize to students that a scientific problem must be defined by a clear, specific statement. For example, saying that scientists wanted to "learn about Mars" is too general a statement to be considered a workable scientific problem.

Have students determine which of the following statements are clear definitions of a scientific problem. Then have them explain why the other statements do not define a scientific problem.

• **What is the ocean like?** (No; too general.)

• **What causes ocean tides?** (Yes.)

• **How do stars, planets, and galaxies compare?** (No; too broad and too vague.)

• **Why are days longer in the summer than in the winter?** (Yes.)

REINFORCEMENT/RETEACHING

Using seven index cards, write one of the steps of the scientific method on each card. Have students take turns picking the cards at random. Challenge each student to describe the importance of the step he or she has chosen and to give an example of how it might be used in an actual investigation.

Then review the following concepts relating to experimental procedures.

• **What is a variable?** (A variable is some-

thing that might change the results of the experiment.)

• **Why is it important to have only one variable?** (If there were more than one variable, you wouldn't know which variable caused the result.)

• **What would happen if we experimented without a control setup?** (Students might suggest that too many things could go wrong or that we wouldn't know what caused what to happen.)

Activity Bank

What Do Seeds Need to Grow?, p.102

The Scientific Method—Not Always So Orderly

By now it must seem as if science is a fairly predictable way of studying the world. After all, you state a problem, gather information, form a hypothesis, run an experiment, and determine a conclusion. It certainly sounds all neat and tidy. Well, sometimes it is—and sometimes it isn't!

In practice, scientists do not always follow all the steps in the scientific method. Nor do the steps always follow the same order. For example, while doing an experiment a scientist might observe something unusual or unexpected. That unexpected event might cause the scientist to discard the original hypothesis and suggest a new one. In this case, the hypothesis actually followed the experiment. In other cases, the problem to be studied might not be where the scientist begins. Let's go back to those unexpected results. Those results might cause the scientist to rethink the way she or he looks at the world. They might suggest new problems that need to be considered. In this case, the problem followed the experiment.

As you already learned, a good rule to follow is that all experiments should have only one variable. Sometimes, however, scientists run experiments with

Figure 1–15 *Why would it be difficult to study the effects of a single variable on these East African lions?* ①

CONTENT DEVELOPMENT

Point out that once a hypothesis is developed, the scientist must continue research and must perform activities that will prove the hypothesis to be right or wrong. Explain that all activities and/or observations must be "for" or "against" the hypothesis to be of any service. If experiments support the hypothesis, the hypothesis is strengthened. If experiments contradict the hypothesis, the hypothesis must be reviewed and possibly changed.

Prefix	Meaning	Prefix	Meaning	Suffix	Meaning
anti-	against	herb-	pertaining to plants	-cyst	pouch
arth-	joint, jointed	hetero-	different	-derm	skin, layer
auto-	self	homeo-	same	-gen	producing
bio-	related to life	macro-	large	-itis	inflammation
chloro-	green	micro-	small	-logy	study
cyto-	cell	multi-	consisting of many units	-meter	measurement
di-	double	osteo-	bone	-osis	condition, disease
epi-	above	photo-	pertaining to light	-phage	eater
exo-	outer, external	plasm-	forming substance	-phase	stage
gastro-	stomach	proto-	first	-pod	foot
hemo-	blood	syn-	together	-stasis	stationary condition

Figure 1–16 *A working knowledge of prefixes and suffixes used in science vocabulary will be of great help to you. According to this chart, what is the meaning of the term arthropod?* ❷

several variables. Naturally, the data in such experiments are much more difficult to analyze. For example, suppose scientists want to study lions in their natural environment in Africa. It is not likely they will be able to eliminate all the variables in the environment and concentrate on just a single one. So although a single variable is a good rule—and one that you will follow in almost all of the experiments you design or perform—it is not always practical in the real world.

There is yet another step in the scientific method that cannot always be followed. Believe it or not, many scientists search for the truths of nature without ever performing experiments. Sometimes the best they can rely on are observations and natural curiosity. Here's an example. Charles Darwin is considered the father of the theory of evolution (how living things change over time). Much of what we know about evolution is based on Darwin's work. Yet Darwin did not perform a single experiment! He based his hypotheses and theories on his observations of the natural world. Certainly it would have been better had Darwin performed experiments to prove his theory of evolution. But as the process of evolution generally takes thousands, even millions of years, performing an experiment would be a bit too time consuming!

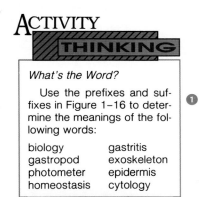

ACTIVITY
THINKING

What's the Word?

Use the prefixes and suffixes in Figure 1–16 to determine the meanings of the following words: ❶

biology	gastritis
gastropod	exoskeleton
photometer	epidermis
homeostasis	cytology

A ■ 27

ACTIVITY
DISCOVERING

A ROCKY OBSERVATION

Discovery Learning

Skills: Making observations, making comparisons

Materials: 4 rocks, masking tape

Through this activity students will gain experience in using observational skills. Students will discover which features of a rock are of most help when describing that rock to another person and which observations are of little help in aiding an outside observer to identify an unknown sample on the basis of its characteristics.

Integration: Use this Activity to integrate geology into your lesson.

1–2 (continued)

FOCUS/MOTIVATION

Students may enjoy applying the steps of the scientific method to the solution of everyday problems.

• **How could the steps of the scientific method be applied to fixing a broken bicycle?** (Answers may vary. The scientific method could help in diagnosing the problem and its cause, as well as in testing possible solutions to the problem.)

• **How might you apply the scientific method to the problem of reducing heating costs in your home?** (Answers may vary. The scientific method could include gathering information about energy costs and conservation, forming a hypothesis as to what measures would save money, and then experimenting to

---

ACTIVITY
DISCOVERING

A Rocky Observation

To be useful, one person's observations must give meaningful information to another person.

1. Obtain four rocks of about equal size.

2. Place a small piece of masking tape on each rock and number the rocks 1 through 4.

3. On a sheet of paper, write down as many observations as you can about each rock next to its number.

4. Rewrite your observations without numbers on another sheet of paper. Give this sheet of paper and the rocks to a classmate.

5. Ask your classmate to match the observations to the rocks.

■ Did your classmate make correct matches? Why or why not?

The Scientific Method in Your World

A common question often asked by students is "Why are we studying science? What does it have to do with my world?" The answer is—plenty! Perhaps you have no real interest in the reason why fresh water freezes at a higher temperature than sea water. Maybe you live in a city or in a part of the country far removed from a beach. But regardless of where you live, people probably drive cars. And that means they may worry about the water in the car's radiator freezing in the winter and boiling over in the summer. How do we prevent these events from occurring? You probably know the answer—we add antifreeze to the radiator.

The principles behind the actions of antifreeze are exactly the same as the principles behind the fresh and salt water experiment. Adding antifreeze lowers the temperature at which the water freezes—an important point to know during the cold winter months. And, strangely enough, in much the same way antifreeze increases the boiling temperature of water so that cars are not as likely to overheat during the hot summer months.

You should keep this example in mind whenever you study science. For very often the concepts you are learning about have very practical applications in your world. When possible, we will point out the relevance of the material you are studying. But that may not always be practical. So it's up to you to remember that science is not just for laboratory workers in white coats. Science affects all of us—each and every day of our lives.

1–2 Section Review

1. List and describe the steps in the scientific method.
2. Explain the importance of running both an experimental setup and a control setup.

Connection—*You and Your World*

3. One morning you wake up and discover that your radio no longer works. How might you apply the steps of the scientific method to determine the cause of the problem?

---

determine which measures actually would cut costs.)

Remind students that the scientific method is a logical approach to problem solving. Although the steps of the scientific method may not fit everyday problems exactly, the idea of approaching problems in a logical and an orderly way is an important skill that can be learned from the scientific method.

Media and Technology

Using the Interactive Videodisc/CD ROM called Paul ParkRanger and the Mystery of the Disappearing Ducks, students can begin to relate the concepts they have learned regarding the scientific method with an actual scientific mystery. Searching through Paul ParkRanger's cabin for clues, as well as interviewing experts and performing simulated experiments, students will begin to develop a hypothesis regarding the missing ducks.

CONNECTIONS

Messages From Outer Space? ❷

Have we been receiving radio messages from outer space? In 1933, people believed we were. They were wrong, but their mistake is an interesting example of how luck, or serendipity, plays a role in science and, in this case, can shake up society for a little while.

Here's how it all happened. In 1931, Bell Telephone scientists wanted to find out what was causing static on some radio telephone lines. The scientists suspected (hypothesized) that the static might be caused by thunderstorms. They asked a young scientist named Karl Jansky to see if he could find out whether this was true. Jansky built a special antenna to try to solve the problem. He mounted his antenna on some wheels from an old car so that he could aim the antenna at any part of the sky. Because it could be turned around, Jansky's invention was nicknamed "the merry-go-round."

Jansky found that almost all of the static was indeed caused by radio waves from thunderstorms. But his an-

tenna had also picked up a faint hissing sound that he could not explain. Jansky could have shrugged his shoulders and ignored this hissing sound, but his curiosity got the best of him. So he decided to investigate. He would try to track down the hissing sounds.

Jansky carried on observations for two years. Eventually, he found that the hiss moved across the sky, as did the stars. In 1933, Jansky announced that the radio waves producing the hissing sound were actually coming to Earth from outer space! Jansky's discovery that radio waves were coming from space became an overnight sensation. Newspaper headlines throughout the world reported the finding. But after only a few weeks, most people seemed to forget Jansky's discovery.

Then, in 1937, an amateur radio operator named Grote Reber had a hunch that Jansky's discovery was important. So Reber built a 10-meter dish antenna in his backyard to capture the radio waves from space. This instrument became the world's first radio telescope. Jansky's unexpected discovery and Reber's hunch gave astronomers a new way of exploring the sky. The science of *radio astronomy,* which would produce many exciting discoveries of its own, had been born.

CONNECTIONS
MESSAGES FROM OUTER SPACE?

The Connections activity describes the beginnings of radio astronomy. In this field astronomers use radio waves rather than light waves to explore and interpret outer space.

Using his homemade radio telescope, Reber was the first to prepare a radio map of the sky. For several years, Reber was the only radio astronomer in the world.

The first really large radio telescope was not built until the 1950s. Constructed at Jodrell Bank Experimental Station in Great Britain under the leadership of the British astronomer Bernard Lovell, the telescope took six years to build. It was then used to track the Soviet satellite *Sputnik* as it revolved about the Earth in 1957.

If you are teaching thematically, you may want to use the Connections feature to reinforce the themes of scale and structure and systems and interactions.

Integration: Use the Connections feature to integrate astronomy into your lesson.

Point out to students that the correct answer to the mystery—if there is one—is less important than the ways in which they go about exploring this mystery of nature.

INDEPENDENT PRACTICE

Section Review 1–2

1. The basic steps in the scientific method are stating the problem, gathering information on the problem, forming a hypothesis, performing experiments to test the hypothesis, recording and analyzing data, stating a conclusion, and repeating the work.

2. An experiment must have only one variable. The control setup should differ from the experimental setup in just one way—the variable being investigated should be absent. In this way, a scientist can be fairly certain that the variable does or does not cause the results.

3. Answers will vary. Students might start by investigating the source of power. Is the radio powered by electricity or battery? If electricity, are any other electrical devices not working? Perhaps the problem is in the wall outlet. If so, try plugging the radio into another outlet. If the radio is battery-operated, try replacing the battery.

REINFORCEMENT/RETEACHING

Review students' responses to the Section Review questions. Reteach any material that is still unclear, based on their responses.

CLOSURE

▶ *Review and Reinforcement Guide*

Have students complete Section 1–2 in their *Review and Reinforcement Guide.*

1-3 Science and Discovery

MULTICULTURAL OPPORTUNITY 1-3

Encourage students to research the work of famous minority scientists. Have students tell how luck, as well as hard work and preparation, played a role in their discoveries. There are many books about the life and work of such important African-American scientists as George Washington Carver and Benjamin Banneker. Suggest that students consult *The Negro Almanac: A Reference Work on the African-American* edited by Harry Ploski or *The Encyclopedia of Black Americans* edited by W. A. Low and Virgil Clift.

ESL STRATEGY 1-3

Give students the names of several scientists whose discoveries were a result of serendipity. Have them choose one scientist to research. Ask volunteers to share their findings with their classmates by giving brief oral reports.

ANNOTATION KEY

Integration
❶ Life Science: Evolution. See *Evolution*, Chapter 1.
❷ Language Arts

TEACHING STRATEGY 1-3

FOCUS/MOTIVATION

Ask students to think about the last time that luck played a beneficial role in their lives. Have a few volunteers share their experiences with the class.

CONTENT DEVELOPMENT

One of the best-known instances of the role of luck in scientific discovery is that of vulcanized rubber. Natural rubber was not very stable when the temperature changed. When too cold, it stiffened and

---

1-3 Science and Discovery

Scientific discoveries are not always made by following the scientific method. **Sometimes a discovery is made because of luck, a hunch, or a new way of looking at (observing) the world.** Remember, the most important trait of any scientist is curiosity. And some of the greatest sparks of curiosity have been experienced when they were least expected.

Recently, two American biologists, Dr. Patricia Bonamo and Dr. James Grierson, discovered a special group of fossils. Fossils are the remains of organisms that lived in the past. While looking for extinct plant specimens in rocks from northern New York, these scientists found something different and unexpected. Instead of plant fossils, the scientists discovered fossils of some of the first land animals. Fossilized centipedes, shells and claws of spiderlike creatures, and a single mite were discovered.

There was much that was amazing about this discovery. The centipede, only 2.54 centimeters long, had its many pairs of legs well preserved. The sense organs of several of the spiderlike creatures were easily recognizable.

Scientists described the fossils as looking as though "they might have died yesterday." But these organisms had not died "yesterday," and that was the most amazing discovery of all. Tests showed that the animals had died about 380 million years ago! Until this discovery, the earliest totally land-living

Figure 1–17 *An artist's concept of what Earth's forests looked like some 350 million years ago.*

---

became brittle. And when it became too hot, it grew soft and sticky.

Then in 1839, the American inventor Charles Goodyear (1800–1860) had a stroke of luck. He was trying to add sulfur to rubber when some of the mixture accidentally came into contact with a hot stove.

• **What do you think most people would have done in Goodyear's place?** (Answers will vary. Students might suggest that they would have thrown away the burned mess and started over.)

To Goodyear's astonishment, pieces of rubber that weren't scorched too badly became dry and flexible. He began to experiment by heating the rubber-sulfur mixture to higher temperatures than anyone else had tried and thus obtained vulcanized rubber.

● ● ● ● **Integration** ● ● ● ●

Use the discussion of the fossils of land animals to integrate the concept of evolution into your lesson.

animals ever discovered had been 300 million years old. Drs. Bonamo and Grierson had turned back the birthday of such animals by 80 million years.

"When we first saw the animals in our samples, we thought they might have fallen in by accident, from the light fixtures or cracks in the wall. But one spiderlike animal had its legs still embedded in the rock." This statement by Drs. Bonamo and Grierson shows how their fossil discovery was an exciting piece of good luck. But it is also an example of scientists recognizing something special when they see it.

1–3 Section Review

1. The term serendipity means making a fortunate discovery through an accident. What role does serendipity play in science?

Critical Thinking—*Making Generalizations*
2. What does this fossil discovery indicate about the appearance of land-living animals?

1–4 Safety in the Science Laboratory

The scientific laboratory is a place of adventure and discovery. Some of the most exciting events in scientific history have happened in the laboratory. For example, the structure of DNA, the blueprint of life, was discovered by scientists in the laboratory. The plastics used today for clothing and other products were first made by scientists in a laboratory. And the laboratory was where scientists discovered the relationship between electricity and magnetism. The list goes on and on.

To better understand the concepts you will read about in science, it is likely you will work in the laboratory too. If you follow instructions and are as careful as a scientist would be, the laboratory will turn out to be an exciting experience for you.

Scientists know that when working in the laboratory, it is very important to follow safety procedures.

ACTIVITY READING

An Unexpected World

You would be amazed at the microscopic creatures that share your home with you. If you are interested in these strange organisms, read *The Secret House,* by David Bodanis. You will never look at your room in quite the same way again!

Guide for Reading

Focus on this question as you read.

▶ *What important safety rules must you follow when working in the laboratory?*

1-4 Safety in the Science Laboratory

MULTICULTURAL OPPORTUNITY 1-4

Have students work in small groups to identify some of the safety rules that they use in their daily lives; for example, "Look both ways before crossing the street" and "Don't accept rides from strangers."

If you have students from different countries in your class, ask them to tell the class some of the safety rules used in their countries. Note that international safety signs exist and are often used.

ESL STRATEGY 1-4

Explain the Safety Rules and Symbols Chart to students. Use gestures to clarify significant features of each rule. Mention that the symbol for glassware is called a flask; however, test tubes, beakers, and bottles are also considered glassware and can be broken easily.

ACTIVITY READING

AN UNEXPECTED WORLD

In this activity students will discover some of the interesting facts about microscopic animals. Point out that the public library contains many books and magazines dealing with popular science. **Integration:** Use this Activity to integrate language arts into your science lesson.

INDEPENDENT PRACTICE

▶ *Product Testing Activity*

Have students perform the product test on shampoo from the Product Testing Activity worksheets. Discuss how a knowledge of the scientific method may help them become more knowledgeable consumers.

INDEPENDENT PRACTICE

Section Review 1–3
1. Serendipity sometimes results in new scientific discoveries or inventions—as long as the scientist is alert and curious when unexpected events occur.
2. The fossils suggest that land-living animals existed earlier in history than was previously thought.

REINFORCEMENT/RETEACHING

Review students' responses to the Section Review questions. Reteach any material that is still unclear, based on their responses.

CLOSURE

▶ *Review and Reinforcement Guide*

Have students complete Section 1–3 in their *Review and Reinforcement Guide.*

TEACHING STRATEGY 1–4

FOCUS/MOTIVATION

Display some or all of the following items: safety goggles, heat-resistant gloves, fire extinguisher, laboratory apron, first-aid kit.

• **What do you think these items have to do with work in the scientific laboratory?** (Answers may vary; guide students to recognize that these items relate to laboratory safety.)

CONTENT DEVELOPMENT

Continue the Motivation discussion by emphasizing to students the need for laboratory safety.

• **What are some laboratory safety rules that you already know?** (Answers will vary.)

Make a transparency and/or enlarged photocopy of each of the eight safety-precaution symbols. Use the copy as a focal point during a discussion of laboratory safety rules, precautions, and emergency procedures. Point out and quiz students on each listed safety precaution. In addition to the items listed, you might ask (or explain) the following questions:

• **What should you do if you accidentally get cut with broken glass?** (Accept all logical answers and explain the procedures for your school.)

• **Where is the closest fire extinguisher? How is it used in an emergency?** (Accept all logical answers and explain the procedures for your school.)

• **Where is the closest fire blanket? How is it used in an emergency?** (Accept all logical answers and explain the procedures for your school.)

• **How should we report a fire?** (Accept all logical answers and explain the procedures for your school.)

• **Where would you find the heat-resistant gloves?** (Accept all logical answers

Figure 1–18 *It is important to always point a test tube that is being heated away from yourself and your classmates (right). What two safety precautions is this student taking before picking up a hot beaker (left)?* ①

The most important safety rule is to always follow your teacher's directions or the directions in your textbook exactly as stated. You should never try anything on your own without asking your teacher first. And when you are not sure what you should do, always ask first.

As you read the laboratory investigations in your textbook, you will see safety alert symbols. These symbols indicate that special safety precautions must be taken. Look at Figure 1–19 to learn the meanings of these safety symbols and the important safety procedures you should take.

In addition to the safety procedures listed in Figure 1–19, there is a more detailed list of safety procedures in Appendix B on page 112 at the back of this textbook. Before you enter the laboratory for the first time, make sure you have read each rule carefully. Then read all the rules over again, making sure you understand each rule. If you do not understand a rule, ask your teacher to explain it. You may even want to suggest further rules that apply to your particular classroom.

1–4 Section Review

1. What is the most important general rule to follow when working in the laboratory?
2. Suppose your teacher asks you to boil some water in a test tube. What precautions should you take to make sure this activity is done safely?

Connection—*You and Your World*

3. How can you apply the safety rules in Figure 1–19 to rules that should be followed when working in a kitchen? In a machine shop?

and explain the procedures for your school.)

• **What should you do if you accidentally burn your fingers or hands?** (Accept all logical answers and explain the procedures for your school.)

• **What should you do if a chemical is accidentally spilled on your face, skin, or clothing?** (Accept all logical answers and explain the procedures for your school. Point out the location of the nearest shower and eye-wash station.)

• **What should you do if your face or eyes are accidentally injured?** (Accept all logical answers and explain the procedures for your school. Point out the location of the nearest shower and eye-wash station.)

• **What should you do if you accidentally cut yourself?** (Accept all logical answers and explain the procedures for your school.

• **What should you do if you see an electric cord close to spilled water?** (Accept

Glassware Safety

1. Whenever you see this symbol, you will know that you are working with glassware that can easily be broken. Take particular care to handle such glassware safely. And never use broken or chipped glassware.
2. Never heat glassware that is not thoroughly dry. Never pick up any glassware unless you are sure it is not hot. If it is hot, use heat-resistant gloves.
3. Always clean glassware thoroughly before putting it away.

Fire Safety

1. Whenever you see this symbol, you will know that you are working with fire. Never use any source of fire without wearing safety goggles.
2. Never heat anything—particularly chemicals—unless instructed to do so.
3. Never heat anything in a closed container.
4. Never reach across a flame.
5. Always use a clamp, tongs, or heat-resistant gloves to handle hot objects.
6. Always maintain a clean work area, particularly when using a flame.

Heat Safety

Whenever you see this symbol, you will know that you should put on heat-resistant gloves to avoid burning your hands.

Chemical Safety

1. Whenever you see this symbol, you will know that you are working with chemicals that could be hazardous.
2. Never smell any chemical directly from its container. Always use your hand to waft some of the odors from the top of the container toward your nose—and only when instructed to do so.
3. Never mix chemicals unless instructed to do so.
4. Never touch or taste any chemical unless instructed to do so.
5. Keep all lids closed when chemicals are not in use. Dispose of all chemicals as instructed by your teacher.

6. Immediately rinse with water any chemicals, particularly acids, that get on your skin and clothes. Then notify your teacher.

Eye and Face Safety

1. Whenever you see this symbol, you will know that you are performing an experiment in which you must take precautions to protect your eyes and face by wearing safety goggles.
2. When you are heating a test tube or bottle, always point it away from you and others. Chemicals can splash or boil out of a heated test tube.

Sharp Instrument Safety

1. Whenever you see this symbol, you will know that you are working with a sharp instrument.
2. Always use single-edged razors; double-edged razors are too dangerous.
3. Handle any sharp instrument with extreme care. Never cut any material toward you; always cut away from you.
4. Immediately notify your teacher if your skin is cut.

Electrical Safety

1. Whenever you see this symbol, you will know that you are using electricity in the laboratory.
2. Never use long extension cords to plug in any electrical device. Do not plug too many appliances into one socket or you may overload the socket and cause a fire.
3. Never touch an electrical appliance or outlet with wet hands.

Animal Safety

1. Whenever you see this symbol, you will know that you are working with live animals.
2. Do not cause pain, discomfort, or injury to an animal.
3. Follow your teacher's directions when handling animals. Wash your hands thoroughly after handling animals or their cages.

Figure 1–19 *You should become familiar with these safety symbols because you will see them in the laboratory investigations in this textbook.*

A ■ 33

SAFETY ACTIONS FOR TEACHERS

The following checklist may help you in setting up proper safety procedures for laboratory investigations.

1. Inspect the laboratory area frequently.

2. Report hazards promptly and in writing. Keep a copy of your report.

3. Report all defective equipment to the administration. Never use defective equipment.

4. Always supervise student activities, moving from point to point during the class period.

5. Secure a supply of first-aid materials. Know how to administer first aid.

6. Provide a fire bucket, a fire blanket, a fire extinguisher, and a safety shower in the laboratory.

7. Post all emergency phone numbers that might be needed in an accident situation. Install a telephone, if possible.

curacy and clarity in the Chapter 1 activity called Organizing Data.

INDEPENDENT PRACTICE

Section Review 1–4

1. Always follow your teacher's directions or the directions in your textbook exactly as stated.

2. Wear safety goggles, heat water in an open container, never reach across the flame, use clamp or tongs or heat-resistant gloves, keep work area clean, don't wear loose clothing.

3. The safety rules for glassware, fire, heat, and sharp instruments would apply in a kitchen. In a machine shop, the rules for sharp instruments and electrical safety would be most important.

REINFORCEMENT/RETEACHING

Review students' responses to the Section Review questions. Reteach any material that is still unclear, based on their responses.

CLOSURE

▶ *Review and Reinforcement Guide*

Have students complete Section 1–4 in their *Review and Reinforcement Guide.*

---

all logical answers and explain the procedures for your school.)

• **Why is it important not to cause pain, discomfort, or injury to a laboratory animal?** (Accept all logical answers.)

• **Why is it important to wash your hands after handling animals or animal cages?** (Accept all logical answers.)

Ask your local humane society about information such as pamphlets and booklets that describe humane treatment of animals used in the laboratory. Some humane societies in cities may provide a consultant to visit your classes and discuss appropriate laboratory animal procedures.

Place copies of the safety-precaution page in conspicuous places around the laboratory. Reinforce and/or explain the safety precautions as appropriate for each laboratory investigation.

REINFORCEMENT/RETEACHING

▶ *Activity Book*

Students are shown the importance of organizing and displaying data with ac-

Laboratory Investigation

A MOLDY QUESTION

BEFORE THE LAB

1. Gather all materials at least one day prior to the investigation. You should have enough supplies to meet your class needs, assuming six students per group. Note that water must be available to each group.

2. Make sure all bread used is of the same type. Ordinary commercial white bread works well.

3. Note that the first part of this activity will require about 15 minutes the first day, then about 5 minutes every few days during the next two weeks. Each of the other experiments (steps 4 and 5) will require about the same amount of time.

PRE-LAB DISCUSSION

The focus of this activity is to give students hands-on experience with the scientific method, particularly in terms of identifying variables and designing an experiment. Before beginning the Pre-Lab Discussion, have students read the Laboratory Investigation carefully.

• **What is the scientific problem presented in this lab?** (What factors affect the growth of bread mold?)

• **According to step 1 of the Procedure, what factors about the two slices of bread will be kept the same during the experiment?** (Both will be in closed jars; both will have the same amount of water added.)

• **What is the advantage of using the medicine dropper to put the water on the bread?** (Using the medicine dropper helps to make sure the same amount of water is added to each setup.)

• **What will be different about the two slices of bread?** (One will be placed in a dark closet, while the other will be placed in the sun.)

SAFETY TIPS

Remind students of the safety rules for handling glassware.

Laboratory Investigation

A Moldy Question

Problem

What variables affect the growth of bread mold?

Materials (per group)

2 jars with lids
2 slices of bread
1 medicine dropper

Procedure ⚗

1. Put half a slice of bread into each jar. Moisten each half slice with ten drops of water. Cap the jars tightly. Keep one jar in sunlight and place the other in a dark closet.

2. Observe the jars every few days for about two weeks. Record your observations. Does light seem to influence mold growth? Include your answer to this question (your conclusion) with your observations.

3. Ask your teacher what scientists know about the effect of light on mold growth. Was your conclusion correct? Think again: What other variables might have affected mold growth? Did you think of temperature? How about moisture? Light, temperature, and moisture are all possible variables in this investigation.

4. Design a second experiment to retest the effect of light on mold growth. Record your procedure, observations, and conclusions.

5. Design another experiment to test one of the other variables. Test only one variable at a time. Work with other groups of students in your class so that each group tests one of the other two variables. Share your results and draw your conclusions together.

Medicine dropper
Water
Bread
Jar 1 (in sunlight)
Jar 2 (in darkness)

Observations

Study the class data for this experiment. What variables seem to affect mold growth?

Analysis and Conclusions

1. In each of your additional experiments, what variable were you testing? Did you have a control setup for each experiment? If so, describe it.

2. Juanita set up the following experiment: She placed a piece of orange peel in each of two jars. She added 3 milliliters of water to jar 1 and placed it in the refrigerator. She added no water to jar 2 and placed it on a windowsill in the kitchen. At the end of a week, she noticed more mold growth in jar 2. Juanita concluded that light, a warm temperature, and no moisture are ideal conditions for mold growth. Discuss the accuracy of Juanita's conclusion.

TEACHING STRATEGY

1. Have the teams follow the directions carefully as they work in the laboratory. When you are asked the question in step 3, tell students that light does not influence mold growth. Point out that there must have been some hidden variables, which is the primary lesson to be learned in this investigation.

2. In step 4 of the Procedure, students are to repeat the same experiment as exactly as they can.

3. For step 5 of the Procedure, you may want to assign a different variable to each group of students.

DISCOVERY STRATEGIES

Discuss how the investigation relates to the chapter ideas by asking open questions similar to the following.

• **Can you offer a hypothesis to the problem?** (Accept all answers.)

• **What is the obvious variable of these two environments?** (Light.)

Study Guide

Summarizing Key Concepts

1–1 Science—Not Just for Scientists

▲ The goal of science is to understand the world around us.

▲ Scientists use facts as clues to the large mysteries of nature.

▲ A theory is the most logical explanation for events that occur in nature. A theory is a time-tested concept that makes useful and dependable predictions about the natural world.

▲ The three main branches of science are life science, earth science, and physical science.

▲ Life scientists study living things and their parts and actions.

▲ Earth scientists study the features of the Earth, which include rocks, oceans, volcanoes, earthquakes, and the atmosphere. Astronomy, which is a part of earth science, is the study of objects such as stars, planets, and moons.

▲ Physical scientists study matter and energy. Physical science can be further divided into chemistry and physics. The study of substances and how they change and combine is the focus of chemistry. The study of energy is the focus of physics.

▲ Within any branch of science, most scientists specialize in a particular area of study.

1–2 The Scientific Method—A Way of Problem Solving

▲ The scientific method is the systematic way of problem solving used by scientists.

▲ The basic steps in the scientific method are stating the problem, gathering information, forming a hypothesis, experimenting, recording and analyzing data, stating a conclusion, and repeating the work.

▲ A hypothesis is a proposed solution to a scientific problem.

▲ A variable is the one factor that is being tested in an experiment.

▲ Scientists run an experimental setup and a control setup, or experiment without the variable, to make sure the results of the experiment were caused by the variable and not some hidden factor.

1–3 Science and Discovery

▲ Not all scientific discoveries are made through the scientific method. Sometimes luck or a hunch leads to an important discovery.

1–4 Safety in the Science Laboratory

▲ When working in the laboratory, it is important to heed all necessary safety precautions. These include using safety equipment and following all instructions carefully.

Reviewing Key Terms

Define each term in a complete sentence.

1–1 Science—Not Just for Scientists
theory
law

1–2 The Scientific Method—A Way of Problem Solving
scientific method
hypothesis
variable
control
data

ANALYSIS AND CONCLUSIONS

1. The variable chosen will vary. The control will be a similar jar and piece of bread that do not contain the variable (moisture, for example) but are otherwise identical to the other experimental setup.

2. The experiment was not well designed because Juanita varied more than one condition at the same time and therefore could not tell which variable was responsible for the difference in mold growth. The experiment should thus be redesigned, and it should also be repeated several times.

GOING FURTHER: ENRICHMENT
Part 1
Have students carry out the same activity using different types of bread, particularly those with and without preservatives.

Part 2
Mold is a growth produced by a fungus. Have students find out more about the characteristics of fungi and the different types of conditions in which they grow.

• **What is a less obvious variable?** (Temperature.)

• **Do you foresee a problem in carrying out an experiment with two variables? If so, why?** (Yes. It may be hard to tell which variable has caused the results of the experiment.)

• **What unit of measurement should you use to describe the amount of mold on each piece of bread?** (Accept all logical answers. Square centimeters would work well.)

OBSERVATIONS

Moisture and high (but not too high) temperatures have a positive effect on mold growth.

Chapter Review

ALTERNATIVE ASSESSMENT

The *Prentice Hall Science* program includes a variety of testing components and methodologies. Aside from the Chapter Review questions, you may opt to use the Chapter Test or the Computer Test Bank Test in your *Test Book* for assessment of important facts and concepts. In addition, Performance-Based Tests are included in your *Test Book*. These Performance-Based Tests are designed to test science process skills, rather than factual content recall. Since they are not content dependent, Performance-Based Tests can be distributed after students complete a chapter or after they complete the entire textbook.

CONTENT REVIEW

Multiple Choice
1. d
2. b
3. a
4. d
5. c
6. b
7. c
8. b

True or False
1. F, closed
2. F, data
3. T
4. F, hypothesis
5. F, one variable
6. T
7. T

Concept Mapping
Row 1: Understand world around us
Row 2: Life science, Earth science,
   Physical science

CONCEPT MASTERY

1. An experiment must have only one variable so that the experimenter can be sure the results obtained are due to that single variable. A control setup is exactly like the experimental setup except that it does not contain the variable to be tested. If the results occur in the experimental setup and not in the control setup, the experimenter can be fairly sure the variable is causing the results.

Content Review

Multiple Choice

Choose the letter of the answer that best completes each statement.

1. An orderly, systematic approach to problem solving is called the
   a. experiment.
   b. conclusion.
   c. hypothesis.
   d. scientific method.
2. The factor being tested in an experiment is the
   a. hypothesis.   c. control.
   b. variable.   d. problem.
3. Recorded observations and measurements are called
   a. data.   c. conclusions.
   b. graphs.   d. variables.
4. The most important laboratory safety rule is to
   a. have a partner.
   b. wear a lab coat.
   c. wear safety goggles.
   d. always follow directions.

5. The branch of science that deals with the study of ocean currents is
   a. life science.   c. earth science.
   b. chemistry.   d. physics.
6. Scientists must analyze the results of an experiment before they form a
   a. hypothesis.   c. data table.
   b. conclusion.   d. variable.
7. A time-tested concept that makes useful and dependable predictions about the world is called a(an)
   a. hypothesis.   c. theory.
   b. discovery.   d. investigation.
8. A safety symbol in the shape of a flask alerts you to
   a. be careful with lab animals.
   b. be careful with glassware.
   c. wear safety goggles.
   d. wear heat-resistant gloves.

True or False

If the statement is true, write "true." If it is false, change the underlined word or words to make the statement true.

1. Never heat anything in an <u>open</u> container.
2. Recorded observations that often involve measurements are called <u>conclusions</u>.
3. The part of the experiment with the variable is called the <u>experimental setup</u>.
4. The <u>scientific method</u> is a proposed solution to a scientific problem.
5. Most experiments must have <u>two</u> <u>variables</u> to be accurate.
6. The study of heat and light is part of <u>physics</u>.
7. The symbol of a <u>razor blade</u> means you are working with a sharp instrument.

Concept Mapping

Complete the following concept map for Section 1–1. Refer to pages A6–A7 to construct a concept map for the entire chapter.

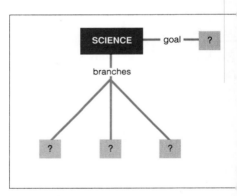

2. Answers will vary. Because all people make observations and wonder about what they have observed, all people are scientists.

3. Answers will vary. Two possible answers are that the scale of the problem is too big (global, astronomical) or that it would be dangerous to threatened species to remove any organisms from their natural environment.

4. The steps are stating the problem, gathering information, suggesting an answer (forming a hypothesis), performing an experiment to see whether the suggested answer makes sense, recording and analyzing the data, stating a conclusion, and repeating the work.

5. Very often a scientist is not looking for a particular event or situation, but when such an event occurs, the scientist must be able to recognize that something has occurred that should be investigated.

6. Answers will vary. You might suggest that students write one question for each of the three branches of science.

Concept Mastery

Discuss each of the following in a brief paragraph.

1. Why should an experiment contain only one variable? What is the purpose of the control in an experiment?
2. List and describe at least three examples of how you act like a scientist.
3. Why are some problems in science impossible to study through laboratory experimentation?
4. Describe the basic steps of the scientific method.
5. What role can luck or chance play in the advancement of science?
6. Describe three science questions that you have an interest in finding an answer to.

Critical Thinking and Problem Solving

Use the skills you have developed in this chapter to answer each of the following.

1. **Following safety rules** Explain the potential danger involved in each of the following situations. Describe the safety precautions that should be used to avoid injury to you or your classmates.
   a. Pushing a rubber stopper far down into a test tube
   b. Pouring acid into a beaker while sitting at your lab table
   c. Tasting a white powder to see if it is salty
   d. Heating a stoppered test tube of water
   e. Deciding on your own to mix two chemicals together
2. **Applying concepts** Explain how the scientific method could be used by a mechanic to determine why a car won't start on a cold morning.
3. **Designing an experiment** The following hypothesis is suggested to you: Water will heat up faster when placed under the direct rays of the sun than when placed under indirect, or angled, rays of the sun. Design an experiment to test this hypothesis. Make sure you have both a variable and a control setup. With your teacher's permission, conduct the experiment and draw a conclusion about the hypothesis.
4. **Making predictions** Develop a time line in which you predict some of the major advances in science during the twenty-first century.
5. **Making charts** Construct a picture chart that shows the fields of study included in the three main branches of science.
6. **Designing an experiment** Design an experiment to determine the best place to grow flowers in your classroom. With your teacher's permission, conduct the experiment and draw a conclusion.
7. **Using the writing process** Write a short story that begins, "It was a dark and eerie night. As the lost hikers knocked on the door of the scientist's laboratory, they suddenly realized . . ."

same way in each container should be noted. The final step would be to place a light source directly above the water and angled at the other container of water. If carried out, students will determine that the hypothesis was correct.

4. Answers will vary. Ask students to include possible advances in all three branches of science.

5. Answers will vary. Students should include the information in Section 1–1 in their charts.

6. Check students' designs for accuracy and to make sure they follow the scientific method. Most designs will include plants and soil conditions that are the same in both the control and experimental setups. Possible variables might be light, temperature, and heat.

7. Answers will vary. Have students include the use of the scientific method somewhere in their story.

KEEPING A PORTFOLIO

You might want to assign some of the Concept Mastery and Critical Thinking and Problem Solving questions as homework and have students include their responses to unassigned questions in their portfolio. Students should be encouraged to include both the question and the answer in their portfolio.

ISSUES IN SCIENCE

The following issues can be used as springboards for discussion or given as writing assignments.

1. It has often been said that students in the United States are less well educated in science than students in Europe and Asia are. Do you think this is true? Find out what type of science education students receive in such countries as Japan, the Soviet Union, England, and Germany. Also find out what American educators have to say on the issue.

2. Explain why scientists should try to understand mistakes that happen during experimentation.

3. It is said that science investigation is like detective work. Write your own science detective story entitled "Fact or Fiction: Bats Fly Only at Night."

CRITICAL THINKING AND PROBLEM SOLVING

1. (a) Test tube is fragile and may break and cut the hand. Lubricate the stopper and do not push too hard. (b) Acid might spill on table, clothing, or skin. Pour acids near the sink or a source of water so that acid can immediately be rinsed off any object on which it spills. (c) Powder could be poisonous. Never taste an unknown substance unless instructed to do so. (d) Gases can build up in the test tube and cause it to explode. Never heat a stoppered test tube. (e) Chemicals could be dangerous when mixed. Never mix chemicals unless instructed to do so.

2. Using experience, the mechanic might identify the three or four most common reasons for a car not starting. Then each reason (hypothesis) can be tested in turn.

3. Check students' designs for accuracy and to make sure they follow the scientific method. Most designs will include a body of water that is the same in both the control and experimental setups. The same type of thermometer placed in the

SECTION	HANDS-ON ACTIVITIES
2–1 The Metric System pages A38–A52 Multicultural Opportunity 2–1, p. A38 ESL Strategy 2–1, p. A38	**Student Edition** ACTIVITY (Doing): Create a Measurement System, p. A40 ACTIVITY (Discovering): A Milliliter By Any Other Name, p. A45 ACTIVITY (Discovering): Does Air Have Mass and Weight? p. A47 ACTIVITY (Discovering): Charting Growth, p. A41 ACTIVITY BANK: Calculating Density, p. A104 ACTIVITY BANK: Dazzling Displays of Densities, p. A106 **Activity Book** CHAPTER DISCOVERY: For Good Measure, p. A37 ACTIVITY: Making a Metric Conversion "Machine," p. A61 ACTIVITY: Using a Metric Conversion "Machine," p. A63 **Teacher Edition** Comparing Measurement Systems, p. A38d Working With Powers of Ten, p. A38d
2–2 Measurement Tools pages A52–A57 Multicultural Opportunity 2–2, p. A52 ESL Strategy 2–2, p. A52	**Student Edition** ACTIVITY (Doing): Metric Measurements, p. A53 LABORATORY INVESTIGATION: Uncertainty of Measurements, p. A58 **Activity Book** ACTIVITY: Practicing Measurement Skills, p. A47 ACTIVITY: Measuring Liquid Volume With a Graduated Cylinder, p. A65 **Product Testing Activity** Testing Breakfast Cereals **Laboratory Manual** Metric Measurement: Length, p. A21 Metric Measurement: Mass, p. A25 Metric Measurement: Volume and Temperature, p. A29
Chapter Review pages A58–A61	

OUTSIDE TEACHER RESOURCES

Books

Adler, Peggy, and Irving Adler. *Metric Puzzles*, Franklin Watts.

Baird, Eva-Lee, and Rose Wyler. *Going Metric the Fun Way*, Doubleday.

Kelly, Brendan. *Metric Measurement*, EDC Publishing Company.

Whitman, Nancy C., and Frederick G. Brown. *The Metric System: A Laboratory Approach for Teachers*, Wiley.

Audiovisuals

Introduction to Biological Measurements: A General Introduction to the Metric System, sound filmstrip, Ward

The Metric System, courseware, HRM Software (Queue)

Real World Measurement, filmstrip, Society for Visual Education

OTHER ACTIVITIES	MEDIA AND TECHNOLOGY
Activity Book ACTIVITY: Thinking in Metrics, p. A41 ACTIVITY: Little Millie Metric, p. A43 ACTIVITY: Metric Units and Quantities, p. A45 ACTIVITY: Say It in Metric, p. A51 ACTIVITY: Density Determination, p. A53 ACTIVITY: Gathering Information From Graphs, p. A55 ACTIVITY: Scientific Measurements, p. A57 ACTIVITY: Dimensional Analysis, p. A59 ACTIVITY: That's Incredible, p. A67 **Review and Reinforcement Guide** Section 2–1, p. A15	**English/Spanish Audiotapes** Section 2–1
Student Edition ACTIVITY (Thinking): How Good Is Your Guess? p. A55 ACTIVITY (Calculating): Metric Conversions, p. A56 **Activity Book** ACTIVITY: Percentage Error, p. A69 **Review and Reinforcement Guide** Section 2–2, p. A19	**English/Spanish Audiotapes** Section 2–2
Test Book Chapter Test, p. A35 Performance-Based Tests, p. A75	**Test Book** Computer Test Bank Test, p. A41

*All materials in the Chapter Planning Guide Grid are available as part of the Prentice Hall Science Learning System.

CHAPTER OVERVIEW

Experiments are an important part of the scientific method. Most experiments require and generate data in the form of measurements. Because these scientific measurements must be accurate and easily communicated to other people, science uses a universal system of measurement called the metric system.

Any system of measurement needs tools to perform measurements, and scientists use a wide variety of measurement tools. These tools can be rather complex or relatively simple. Basic lab-oratory tools include the metric ruler, triple-beam balance, graduated cylinder, and Celsius thermometer.

Use of the metric system of measurement is not reserved exclusively for scientists. Although they use it frequently to measure things like length, volume, mass, weight, density, and temperature, people other than scientists also use the metric system of measurement. The need to know the metric system of measurement will only become greater in the lives of students.

2–1 THE METRIC SYSTEM

THEMATIC FOCUS

The purpose of this section is to explain the basic units of measurement in the metric system. Students will learn that the basic unit of metric length is the meter (m). Larger units of length include the kilometer (km), and smaller units include the centimeter (cm) and millimeter (mm). Volume is the amount of space an object occupies, and the basic metric unit of liquid volume is the liter (L). Smaller units of liquid volume are measured in milliliters (mL). The basic metric unit of solid volume is the cubic centimeter (cm^3 or cc). Mass is a measure of the amount of matter in an object, and the basic unit of mass in the metric system is the kilogram (kg). Smaller units of mass include the gram (g) and the milligram (mg). Weight is a measure of the attraction between two objects due to gravity, and the basic unit of metric weight is the newton (N). Density is the relationship between the mass and volume of a substance, or its mass per unit volume. When compared to water, the density of an object is given as grams per milliliter (g/mL). The basic unit of metric temperature is Celsius degrees (°C).

Students will also learn the skill of dimensional analysis, or converting from one metric unit to another. Two essential ingredients of scientific measurements are accuracy and ease of communication to other people. The metric system is a universal system of measurement and is often called the International System of Units, or SI. This system allows scientists and people from all over the world to compare and analyze data.

The themes that can be focused on in this section are scale and structure, systems and interactions, patterns of change, and stability.

*Scale and structure: Point out that the metric system is a decimal system in which units increase or decrease by powers of 10. Inform students that some of our ways of counting money are somewhat analogous to the metric powers of ten. In our system of money, one penny represents 10^0 cents. One dime represents 10^1 cents. One dollar represents 10^2 cents. Ten dollars represents 10^3 cents. One hundred dollars represents 10^4 cents. Remind students that other money denominations we use are quite unlike these powers of ten, dividing five dollars into five singles and one dollar into four quarters, for example.

*Systems and interactions: Stress that all objects interact through gravitational forces that exist between them. The strength of these gravitational forces is directly proportional to the mass of the objects and inversely proportional to their distance apart.

Patterns of change: Although the mass of an object remains constant, its weight changes as its location changes. Make sure students realize that the weight of a person is a measure of the Earth's force of gravity on him or her. They can increase their weight by digging a deep hole into the Earth and weighing themselves at the bottom of it. Their mass has not changed, but because they are closer to the center of gravity, its force is stronger and their weight will show an increase. The op-posite is true also. Weighing themselves at the top of Mount Everest would place them farther away from the center of gravity, and a weight decrease would result, even though their mass has not changed.

Stability: Sometimes scientists must compare substances based on their mass and volume. The relationship between mass and volume is called density, and the density of a substance is constant. If students have difficulty with the concept of density, you might choose to explain the substitution of simple numbers into the formula $D = M/V$, where D is density, M is mass, and V is volume. Then compare the computed density of the substance to the density of water, which is 1 g/mL. If the computed density of the substance is greater than 1 g/mL, the substance will sink in water. If the computed density of the substance is less than 1 g/mL, the substance will float on water.

PERFORMANCE OBJECTIVES 2–1

1. Explain the importance of a universal language of measurement.
2. Identify the metric units used in scientific measurements.
3. Use dimensional analysis to convert one metric unit to another.

SCIENCE TERMS 2–1

metric system p. A40
meter p. A41
centimeter p. A41
millimeter p. A42
kilometer p. A43
light-year p. A43
liter p. A44
milliliter p. A44

2-2 MEASUREMENT AND TOOLS

THEMATIC FOCUS

The purpose of this section is to explain the laboratory tools used to measure length, mass, volume, and temperature of an object. Students will manipulate these tools to measure the metric length, mass, volume, and temperature of various objects and substances.

The themes that can be focused on in this section are unity and diversity and systems and interactions.

*Unity and diversity: Stress that all objects, regardless of their disparities, share the properties of length, mass, volume, density, and temperature. Depending on the object(s) chosen, measuring these properties might be relatively simple or rather complex. Regardless, each of these properties could be measured or approximated for any object because all objects possess these properties.

*Systems and interactions: Lead students to understand that many systems combine to form the world that they live in. All these systems interact within themselves and between one another. It is the understanding of these systems and interactions and the application of this understanding that drive scientists to help create a better world.

PERFORMANCE OBJECTIVES 2-2

1. Describe laboratory tools used to measure length, mass, volume, and temperature.

2. Choose appropriate tools and metric units to measure given substances.

Discovery *Learning*

TEACHER DEMONSTRATIONS MODELING

Comparing Measurement Systems

You may wish to begin by writing this on the chalkboard: 15 miles = ? inches.
• **Describe some ways we could change 15 miles into inches.** (Responses might include multiplying by 5280 to find the number of feet, then multiplying by 12 to find the number of inches; or multiplying by 1760 to find the number of yards, then multiplying by 36 to find the number of inches.)

Have each student choose a method and use paper and pencil to compute the actual number of inches in 15 miles. Also have them time themselves to find how long the computation took.
• **How many inches are equal to 15 miles?** (950,400.)
• **About how long did your computation take?** (Answers will vary.)

Explain that they have converted from our most common unit of measuring large distances on Earth to our most common unit of measuring small distances.

Ask for a volunteer to go to the chalkboard and write a very large number, writing the unit abbreviation "km" after that number. Explain that the kilometer is the most common unit of measuring large distances in the metric system and that the millimeter is the most common unit of measuring small distances. Reminding students of how long their computation took in our system, walk to the chalkboard and move the decimal of the number six places to the right, erase the "km," and insert an "mm" in its place for the abbreviation.
• **What metric conversion have I just performed?** (Lead students to realize that you have just performed a conversion from the largest unit of metric dis-

tance to the smallest, much like the previous example of changing miles to inches in our system.
• **Why is a conversion in the metric system so much faster than our system?** (Lead students to realize that the metric system is a decimal system in which units increase by powers of ten and that multiplication or division by powers of ten is quite fast when compared with our system of measurement.)

Working With Powers of Ten

Ask for volunteers to name some units in the customary measuring system such as inches, feet, yards, gallons, quarts, teaspoons, etc.

Write a large 10 on the chalkboard.
• **Multiply this number by ten. What is the result?** (100.) Remind students to simply write a 0 after the 10, making it 100.
• **Multiply 100 by 10. What is the result?** (1000.) Remind students again to simply write a 0 after the 100, making it 1000.

Repeat the process of multiplying by 10 until you have ten zeros after the 1. The number should read 10,000,000,000. Then have students reverse the process.
• **Divide your number by 10. What is the result?** (1,000,000,000.) Remind students to simply erase or strike the last zero from the number, making it 1,000,000,000.

Repeat the process of dividing by 10 until only the whole number 1 remains.
• **Would you like all of your multiplication and division to be this easy?** (Yes.)
• **Why?** (Accept all logical answers.)

Point out that students have just experienced what it is like to make conversions in the metric system of measurement.

CHAPTER 2
Measurement and the Sciences

INTEGRATING SCIENCE

This chapter provides you with numerous opportunities to integrate any area of science, as well as other disciplines, into your curriculum. Blue numbered annotations on the student page and integration notes on the teacher wraparound pages alert you to areas of possible integration.

In this chapter you can integrate language arts (p. 40), mathematics (pp. 41, 47, 51, 56), earth science and astronomy (p. 43), physical science and mechanics (p. 48), and social studies (p. 57).

SCIENCE, TECHNOLOGY, AND SOCIETY/COOPERATIVE LEARNING

Measurements of speed, distance, height, weight, and time are constantly being taken in many different kinds of sporting events. One of the most frequently used measures in sports is the second. Competitions of all kinds have been won or lost in a single second, sometimes even a fraction of a second.

One second may not seem like a lengthy amount of time. A basketball player can catch a pass and shoot a game-winning shot in less than one second. A sprinter can run 100 meters in less than ten seconds. That runner covers approximately 10.1 meters during each one-second span. Speed skaters can cover 15 meters in a single second because they are competing on the nearly frictionless surface of ice. Downhill skiers win or lose by fractions of a second. A skier who loses a race by one second can lose the race by as much as 30 meters. Professional baseball pitchers can throw a ball toward the batter at speeds close to 45 meters per second. The batter must react to the pitch and begin to swing within 0.25 second of the release of the ball in order to have any chance of hitting it.

INTRODUCING CHAPTER 2

DISCOVERY LEARNING

▶ *Activity Book*

Begin your teaching of the chapter by using the Chapter 2 Discovery Activity from your *Activity Book*. Using this activity, students will discover that many different properties of an object can be measured.

USING THE TEXTBOOK

Have students observe the photograph on page A38.
• **What do you predict is happening in the photograph?** (A Space Shuttle is releasing an object into space.)

Explain that a robotic arm on the *Space Shuttle Discovery* is releasing the *Hubble Space Telescope*.
• **Why would we put a telescope in space instead of building another telescope for the surface of the Earth?** (Responses

Measurement and the Sciences

Guide for Reading

After you read the following sections, you will be able to

2–1 The Metric System
- Discuss the importance of a universal language of measurement.
- Identify the metric units used in scientific measurements.
- Use dimensional analysis to convert one metric unit to another.

2–2 Measurement Tools
- Identify the common laboratory tools used to measure length, volume, mass, and temperature.

Slowly, ever so carefully, the robot arm of the *Space Shuttle Discovery* released the *Hubble Space Telescope* into orbit above the Earth on April 25, 1990. The *Hubble Space Telescope* had been more than a decade in the making at a cost of several billion dollars. The 2.4-meter primary mirror was the most carefully constructed and most expensive mirror ever built. The development of the primary mirror was a monumental scientific achievement—or was it?

Soon after its launch, scientists discovered a problem with the primary mirror. Light striking the outer edge of the mirror was brought to a focus about 4 centimeters behind light striking the center of the mirror. As a result, the images produced by the telescope were fuzzy and not as clear as expected. A slight miscalculation in measurement had been built into the mirror's design.

The *Hubble Space Telescope* will be repaired. In time it will bring us pictures of the universe we can only dream about today. But until that day, it stands as a reminder to all scientists—and those who would be scientists—that careful and precise measurements can be the difference between scientific success and failure.

Journal *Activity*

You and Your World Pick a type of measurement. Perhaps length is your favorite. Or you may prefer temperature or volume. Whatever type of measurement you choose, make an entry in your journal each time you use that type of measurement on a particular day.

The Hubble Space Telescope *being released by the robot arm on the* Space Shuttle Discovery.

A ■ 39

Cooperative learning: Using preassigned lab groups or randomly selected teams, have each group complete one of the following assignments.

• Design and conduct an experiment to determine how far a volunteer group member runs in one second. Remind groups to follow the scientific method in designing their experiment and to make accurate measurements when conducting their experiment.

• Some people have repeated the word *Mississippi* to help measure time when a stopwatch or second hand was unavailable. Have groups design and conduct an experiment that determines the accuracy of using the counting method "one-Mississippi, two-Mississippi," etc., as a means of measuring the length of a second. You may want to suggest that the groups perform their experiment several times and then average their results.

See Cooperative Learning in the *Teacher's Desk Reference.*

JOURNAL ACTIVITY

You may want to use the Journal Activity as the basis of a class discussion. As students discuss the entries they made in their journals, lead them to the idea that measurement is used much more frequently than they might realize in their lives, and life in general would be completely chaotic if we did not have consistent ways of measuring things. Students should be instructed to keep their Journal Activity in their portfolio.

---

might include diminished visibility from Earth's surface because of atmospheric pollutants.)

Have students read the chapter introduction on page A39. Then explain to them that even though it took years to develop and manufacture, the *Hubble Space Telescope* was not tested on Earth before it was sent into space. It worked, but it worked only on paper.

• **Why do you think the *Hubble Space Telescope* was not tested on Earth before it was put into space?** (Students might suggest that budget constraints or the high cost of duplicating space conditions on Earth may have prevented a test before launch.)

• **List some methods that scientists might use to try to repair the telescope.** (Accept all logical responses.)

• **What kind of measurements might the *Hubble Space Telescope* one day make?** (Responses might include distances to and sizes of other objects.)

• **How can the information gathered by the *Hubble Space Telescope* affect our lives?** (Responses might include answers about the origin of our universe will help us plan for the future on Earth.)

Remind students to remember the lessons learned from the *Hubble Space Telescope* as they complete this chapter about measurement and the sciences. Careful and precise measurements can be the difference between scientific success and failure.

2-1 The Metric System

If you have students from different countries in your class, you may want to ask volunteers to tell the class about the measurement systems used in their countries of origin. Interested students may want to research the origin and development of suggested systems.

ESL STRATEGY 2-1

Working in small groups, have students record the statements that you dictate to them. Then one student from each group reads a statement. Another student responds to it, and a third student confirms or corrects the response. Repeat the process, using different volunteers each time.

1. List the scientific measurement uses of the metric system.

2. Give the names of the basic metric units for measuring length and volume.

3. Attach the prefixes *milli-, centi-,* and *kilo-* to the length unit *meter* to indicate how its value changes depending on the prefix used.

4. Indicate the names of the units for liquid and solid volume measurements.

TEACHING STRATEGY 2-1

FOCUS/MOTIVATION

Write the following "recipe" on the chalkboard.

OATMEAL TREATS

Combine together these ingredients:

some butter   a bunch of nuts
some sugar   a whole lot of oatmeal
a little salt   a little baking power
a lot of flour

Mix well, heat up the oven, and bake for a long time.

• **What is wrong with this recipe?** (You cannot tell how much of each ingredient to use, how long the treats should be baked, or at what temperature to set the oven.)

CONTENT DEVELOPMENT

Inform students that measurements are important because we often need to know exact quantities or dimensions.

ACTIVITY
DOING

Create a Measurement System

Using objects found in your classroom as standards, create your own measurement system for length, mass, and volume. For each type of measurement, try to include units of several different sizes. Keep in mind that your "standards" must be things that will remain constant over time. Also keep in mind that you should be able to convert easily from one unit to another.

Once your measurement system is established, create a display of your standard objects and the units they represent. Then challenge members of your class to use your system to make measurements of various objects and distances.

• **Describe a time when you needed to know an exact quantity or dimension.** (Responses might include cooking by following a recipe.)

Exact quantities or dimensions also need to be communicated to other people.

• **Describe a time when you needed to communicate an exact quantity or dimension.** (Responses might include telling a friend how to cook your favorite recipe or making a treasure map.)

2-1 The Metric System

Magnum est ut inter sese colloqui possint periti in scientiae rebus.

Having trouble reading the sentence written above? Don't worry, it's not a string of new vocabulary words you have to memorize. Actually, it is a very clear and concise sentence. It just happens to be written in a language you probably don't understand. And it's been included to make a simple but important point. Science is a worldwide topic, and scientists come from every country on Earth. If they are to work together and know what each other is doing, scientists must be able to communicate—in a sense, to speak the same language. In case you're wondering, the sentence above is in Latin. Its translation is:

It is important that scientists can communicate with each other.

Metrics—The Universal Language of Measurement

In Chapter 1 you learned that experiments are an important part of the scientific method. You also learned that most experiments require data in the form of measurements. It is important that measurements be accurate and easily communicated to other people. So a universal system of measurement having standard units must be used. You can imagine the confusion that would result if measurements were made without standard units. For example, suppose you ask a friend how far it is to his house, and his response is five. You do not know if he means five blocks, five kilometers, or that it takes about five minutes to get there. Obviously, such a response would be of little help to you—and you probably would not accept that answer.

Scientists are ordinary people just like you. In order to make sure there is little confusion about their work, all scientists use the same standard system of measurement. The scientific system of measurement is called the **metric system.** The metric system is often referred to as the International System

---

● ● ● ●   **Integration**   ● ● ● ●

Use the Latin sentence and the information about the need of scientists to communicate effectively to integrate language arts into your lesson.

Use the discussion on counting money to integrate mathematics and decimal systems into your lesson.

REINFORCEMENT/RETEACHING

▶ *Activity Book*

Students who need practice on the concept of measuring systems should

COMMON METRIC UNITS

Length	Mass
1 meter (m) = 100 centimeters (cm) 1 meter = 1000 millimeters (mm) 1 meter = 1,000,000 micrometers (µm) 1 meter = 1,000,000,000 nanometers (nm) 1 meter = 10,000,000,000 angstroms (Å) 1000 meters = 1 kilometer (km)	1 kilogram (kg) = 1000 grams (g) 1 gram = 1000 milligrams (mg) 1000 kilograms = 1 metric ton (t)
Volume	**Temperature**
1 liter (L) = 1000 milliliters (mL) or 1000 cubic centimeters (cm^3)	0°C = freezing point of water 100°C = boiling point of water
kilo- = one thousand centi- = one hundredth milli- = one thousandth	micro- = one millionth nano- = one billionth

Figure 2–1 *The metric system is easy to use because it is based on units of ten. How many centimeters are there in 10 meters?* ❶

of Units, or SI. Using the metric system, scientists all over the world can compare and analyze their data.

The metric system is a simple system to use. Like our money system, the metric system is a decimal system; that is, it is based on the number ten and multiples of ten. (There are ten pennies in a dime, ten dimes in a dollar, and so on.) In much the same way, each unit in the metric system is ten times larger or ❷ ten times smaller than the next smaller or larger unit. So calculations with metric units are relatively easy.

Scientists use metric units to measure length, volume, mass, weight, density, and temperature. Some frequently used metric units and their abbreviations are listed in Figure 2–1.

Length

The basic unit of length in the metric system is the **meter** (m). A meter is equal to 39.4 inches, or a little more than a yard. Your height would be measured in meters. Most students your age are between 1.5 and 2 meters tall.

To measure the length of an object smaller than a meter, scientists use the metric unit called the **centimeter** (cm). The prefix *centi-* means one-hundredth. As you might guess, there are 100 centimeters in a meter. The height of this book is about 26 centimeters.

ACTIVITY DISCOVERING

Charting Growth

Make a height recorder in your classroom. Place a meterstick vertically 1 meter above the floor. Use transparent tape to secure the meterstick to the wall. Measure your height using the meterstick. Measure the heights of your classmates in the same way. Do not forget to add 100 cm (1 m) to every measurement you take! Keep growth records for each member of the class for the duration of the school year. Keep in mind that everyone grows at a different rate.

■ At the end of the year, calculate the growth of each student. Add up the total growth of the class in centimeters. Are you impressed?

complete the chapter activity Metric Units and Quantities.

▶ *Activity Book*

Students will be challenged by the Chapter 2 activity in the *Activity Book* called That's Incredible. Students will convert English system measurements to metric measurements in this activity that focuses on amazing facts about animals.

ANNOTATION KEY

Answers

❶ 1000. (Making conversions)

Integration

❶ Language Arts

❷ Mathematics

ACTIVITY DOING

CREATE A MEASUREMENT SYSTEM

Skills: Making observations, making calculations

Materials: common objects

As students are selecting objects to represent "standard" units, remind them that the choosing of a relatively common object will help to ensure that other people will also be able to use their measurement system. Uncommon or unique objects will create a measurement system that few other people could use.

Also remind students that careful and precise measurements can represent the difference between success and failure in an experiment.

ACTIVITY DISCOVERING

CHARTING GROWTH

Discovery Learning

Skills: Making comparisons

Materials: meterstick, transparent tape

This simple activity will enable students to both use their measurement skills and make growth comparisons. Make sure students are aware that growth varies from person to person and each person's growth is normal for that person.

The first international standard of length was a bar of platinum-iridium alloy called the standard meter. Two fine lines were engraved on this bar, and when the bar was held at a temperature of 0°C and supported mechanically in a prescribed way, the distance between those two engraved lines was said to be one meter. Students will recall that a meter was intended to be one ten-millionth of the distance from the equator to the North Pole along the meridian line through Paris. This distance was shown to differ by about 0.023 percent from its intended value after the standard meter bar was constructed.

HISTORICAL NOTE
THE METRIC SYSTEM

The French Revolution brought a new government to power that decided to produce a rational set of units for all measurements—the everyday as well as those used in science and technology. They called their system the metric system. The base unit of length was the meter (from the Greek word *metron*, meaning "to measure"). They chose the meter to be one ten-millionth of the distance between the equator and the North Pole.

2-1 (continued)

CONTENT DEVELOPMENT

Remind students that in order to communicate effectively, scientists must speak the same measurement language. The common language of measurement in science all over the world is the metric system. The metric system is based on powers of ten. Calculations with the metric system are convenient to make because each unit is ten times larger or ten times smaller than the next unit.

Write "meter (symbol m)" on the chalkboard. Point out that the meter is the basic unit of length in the metric system.

Show the students a meterstick. Explain that to measure distances much greater than a meter, scientists use kilo-

Figure 2-2 *Which metric unit of length would be most appropriate when measuring the height of the Matterhorn in Switzerland or giraffes in Kenya?* ❶

Figure 2-3 *The length of bacteria (right) are measured in micrometers or nanometers. What unit of length is used when measuring atoms such as these silicon atoms (left)?* ❸

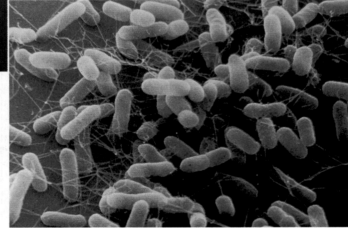

To measure even smaller objects, the metric unit called the **millimeter** (mm) is used. The prefix *milli-* means one-thousandth. So there are 1000 millimeters in a meter. In bright light, the diameter of the pupil of your eye is about 1 millimeter. How many millimeters are there in a centimeter? ❷

Even millimeters are too large to use when describing the sizes of microscopic organisms such as bacteria. Bacteria are measured in micrometers, or millionths of a meter, and nanometers, or billionths of a meter. That may seem small enough for any measurement, but it's not. To describe the size of

---

meters, or km. The prefix *kilo-* means 1000, and a kilometer is equal to 1000 meters. Write "1000 m = 1 km" on the chalkboard.

Point out that to measure distances less than a meter, scientists use the centimeter, cm, and the millimeter, mm. Explain that the prefix *centi-* means one hundredth and that a centimeter is ¹⁄₁₀₀ of a meter. The prefix *milli* means one thousandth, and a millimeter is ¹⁄₁₀₀₀ of a meter. Write "1 m = 100 cm" and "1 m = 1000 mm" on the chalkboard.

● ● ● ● **Integration** ● ● ● ●

Use the discussion of light-years and astronomy to integrate earth science into your lesson.

INDEPENDENT PRACTICE

▶ *Activity Book*

Students who need practice on the concept of finding conversions should complete the chapter activity Making a Metric Conversion Machine.

Figure 2–4 *To measure the length of long rivers, scientists would choose the unit of length called the kilometer.*

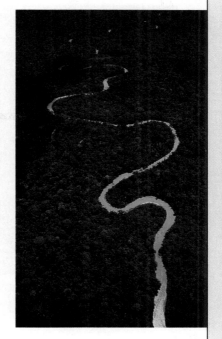

atoms, the building blocks of matter, scientists use the metric unit called the angstrom. An angstrom is equal to one ten-billionth of a meter!

Sometimes scientists need to measure large distances, such as the length of the Nile River in Africa. Such lengths can be measured in meters, centimeters, or even millimeters. But when measuring large distances with small units, the numbers become very difficult to work with. For example, the length of the Nile River is about 6,649,000,000 millimeters—not an easy number to use! To avoid such large numbers, scientists use the metric unit called the **kilometer** (km). The prefix *kilo-* means one thousand. So there are 1000 meters in a kilometer. The length of the Nile River is about 6649 kilometers. How many meters is this? ❹

On Earth, meters and kilometers are very useful units of measurement. But in space, distances are often too great to be measured in kilometers. (Again, the numbers start getting very large.) To measure long distances in space, astronomers use a unit of distance called the **light-year.** A light-year is the distance light travels in one year. As you probably know, light travels mighty fast—about 300,000 kilometers per second. A light-year, then, is about 9.5 trillion kilometers. No, we won't ask you how many millimeters are in a light-year, but you might have fun figuring it out on your own. You can think of a light-year as a ruler made of light. But keep in mind that a light-year measures distance, not time.

A light-year may seem like an enormous distance, but in space, it is not very far at all. The closest star system to the Earth is over 4 light-years away. It takes the light from that star system over four years to reach the Earth. Yet even that distance seems quite short when compared to the distance of the farthest known star system, which is about 12 billion light-years away. The light from these most distant stars may take more than 12 billion years to reach Earth. Unbelieveable as it may seem, the light began its long journey toward Earth before the Earth had even formed.

FACTS AND FIGURES
HOOF-AND-MOUTH DISEASE

One of the smallest germs known to scientists is the virus that causes hoof-and-mouth disease in cattle, sheep, and pigs. This virus is about 10 nanometers, or ten billionths of a meter, in diameter.

GUIDED PRACTICE

Skills Development

Skill: Applying concepts

Divide students into teams of four to six students per team. The list below contains ten objects or distances varying in size from microscopic to enormous. Write the list on the chalkboard.

—the distance from Earth to our nearest star
—the size of a bacterium
—the width of a penny
—the height of our school building
—the length of a bond between two atoms in a molecule
—the width of a fingernail
—the distance from New York to Florida
—your height
—the width of a postage stamp
—the length of a soccer field

Have teams discuss which unit of metric measure would be most useful in measuring each object or distance. Then discuss team results as a class.

When the discussion is complete, have each team create a new list of ten objects or distances varying in size from microscopic to enormous. Have teams exchange lists and repeat the activity.

INDEPENDENT PRACTICE

▶ *Activity Book*

Students who need practice on the concept of making conversions should complete the chapter activity Using a Metric Conversion Machine.

MATHEMATICS

Gather objects (such as cylinders, cones, and spheres) that represent common solids other than rectangular prisms. Although solid volumes can be determined by the liquid displacement method, formulas represent a more convenient method of determining volume.

You may want to divide students into teams. Distribute various solids, measuring tools, and volume formulas from the list below to each team.

Cylinder: $V = Bh$
Cone: $V = Bh/3$
Sphere: $V = 4\pi r^3/3$

Reminding each team that the capital letter B in these formulas represents base area, have each team calculate the volume of the given solids. When the activity is complete, you may wish to have teams check their answers using the displacement method, if possible.

COMMON ERRORS

When calculating the volume of solids without given measures, it is essential that students perform accurate measurements of each solid. Sometimes students measure using units that are too large to yield exact dimensions of the object, resulting in inaccurate volume determinations. Stress that students measure using the most precise units available to them.

Figure 2–5 *What unit of length is used to measure distant objects in space, such as this galaxy?* ❶

Figure 2–6 *A cubic centimeter (cm³ or cc) is the volume of a cube that measures 1 cm by 1 cm by 1 cm. How many milliliters are in a cubic centimeter?* ❸

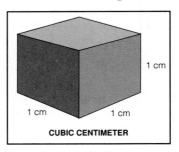

1 cm
1 cm 1 cm
CUBIC CENTIMETER

Volume

Volume is the amount of space an object takes up. In the metric system, the basic unit of volume is the **liter** (L). A liter is slightly larger than a quart. To measure volumes smaller than a liter, scientists use the **milliliter** (mL). Recall that the prefix *milli-* means one-thousandth. So there are 1000 milliliters in a liter. An ordinary drinking glass holds about 200 milliliters of liquid. How many milliliters are there in 10 liters? ❷

Liters and milliliters are used to measure the volume of liquids. Of course, both you and scientists may need to measure the volume of solids as well. The metric unit used to measure the volume of solids is called the **cubic centimeter** (cm³ or cc). A cubic centimeter is equal to the volume of a cube that measures 1 centimeter by 1 centimeter by 1 centimeter. It just so happens that a cubic centimeter is exactly equal in volume to a milliliter. (We told you the metric system is easy to use.) In fact, cubic centimeters can be used to measure the volume of liquids as well as solids. How many cubic centimeters are there in a liter? ❹

2–1 (continued)

CONTENT DEVELOPMENT

Point out that the amount of space an object takes up or occupies is called volume. Explain that the basic unit of volume in the metric system is called a liter, and another metric system name for the volume of a 10-by-10-by-10-cm cube (1000 cm³) is a liter. The symbol for a liter is L.

Write "L = liter" on the chalkboard. Explain that the metric system uses divisions of the liter to measure smaller volumes.

- **What is the definition of the prefix *milli-* ?** (One thousandth.)
- **One milliliter represents what fraction of one liter?** (¹⁄₁₀₀₀)
- **One liter is equal to how many milliliters?** (1000.)
- **One milliliter represents ¹⁄₁₀₀₀ L. What is the decimal equivalent for the fraction ¹⁄₁₀₀₀?** (0.001.)

GUIDED PRACTICE

Skills Development

Skill: Identifying relationships

Prepare several sets of flashcards that students can use to practice converting units of metric measure. Write the answers for each conversion fact on the back of each card. Some examples of conversions are given below.

1 meter = _____ centimeters (100)
1 meter = _____ millimeters (1000)
1 kilometer = _____ meters (1000)

Figure 2–7 To measure the volume of water rushing over Iguazu Falls in Brazil, scientists would use the unit of volume called the liter. What unit of volume would they use to measure the amount of water in a pet's water dish? ⑤

Mass

Mass is a measure of the amount of matter in an object. For example, there is more matter in a dumptruck than in a mid-sized car. So a dumptruck has more mass than a mid-sized car. Which has more mass, a mid-sized car or a bicycle? ⑥

Keep in mind that mass is different from volume. Volume is the amount of space an object takes up, whereas mass is the amount of matter in the object. The basic unit of mass in the metric system is the **kilogram** (kg).

The kilogram is a useful unit when measuring the mass of large objects. To measure the mass of small objects, such as a nickel, the **gram** (g) is used. If you remember what the prefix *kilo-* means, then you know that a kilogram contains 1000 grams. A nickel has a mass of about 5 grams. How many grams are in 20 kilograms? ⑦

ACTIVITY
DISCOVERING

A Milliliter by Any Other Name

■ Use a graduated cylinder, water, a metric ruler, and a small rectangular solid made of a material that sinks in water to prove that 1 milliliter = 1 cubic centimeter.

A ■ 45

ACTIVITY
DISCOVERING

A MILLILITER BY ANY OTHER NAME

Discovery Learning

Skills: Making observations, applying concepts

Materials: graduated cylinder, metric ruler, 1 cubic centimeter solid

Students should be able to determine that the volume of 1 cubic centimeter is equal to 1 milliliter by measuring the amount of water displacement that occurs when the solid sinks in a graduated cylinder. Students should also realize that the amount of displacement is directly proportional to the volume of the object.

---

1 liter = _____ milliliters (1000)
1 liter = _____ cubic centimeters (1000)
1000 _____ = 1 meter (millimeters)
1000 meters = 1 _____ (kilometer)
1 liter = 1000 _____ (milliliters)
1 kilogram = _____ grams (1000)
1 gram = _____ 1000 (milligrams)

Divide students into teams of two to four students per team. Distribute a set of flashcards to each team and allow them time to practice converting units of metric measure.

REINFORCEMENT/RETEACHING

▶ *Activity Book*

Students who need practice on the concept of making conversions should complete the chapter activity Little Millie Metric.

GUIDED PRACTICE

Skills Development

Skill: Making a model

Divide students into teams of four to six students per team. Have each team

measure and cut out six paper squares that measure 10 cm by 10 cm. Then tell the teams to make a cube by attaching the squares together with tape.

● **How many centimeters is the cube on each side?** (10 cm.)

● **How do we calculate the volume of a rectangular solid?** (Multiply the length times the width times the height.)

● **What unit of volume would we get by multiplying cm times cm times cm?** (Cubic centimeters, or cm³.)

● **What is the volume of the cube?** (1000 cubic centimeters, or 1000 cm³.)

The metric system is often referred to as the International System of Units, or SI. In the SI system, unit force is measured in newtons (N), mass is measured in kilograms (kg), and acceleration is measured in meters per second squared (m/s^2).

Even though the use of SI in scientific circles is widespread, there also exist other applications and systems of mechanical units.

In the Cgs system (centimeter, gram, second), unit force is measured in dynes, mass is measured in grams (g), and acceleration is measured in centimeters per second squared (cm/s^2).

In the British system of units, unit force is measured in pounds (lb), mass is measured in slugs, and acceleration is measured in feet per second squared (f/s^2).

2–1 (continued)

CONTENT DEVELOPMENT

Explain that the amount of matter in an object is called its mass. The base metric unit of mass is the kilogram (kg). One liter of water has a mass of 1 kilogram.

Kilogram units are used to measure the mass of large things, like automobiles. To measure the mass of small things, such as a mouse, scientists need a smaller unit. Things with small masses are measured in grams. A one-dollar bill has a mass of about 1 gram.

Explain that mass is a constant whereas weight is not. A person who weighs a certain amount on Earth would weigh much less on the moon. Weight is less on the moon because the moon's gravitational pull is less than the Earth's gravitational pull. But the mass of a person or object would be the same on Earth as it would be on the moon or on any other planet. The mass of an object does not change when that object is moved to a different location. The weight of an object does change when the force of gravity changes.

Figure 2–8 *The buffalo is one of the largest land animals on Earth. Harvest field mice are the smallest mice on Earth. Which metric unit would be best for measuring the mass of the buffalo? Of field mice?* ❷

As you might expect, scientists often need to measure the mass of objects much smaller than a nickel. To do so, they use the metric unit called the **milligram** (mg). Again, recall that the prefix *milli-* means one-thousandth. So there are 1000 milligrams in a gram. How many milligrams are there in a kilogram? ❶

Weight

Weight is a measure of the attraction between two objects due to gravity. Gravity is a force of attraction. The strength of the gravitational force between objects depends in part on the distance between these objects. As the distance between objects becomes greater, the gravitational force between the objects decreases. On Earth, your weight is a measure of the Earth's force of gravity on you.

The basic unit of weight in the metric system is the **newton** (N), named after Isaac Newton who discovered the force of gravity. The newton is used because it is a measure of force, and weight is the amount of force the Earth's gravity exerts on an object. An object with a mass of 1 kilogram is pulled toward the Earth with a force of 9.8 newtons. So the

46 ■ A

● ● ● ● **Integration** ● ● ● ●

Use the discussion on force and newtons to integrate mathematics into your lesson.

REINFORCMENT/RETEACHING

▶ *Activity Book*

Students who need practice on the concept of metric and customary units should complete the chapter activity Thinking in Metrics.

GUIDED PRACTICE

Skills Development

Skill: Identifying relationships

Show the class an object with a mass of 1 kilogram. Point out that the object has a mass of 1 kilogram anywhere in the universe. Hang the object on a weak spring or rubber band.

• **What happened?** (The spring stretched.)

• **What caused the spring to stretch?** (The pull of gravity on the mass of the object.)

weight of the object is 9.8 N. An object with a mass of 50 kilograms is pulled toward the Earth with a force of 50 × 9.8, or 490 N. That object's weight is 490 N. What is your weight on Earth? ③

Because the force of gravity changes with distance, your weight can change depending on your location. For example, you are farther from the center of the Earth when standing atop a tall mountain than when standing at sea level. And although the change may be small, you actually weigh less at the top of the mountain than you do at sea level. How might your weight change if you went down into a deep mine? ④

We often describe astronauts orbiting above the Earth as being weightless. You now know that this description is not correct. The distance between the astronauts and the center of the Earth is so great that the Earth's gravitational force is less strong. The astronauts appear to be weightless, but they actually are not. They still have weight because they

Figure 2–9 *Although we speak of astronauts as being "weightless," they are not. However, on Earth this astronaut would never have been able to lift this heavy communications satellite. But he was able to lift it with ease while floating above the Earth. Can you explain why?* ⑤

A ■ 47

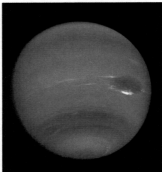

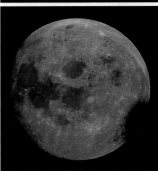

Figure 2–10 *The mass of planet Neptune is much greater than that of Earth, while the moon's mass is only about one sixth that of Earth. How would your weight on Neptune compare with your weight on Earth? On the moon? Is the same true of your mass?*

Activity Bank

Calculating Density, p.104

are still being pulled toward the Earth by the force of gravity.

As you just read, the strength of the gravitational force changes with distance. But it also changes depending on mass. An object with a large mass, such as the Earth, exerts a strong gravitational force on other objects. (Which is why you remain rooted to the ground and don't float off into space.) But any object with mass exerts a gravitational force—and that includes you! There is actually a gravitational force of attraction between you and this textbook. But don't worry, the book will not come flying at you as a result of gravity. Why? Your mass is much too small.

We tend to think of the Earth as being extremely large. But as objects in space go, the Earth is not so big. The mass of the planet Jupiter is more than two and one-half times that of Earth. If you could stand on Jupiter, you would find that your weight would be two and one-half times greater than your weight on Earth. The mass of the moon is about one sixth that of the Earth. How would your weight on the moon compare with your weight on Earth?

It should be clear to you by now that mass remains a constant, but weight can change. The amount of matter in an object does not change regardless of where the object is located. But the weight of an object can change due to its location.

Density

Sometimes scientists need to compare substances based on their mass and volume. The relationship between mass and volume is called **density.**

Density is defined as the mass per unit volume of a substance. That may sound complicated, but it really isn't. Perhaps the following formula, which shows the relationship between density, mass, and volume, will help:

$$\text{Density} = \frac{\text{Mass}}{\text{Volume}}$$

Suppose a substance has a mass of 10 grams and a volume of 10 milliliters. If you divide the mass of

---

2–1 (continued)

CONTENT DEVELOPMENT

You might wish to make a further distinction between mass and weight. Weight is measured in units of force, not units of mass. The unit of force in the metric system is the newton. Weight is calculated by multiplying the mass of an object by the acceleration due to gravity, which is approximately 9.8 meters/second/second (m/s^2) on the Earth's surface. Thus an object of mass 10 kg would have a weight of 9.8×10, or 98 newtons.

To help reinforce the distinction between mass and weight, ask students to find the errors in sentences such as these.
• **This apple weighs 200 grams.** (Grams are a measure of mass, not weight.)
• **Objects of equal mass always weigh the same.** (Only if they are in the same location with respect to gravity.)
• **Gravity can increase a person's mass.** (Mass is constant; gravity can only increase weight.)

● ● ● ● **Integration** ● ● ● ●

Use the discussion of force to integrate physical science into your lesson.

CONTENT DEVELOPMENT

Tell students that sometimes it is useful to know the relationship between the mass and the volume of a substance. This relationship is called density. Explain that the density of a substance is the ratio of its mass to its volume (mass per unit volume). The density of an object is equal

10 grams by the volume of 10 milliliters, you obtain the density of the substance:

$$\frac{10\ g}{10\ mL} = \frac{1\ g}{mL}$$

As it turns out, this substance is water. The density of water is 1 g/mL. Objects with a density less than that of water will float on water. Objects with a density greater than that of water will sink. Does iron have a density less than or greater than 1 g/mL?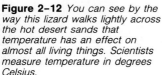

Temperature

In the metric system, temperature is measured on the **Celsius** scale. On this temperature scale, water freezes at 0°C and boils at 100°C. This is not an accident. The metric system of temperature was set up in such a way that there are exactly 100 degrees between the freezing point and boiling point of water. (Remember the metric system is based on units of 10.) Normal body temperature is 37°C. Comfortable room temperature is about 21°C.

Dimensional Analysis

You now know the basic units of measurement in the metric system. But there is still one more thing you must learn—how to go from one unit to another. The skill of converting one unit to another is called **dimensional analysis.** Dimensional analysis involves determining in what units a problem is

Figure 2–11 *To increase her density so that she can sink to the depths of the sea bottom, this scuba diver wears a belt of lead weights.*

Activity Bank
Dazzling Displays of Densities, p.106

Figure 2–12 *You can see by the way this lizard walks lightly across the hot desert sands that temperature has an effect on almost all living things. Scientists measure temperature in degrees Celsius.*

A ■ 49

INDEPENDENT PRACTICE

▶ *Activity Book*

Students who need practice on the concept of finding density should complete the chapter activity Density Determination

GUIDED PRACTICE

Skills Development

Skill: Making calculations

Divide students into teams of four to six students per team. Challenge each team to write five exercises involving the calculation of density. (Students may use the sample problem shown in the text as a model or create their own.) Then have each group trade exercises with another group and solve.

INDEPENDENT PRACTICE

▶ *Activity Book*

Students who need practice on the concept of measurement should complete the chapter activity Scientific Measurements.

to the mass divided by the volume (Density = Mass/Volume).

Explain that if an object is cut into smaller pieces, each piece would have a mass of its own. And the mass and volume of one small piece would be less than the mass and volume of the large object it was cut from. The density of the same pure substance, however, is always the same.

GUIDED PRACTICE

Skills Development

Skill: Applying concepts

Divide students into teams of four to six students per team. Provide each group with two containers of the same volume, some sand, some cotton, and a balance scale. Challenge each team to create a demonstration that illustrates the property of density. Then have each team present its demonstration to the class.

INTEGRATION
MATHEMATICS

Since many temperature measurements are given in degrees Fahrenheit, it may be helpful for students to know the formulas for conversion from Fahrenheit to Celsius and from Celsius to Fahrenheit.

$$°C = (F° - 32) \times \tfrac{5}{9}$$
$$°F = (C° \times \tfrac{9}{5}) + 32$$

Provide students with several Celsius and Fahrenheit temperatures to convert. Then, if you wish, challenge students to write their own exercises involving conversion from Celsius to Fahrenheit and from Fahrenheit to Celsius. These exercises can then be traded with a partner and solved.

COMMON ERRORS

When performing temperature conversions, some students avoid working with fractions by first converting each fraction to its decimal equivalent. In the case of the formula $°C = (F° - 32) \times \tfrac{5}{9}$, using a decimal equivalent for the fraction $\tfrac{5}{9}$ will yield inexact answers, because $\tfrac{5}{9}$ is a repeating decimal, and only its approximation can be used in the calculation. Remind students that the fractions in these formulas can by multipled simply by changing each number in the desired calculation to a fraction, then multiplying the numerators, and then multiplying the denominators.

2–1 (continued)

CONTENT DEVELOPMENT

Many times in science you will need to convert one unit of measurement to another. For example, you might be given a problem in kilometers but need the answer in centimeters. The process of converting one unit to another is called dimensional analysis.

Dimensional analysis involves determining three important facts: the unit in which your measurement is given, the unit in which the answer should be expressed, and what relationship between the units will allow you to make the con-

CAREERS

Science Editor

The staff of a national science magazine has decided to do a series of articles on important advances in science. Choosing topics for scientific articles is part of the job of **science editors.** Science editors must also select the writers who prepare the stories, and then review those stories. This may involve rewriting, correcting errors, and preparing the material for printing. The editors may also select drawings, photos, or charts to be included with the story.

Editorial opportunities are available with book, magazine, and newspaper publishers, as well as with broadcasting companies. To learn more about a career in science editing, write to The Newspaper Fund, Inc., PO Box 300, Princeton, NJ 08540.

given, in what units the answer should be, and the factor to be used to make the conversion from one unit to another. Keep in mind that you can only convert units that measure the same thing. That is, no matter how hard you try, you cannot convert length in kilometers to temperature in degrees Celsius.

To perform dimensional analysis, you must use a **conversion factor.** A conversion factor is a fraction that *always* equals 1. For example, 1 kilometer equals 1000 meters. So the fraction 1 kilometer/ 1000 meters equals 1. You can flip the conversion factor and it still equals 1: 1000 meters/1 kilometer equals 1.

In any fraction, the top number is called the numerator. The bottom number is called the denominator. So in a conversion fraction the numerator always equals the denominator and the fraction always equals 1.

This is probably beginning to sound a lot more complicated than it actually is. Let's see how it all works by using an example. Suppose you are told to convert 7500 grams to kilograms. This means that grams are your given unit and you are to convert grams to kilograms. (Your answer must be expressed in kilograms.) The conversion factor you choose must contain the relationship between grams and kilograms that has a value of 1. You have two possible choices:

$$\frac{1000 \text{ grams}}{1 \text{ kilogram}} = 1 \quad \text{or} \quad \frac{1 \text{ kilogram}}{1000 \text{ grams}} = 1$$

To convert one metric unit to another, you must multiply the given quantity times the conversion factor. Remember that multiplying a number by 1 does not change the value of the number. So multiplying by a conversion factor does not change the value of the quantity, only its units.

Now, which conversion factor should you use to change 7500 grams to kilograms? Since you want the given unit to cancel out during multiplication, you should use the conversion whose denominator has the same units as the units you wish to convert. Because you are converting grams into kilograms, the denominator of the conversion factor you use must be in grams and the numerator in kilograms.

version. The relationship between the units is called a conversion factor. A conversion factor expresses an exact relationship between the original unit and the desired unit. It is a fraction whose unit value is 1. For example,

$$\frac{60 \text{ minutes}}{1 \text{ hour}} \quad \text{or} \quad \frac{1 \text{ liter}}{1000 \text{ milliliters}}$$

Although the numerator (top) of the fraction and the denominator (bottom) of the fraction are different, their actual values are the same—60 minutes is equal to 1 hour, and 1 liter is equal to 1000 milliliters.

Any number can be multipled by one without changing its value. Multiplying a measurement by a conversion factor, then, does not change the value of the measurement. This means that you can convert the given unit to the desired unit by multiplying by an appropriate conversion factor. Point out that students must, however, choose the correct form of the

The first step in dimensional analysis, then, is to write out the given quantity, the correct conversion factor, and a multiplication symbol between them:

$$7500 \text{ grams} \times \frac{1 \text{ kilogram}}{1000 \text{ grams}}$$

The next step is to cancel out the same units:

$$7500 \text{ grams} \times \frac{1 \text{ kilogram}}{1000 \text{ grams}}$$

The last step is to multiply:

$$7500 \times \frac{1 \text{ kilogram}}{1000} = \frac{7500 \text{ kilograms}}{1000}$$

$$\frac{7500 \text{ kilograms}}{1000} = 7.5 \text{ kilograms}$$

PROBLEM Solving

Dimension Convention ❶

You have been selected as your school's representative to the International Dimension Convention. The purpose of the convention is to select the dimensional analysis champion. In order to help you bring home the trophy, your classmates have developed the following problems for you to solve. Keep in mind that the champion will be determined on both speed and accuracy.

Making Conversions
1. Two friends are training for the track team. One friend runs 5000 meters each morning. The other friend runs about 3 kilometers. Which friend is training the hardest?

2. Data from several experiments have been sent to you for analysis. To compare the data, however, you must convert the following measurements to the same units:

      20 kilograms
      700 grams
      0.004 kilograms
      300 milligrams

3. Your cat's bowl holds 0.25 liter. You have about 300 cubic centimeters of milk. Will all the milk fit in the bowl?

4. A recipe calls for 350 grams of flour. You have used 0.4 kilogram. Did you put in too much, too little, or just the right amount?

A ■ 51

---

conversion factor. The unit to be converted must cancel out, and the desired unit must remain. Thus, the denominator of the conversion factor must contain the same unit as the unit given to enable them to be canceled. Similarly, the numerator must contain the unit of the target answer.

INDEPENDENT PRACTICE

▶ *Activity Book*

Students who need practice on the concept of unit conversion should complete the chapter activity Dimensional Analysis.

• **How many kilograms are equal to 1357 grams?** (1357 g × 1 kg/1000 g = 1.357 kg.)

• **How many kilograms are equal to 791 grams?** (791 g × 1 kg/1000 g = 0.791 kg.)

PROBLEM SOLVING
DIMENSION CONVENTION

This feature enables students to relate the concept of dimensional analysis to a real-life situation: You are a representative to the International Dimension Convention. As students work, circulate around the classroom to help those who are having trouble finding the correct conversion factor or who are having difficulty multiplying and canceling the fractions.
1. The friend who runs 5000 meters each morning is training hardest.
2. 20,000 g; 700 g; 4 g; 0.3 g
3. No.
4. Too much.
Integration: Use the Problem Solving feature to integrate mathematics concepts into your lesson.

• **How many grams are equal to 3.184 kilograms?** (3.184 kg × 1000 g/1 kg = 3184 g.)
• **How many grams are equal to 0.31 kilograms?** (0.31 kg × 1000 g/1 kg = 310 g.)

INDEPENDENT PRACTICE

▶ *Activity Book*

Students who need practice on the concept of graphing conversions should complete the chapter activity Gathering Information From Graphs.

GUIDED PRACTICE

Skills Development

Skill: Making calculations

Have students make additional conversions between grams and kilograms. If necessary, write the conversion factor on the chalkboard and show both the cancellation and multiplication for each problem. Encourage students to use the symbols g and kg.

A ■ 51

2-2 Measurement Tools

MULTICULTURAL OPPORTUNITY 2-2

In small groups, have students brainstorm a list of the various tools that they use on a daily basis to make measurements; for example, measuring cup, teaspoon, bathroom scale, alarm clock, ruler. Have each group then indicate the tool and its corresponding type of measurement, such as thermometer—temperature.

Students may want to research the various tools used in different countries to make measurements. Discussing the everyday tools used for measurement may lead to a discussion on how basic systems of measurements evolved in different cultures. The ancient Chinese system of weights and measures, for example, included an acoustical dimension to measurement—the quantity of content in a vessel was defined not only by weight, but by the pitch that sounded when the object was struck.

ESL STRATEGY 2-2

Have students illustrate and label the scientific measurement tools used to determine length, volume, and mass. They should list the purpose and specific unit of measurement for each tool, as well as the unit symbol. Then ask students to exchange their work with a classmate and check for accuracy.

2-1 (continued)

INDEPENDENT PRACTICE

Section Review 2-1

1. Meter; liter; kilogram; newton; degree Celsius.
2. Mass is the amount of matter in an object. Weight is a measure of the gravitational attraction between objects.
3. Celsius scale; freezing point of water, 0°C; boiling point of water, 100°C.
4. Kilometers. The distance is so large that using smaller units would involve very large numbers, and a larger unit (light-year) would involve a very small number.
5. By determining its density. If the ob-

2-1 Section Review

1. What are the basic units of length, volume, mass, weight, and temperature in the metric system?
2. Compare mass and weight.
3. On what scale is temperature measured in the metric system? What are the fixed points on this scale?
4. What metric unit of length would be appropriate for measuring the distance from the Earth to the sun? Why?

Critical Thinking—*Applying Concepts*

5. Without placing an object in water, how can you determine if it will float?

Guide for Reading

Focus on this question as you read.

▶ *What laboratory tools are used to measure length, mass, volume, and temperature?*

2-2 Measurement Tools

Scientists use a wide variety of tools in order to study the world around them. Some of these tools are rather complex; others are relatively simple. In Chapter 3 you will discover more about the specific tools used by Life scientists, Earth scientists, and Physical scientists.

Because all sciences involve measurement, there are certain tools of measurement used by all scientists. You too will have an opportunity to use these tools when you perform activities and laboratory investigations. **The basic laboratory tools that you will learn to use are the metric ruler, triple-beam balance, graduated cylinder, and Celsius thermometer.**

Measuring Length

The most common tool used to measure length is the metric ruler. A metric ruler is divided into centimeters. Most metric rulers are between 15 and 30 centimeters in length. Each centimeter is further divided into 10 millimeters. Figure 2–13 shows a

---

ject has a density of less than 1 g/mL, it will float on water.

REINFORCEMENT/RETEACHING

Monitor students' responses to the Section Review questions. If students appear to have difficulty with any of the questions, review the appropriate material in the section.

CLOSURE

▶ *Review and Reinforcement*

At this point have students complete

Section 2–1 in their *Review and Reinforcement Guide*.

TEACHING STRATEGY 2-2

FOCUS/MOTIVATION

Collect a variety of objects whose length, mass, volume, or temperature can be measured. You might display, for example, a length of ribbon, a paperweight, a glass of cold water, and a wooden block. Ask students to tell what

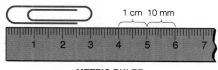

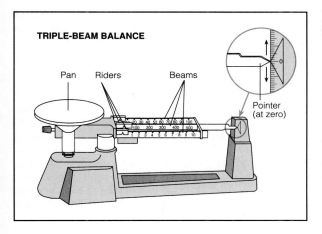

METRIC RULER

Figure 2-13 *A metric ruler is used to measure the length of small objects. What is the length of this paper clip?* ❶

metric ruler and the centimeter and millimeter divisions.

Sometimes you will need to measure objects longer than a metric ruler. To do so, you can use a meterstick. A meterstick is 1 meter long. So there are 100 centimeters in a meterstick. How many millimeters will be marked on a meterstick? Why won't you find angstroms marked off on a meterstick? ❷

Measuring Mass

As you just learned, the kilogram is the basic unit of mass in the metric system. A kilogram is equal to 1000 grams. Most of the measurements you will make in science will be in grams. The most common tool used to measure mass is the triple-beam balance. See Figure 2–14.

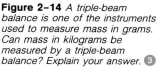

TRIPLE-BEAM BALANCE

Pan   Riders   Beams

Pointer (at zero)

Figure 2–14 *A triple-beam balance is one of the instruments used to measure mass in grams. Can mass in kilograms be measured by a triple-beam balance? Explain your answer.* ❸

A ■ 53

cision of the measuring instrument and scale.

type of measurements they would make for each item. Also display a metric ruler, a triple-beam balance, a graduated cylinder, and a Celsius thermometer. Show the collection of tools to the class and point out that every occupation or skill has its own special tools. Explain that these are the basic tools that scientists use to measure. Ask students to tell which tool they would use to measure the objects displayed.

CONTENT DEVELOPMENT

Point out that each scientific measuring tool performs a different job or function. Explain that when tools are used for measuring, we are measuring directly. In direct measurement, the thing being measured is being compared directly to the standard unit. The accuracy of a measurement depends on three things: (1) the smallest unit on the measuring scale; (2) the ability of the observer to read the scale properly; and (3) the degree of pre-

SI PREFIXES

In 1971, the Fourteenth General Conference on Weights and Measures recommeded the SI prefixes shown in the table below. In all cases, the first syllable in each prefix is accented.

Prefix	Symbol	Factor
exa-	E	10^{18}
peta-	P	10^{15}
tera-	T	10^{12}
giga-	G	10^{9}
mega-	M	10^{6}
kilo-	k	10^{3}
hecto-	h	10^{2}
deka-	da	10^{1}
deci-	d	10^{-1}
centi-	c	10^{-2}
milli-	m	10^{-3}
micro-	μ	10^{-6}
nano-	n	10^{-9}
pico-	p	10^{-12}
femto-	f	10^{-15}
atto-	a	10^{-18}

ECOLOGY NOTE

DIFFERENT METRIC PREFIXES

In addition to the common prefixes, other prefixes exist in the metric system. One hot day during the summer of 1991, the 8 million people of Chicago and its suburbs used 332 gigawatts of electricity. The prefix *giga-* means 10^{9}. With students, discuss the various ways this power may have been generated and the possible environmental impact(s) of these ways.

2-2 (continued)

CONTENT DEVELOPMENT

Remind students that in the metric system, mass is measured in kilograms, whereas weight is measured in newtons (N).

GUIDED PRACTICE

▶ *Laboratory Manual*

Skills Development

Skill: Making calculations

Have students complete the Chapter 2 Laboratory Investigation, Metric Mea-

---

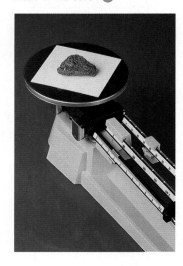

Figure 2-15 *A triple-beam balance is used to determine the mass of an object. What is the mass of the solid?* ❶

On the basis of its name, you probably guessed that a triple-beam balance has three beams. Each beam is marked in grams. The front beam is the 10-gram beam. Markings divide the front beam into 10 segments of 1 gram each. On some triple-beam balances, each 1-gram segment is further divided into units of one-tenth gram. The middle beam, often called the 500-gram beam, is divided into 5 segments of 100 grams each. The back beam, or 100-gram beam, is divided into 10 segments of 10 grams each. Based on this information, what is the largest mass you can measure on a triple-beam balance? ❷

To measure the mass of a solid, such as a small pebble, you should follow these steps. First, place the pebble on the flat pan of the balance. Then slide the rider on the middle beam notch by notch until the pointer drops below zero. Move this rider back one notch. Next, slide the rider on the back beam notch by notch until the pointer drops below zero. Move this rider back one notch. Finally, move the rider on the front beam notch by notch until the pointer points exactly to the zero mark. The mass of the object is equal to the sum of the readings on the three beams.

If you want to find the mass of a powder or of crystals, you will have to place the sample on a sheet of filter paper on top of the pan. You must never place such a sample directly on the pan itself. The mass of the filter paper must first be determined. Once this is done, you can pour the sample onto the filter paper and find the mass of the filter paper and sample combined. Finally, by subtracting the mass of the filter paper from the combined mass of the filter paper and sample, you will get the mass of the sample.

You can use a similar method to find the mass of a liquid. As you might imagine, you must never pour a liquid directly onto the pan of the triple-beam balance. Instead, first place an empty beaker or flask on the pan and find its mass. Then pour the liquid into the container and find the combined mass of the liquid and the container. Now it is a simple process to subtract the mass of the container from the combined mass of the container and liquid. This will give you the mass of the liquid.

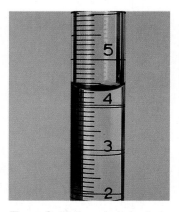

Figure 2-16 *A graduated cylinder is used to measure volume. To get an accurate measurement, where should you read the markings on the graduated cylinder?* ❸

---

surement: Mass, in the *Laboratory Manual*. In the investigation students will learn to measure mass and express the measurement in the proper metric unit.

CONTENT DEVELOPMENT

Hold up a glass of water. Explain that volume is the amount of space an object takes up. When the volume of a container is measured, that measure is called capacity.

• **How could we measure the volume of water in this glass?** (Students might sug-

gest pouring the liquid into a measuring cup or graduated cylinder.)

Tell students that the basic unit for measuring volume in the metric system is the liter (L). Volumes less than 1 liter are measured in milliliters (mL).

Show students a block of wood.

• **How could we find the volume of this piece of wood?** (Most students will say measure it using the formula V = lwh.)

Tell students that the volume of a solid is measured in cubic centimeters (cm^3),

Measuring Volume

As you know, the liter is the basic unit of volume in the metric system. However, most of the measurements you will make in science will be in milliliters or cubic centimeters. Recall that 1 milliliter equals 1 cubic centimeter.

To find the volume of a liquid, scientists use a graduated cylinder. See Figure 2–16. A graduated cylinder is marked off in 1-milliliter segments. Each line on a graduated cylinder is 1 milliliter. To measure the volume of a liquid, pour the liquid into a graduated cylinder. You will notice that the top surface of the liquid is curved. To determine the volume of the liquid, read the milliliter marking at the bottom of the curve. (This curve is called the meniscus.) Suppose a liquid has a volume of 10 mL. How many cubic centimeters is this? ④

To find the volume of a solid that is rectangular in shape, you will use a metric ruler. A rectangular solid is often called a regular solid. The volume of a regular solid is determined by multiplying the length of the solid times the width times the height. The formula you can use to find the volume of a regular solid is:

Volume = length times width times height

or

$$v = l \times w \times h$$

As you might expect, most of the solids you will measure will not be regular solids. Such solids are called irregular solids. Because the solid has an irregular shape, you cannot measure its length, width, or height. Are you stuck? Not really.

To determine the volume of an irregular solid, you will go back to the graduated cylinder. First fill the cylinder about half full with water. Record the volume of the water. Then carefully place the solid in the water. Record the volume of the solid and water combined. Subtract the volume of the water from the combined volume of the water and solid. The result will be the volume of the irregular solid. What units should you use for your answer? ⑤

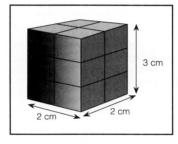

Figure 2–17 *What is the volume of this rectangular block in cubic centimeters?* ⑥

A C T I V I T Y
T H I N K I N G

HOW GOOD IS YOUR GUESS?

Skills: Relating facts, making observations

Students should be able to apply their knowledge and understanding of various metric units (mass, volume, length, distance, and temperature) to the measure of familiar objects. Students may be used to thinking of these objects in terms of English units of measurement. Accept all logical answers.

• **Do you think that this method would work for any irregular object, provided the container of water was large enough to hold it?** (Responses might include yes.)

• **For what types of objects would this method not work?** (Objects that are less dense than water.)

• **Why?** (These objects would float and would not displace an amount of water equal to their own volumes.)

INDEPENDENT PRACTICE

▶ *Activity Book*

Students who need practice in measuring volume should be provided with the Chapter 2 activity called Measuring Liquid Volume With a Graduated Cylinder.

reminding them that 1 cubic centimeter (cm³) is equal to 1 milliliter (mL).

GUIDED PRACTICE

Skills Development

Skill: Making calculations

Begin by showing the class a stone.

• **Do you think we could find the volume of this stone by measuring its dimensions?** (No.)

• **Why not?** (The stone is not a regular shape, and there is no formula for cal-

culating the volume of an irregular solid such as a stone.)

Divide students into teams of four to six students per team. Give each team a graduated cylinder, some water, and a stone. Reminding teams to note the height of the water in the cylinder both before and after the stone is inserted, have them calculate the volume of the stone.

• **Knowing that 1 mL = 1 cm³, what is the volume of your stone?** (Answers will vary.)

Check each conversion for accuracy.
Integration: Use this Activity to integrate mathematics concepts into your lesson.

BACKGROUND INFORMATION

ANCIENT UNITS OF LENGTH

History has recorded units of length used in ancient civilizations.

Cubit: A unit of length based on the length of a forearm, considered to be approximately 43 to 53 centimeters.

Digit: A unit of length based on the width of a finger, considered to be approximately 2 centimeters.

Span: A unit of length based on the distance between the tip of the thumb and the tip of the little finger when the hand is fully extended. A span is considered to be approximately 23 centimeters.

2–2 (continued)

GUIDED PRACTICE

▶ *Laboratory Manual*

Skills Development

Skill: Making calculations

Have students complete the Chapter 2 Laboratory Investigation, Metric Measurement: Volume and Temperature, in the *Laboratory Manual.* In the investigation students will learn to measure volume and temperature and to express these measurements in proper metric units.

CONTENT DEVELOPMENT

Distribute several Celsius thermometers throughout the classroom. Allow students sufficient time to examine the thermometers.

• **What is the air temperature in the classroom?** (Usually about 20° to 25°C, unless it is an unusually hot or cold day.)

Figure 2–18 *A Celsius thermometer is used to measure temperatures such as those experienced by a polar bear in Alaska. What is the temperature of the ice-water mixture in the beaker?* ❶

ACTIVITY

CALCULATING

Metric Conversions

❶ Use conversion factors to make the following metric conversions. *Do not write in this book.*

10 m = _____	km
2 km = _____	cm
250 mL = _____	L
2000 g = _____	kg
10 kg = _____	mg
1500 cc = _____	L

Measuring Temperature

You already know that temperature is measured with a thermometer. In the laboratory you will use a Celsius thermometer for temperature measurements. Each segment on a Celsius thermometer is equal to 1 degree Celsius. Many Celsius thermometers go as low as −25° so that temperatures below the freezing point of water (0°) can be measured.

Within the glass tube of a Celsius thermometer is a colored liquid. The liquid is usually mercury or alcohol. In order to measure the temperature of a substance, place the thermometer in the substance. The liquid in the thermometer will begin to change level (go up or go down). Wait until the liquid stops changing level. Then read the number next to the mark on the thermometer that lines up with the top of the liquid. This number is the temperature of the substance.

2–2 Section Review

1. Identify the instruments used to measure length, mass, volume, and temperature.
2. Each side of a regular solid is 5 centimeters long. What is the volume of the solid?

Critical Thinking—*Relating Concepts*
3. If you want to find the density of an irregular object, what tools will you need? How will you go about making this measurement?

• **What would the thermometer read if the temperature was at the freezing point of water?** (0°C.)

• **What would the thermometer read if the temperature was at the boiling point of water?** (100°C.)

Write the formula $C = (F° - 32) \times \frac{5}{9}$ on the chalkboard.

• **The average temperature of a human being is 98.6 degrees Fahrenheit. In degrees Celsius, what is the average body temperature of a human being?** (37°C.)

Write the formula $F = (C° \times \frac{9}{5}) + 32$ on the chalkboard.

• **A comfortable temperature for bath water is about 45 degrees Celsius. What is a comfortable temperature for bath water in Fahrenheit degrees?** (113°F.)

GUIDED PRACTICE

Skills Development

Skill: Applying concepts

Students may now complete the in-text Chapter 2 Laboratory Investigation

CONNECTIONS

Elbows to Fingertips ❷

Have you complained to your teacher yet that you do not like the metric system? If so, perhaps you should read about some ancient systems of measurement. You might just decide that the metric system makes a lot of sense.

The Egyptians: The Egyptians are credited with having developed the most widespread system of measuring length in the ancient world. Developed around 3000 BC, the Egyptian standard of measurement was the *cubit.* The cubit was based on the length from the elbow to the fingertips. The cubit was further divided into *digits* (the length of

a finger), *palms,* and *hands.* As you can see, body parts were the basis for most measurements.

The cubit may not seem like a very accurate measurement as the length of an arm varies from person to person. To avoid any confusion, a standard cubit made of granite was developed. All cubit sticks used in Egypt were measured against the standard granite cubit. And while this may not seem all that precise, the Egyptians built the great pyramids with incredible accuracy using the cubit!

The Greeks and Romans: Around 1000 BC, the Greeks developed a new system of measuring length. The basic unit of measurement was called the *finger* (again, body parts were popular). Sixteen fingers equaled a *foot* in the Greek system. Over time the influence of the Greeks diminished and the Romans became the dominant culture in the ancient world. The Romans adjusted the Greek system and divided the Greek foot into twelve *inches.* (Although the lengths have changed, we still use feet and inches in the United States.) The Romans then decided that five foots equaled a *pace.* And finally, one thousand paces equaled what they called a *mile.*

So the next time you are asked to measure something in meters or centimeters, remember—it could be worse. You could have to measure the distance from one place to another by placing your arm down over and over again.

A ■ 57

CONNECTIONS
ELBOWS TO FINGERTIPS

Students will be interested by the discussion about ancient systems of measurement. Many students may not have previously realized that civilization did not always have universal, precise standard units of measure. You may want to have students make measurements of objects in the classroom and the school grounds using some of these ancient units.

If you are teaching thematically, you may want to use the Connections feature to reinforce the themes of unity and diversity, systems and interactions, or scale and structure.

Integration: Use the Connections feature to integrate social studies into your lesson.

---

inder; temperature: Celsius thermometer.

2. 125 cm³.

3. To determine the density of an irregular object, find its mass using a triple-beam balance, find its volume using a graduated cylinder, and then use the formula Density = Mass/Volume.

REINFORCEMENT/RETEACHING

Review students' responses to the Section Review questions. Reteach any material that is still unclear, based on their responses.

CLOSURE

▶ *Review and Reinforcement*

Students may now complete Section 2–2 in their *Review and Reinforcement Guide.*

---

called Uncertainty of Measurement. In the investigation students will discover how accurately matter can be measured.

INDEPENDENT PRACTICE

▶ *Product Testing Activity*

Have students perform the product test on breakfast cereals from the Product Testing Activity worksheets. Ask students to relate the measurements to probability and statistics.

ENRICHMENT

▶ *Activity Book*

Students will be challenged by the Chapter 2 activity in the *Activity Book* called Percentage Error. In the activity students will compute the amount of error in measurements as scientists do.

INDEPENDENT PRACTICE

Section Review 2–2

1. Length: meterstick; mass: triple-beam balance; volume: graduated cyl-

Laboratory Investigation

UNCERTAINTY OF MEASUREMENTS

BEFORE THE LAB

1. Divide the class into groups of three to six students.

2. Gather all materials at least one day prior to the investigation.

3. Prepare a class data table so that students can record all class data for each work station.

PRE-LAB DISCUSSION

Have students read the complete laboratory procedure

• **What is the purpose of the laboratory activity?** (To find out about the uncertainty of measurement or how accurately matter can be measured using common laboratory tools.)

• **Station 1: What is the smallest unit shown on the meterstick?** (The smallest unit shown on the meterstick is 1 mm, or 0.1 cm.)

• **Station 2: How do you find the volume of an object when you know its length, width, and height?** (Multiply the length times the width times the height.)

• **Station 3: Which part of the meniscus should be read?** (The bottom curve of the meniscus should be read.)

• **Station 4: Why is it important for the riders to start at zero?** (The riders should start at zero so that you can see that the balance starts even at zero grams.)

• **Station 5: How can we convert milliliters to cubic centimeters?** (One cubic centimeter is equal to 1 mL. Keep the same number and change the unit symbol.)

• **Station 6: What is the smallest unit on this Celsius scale?** (One degree Celsius is the smallest unit on the thermometer scale. **Note:** *Some thermometers may have different graduations.*)

Laboratory Investigation

Uncertainty of Measurements

Problem

How accurately can matter be measured?

Materials   *(per station)*

Station 1: meterstick
Station 2: metric ruler
           regular object
Station 3: graduated cylinder
           beaker with colored liquid
Station 4: triple-beam balance
           small pebble
Station 5: graduated cylinder
           beaker of water
           irregular object
Station 6: Celsius thermometer
           beaker with ice and water
           paper towel

Procedure ⚗

1. Station 1: Use the meterstick to measure the length and width of the desk or lab table. If the table is irregular, measure the shortest width and the longest length. Express your measurements in centimeters.

2. Station 2: Use the metric ruler to find the volume of the regular object. Express the volume in cubic centimeters.

3. Station 3: Use the graduated cylinder to find the volume of the colored liquid in the beaker. Then pour the liquid back into the beaker. Express your measurement in milliliters.

4. Station 4: Place the pebble on the pan of the triple-beam balance. Move the riders

until the pointer is at zero. Record the mass of the pebble in grams. Remove the pebble and return all riders back to zero.

5. Station 5: Fill the graduated cylinder half full with water. Find the volume of the irregular object. Express the volume of the object in cubic centimeters. Carefully remove the object from the graduated cylinder. Pour all of the water back into the beaker.

6. Station 6: Use the Celsius thermometer to find the temperature of the ice water. Record the temperature in degrees Celsius. Remove the thermometer and carefully dry it with a paper towel.

Observations

Your teacher will construct a large class data table for each of the work stations. Record the data from each work station in the class data table.

Analysis and Conclusions

1. Do all the class measurements have the exact same value for each station?

2. Which station had measurements that were most nearly alike? Explain why these measurements were so similar.

3. Which station had measurements that were most varied? Explain why these measurements were so varied.

4. **On Your Own**   Calculate the average (mean) for the class data for each work station.

TEACHING STRATEGY

1. Assign a starting station to each group. After the groups have completed one station, they should proceed to the next station. Allow about five minutes per station.

2. Have the groups follow the directions carefully as they work in the laboratory.

3. You might ask the groups to write down what they guess each measure will be before the actual measurement.

DISCOVERY STRATEGIES

Discuss how the investigation relates to the chapter ideas by asking open questions similar to the following.

• **Describe a way in which the tools at the various stations will yield accurate measurements.** (The measurement is exactly equal to the smallest unit of measure on the scale.)

• **Describe a way in which the tools at the various stations will yield inaccurate measurements.** (The measurement

Study Guide

Summarizing Key Concepts

2–1 The Metric System

▲ The standard system of measurement used by all scientists is the metric system.

▲ The basic unit of length in the metric system is the meter. One meter is equal to 100 centimeters or 1000 millimeters.

▲ One kilometer is equal to 1000 meters.

▲ The basic unit of mass in the metric system is the kilogram. One kilogram is equal to 1000 grams.

▲ Weight is a measure of the force of attraction due to gravity. The basic unit of weight in the metric system is the newton.

▲ Although mass is a constant, weight can change depending on location.

▲ The basic unit of volume in the metric system is the liter. One liter contains 1000 milliliters or 1000 cubic centimeters.

▲ One cubic centimeter is equal in volume to 1 milliliter.

▲ Density is defined as the mass per unit volume of an object.

▲ The basic unit of temperature in the metric system is the degree Celsius.

▲ Dimensional analysis is a method of converting from one unit to another by multiplying the given quantity by a conversion factor whose value is one.

2–2 Measurement Tools

▲ A metric ruler is used to measure length. It is divided into centimeters and millimeters.

▲ A triple-beam balance is used to measure mass.

▲ A graduated cylinder is used to find the volume of a liquid or the volume of an irregular solid.

▲ The volume of a regular solid can be determined by multiplying its length by its width by its height.

▲ A Celsius thermometer is used to measure temperature.

Reviewing Key Terms

Define each term in a complete sentence.

2–1 The Metric System

metric system	kilogram
meter	gram
centimeter	milligram
millimeter	weight
kilometer	newton
light-year	density
liter	Celsius
milliliter	dimensional analysis
cubic centimeter	conversion factor

dents measure the temperature of ice water, will likely have quite different measurements because the ice may melt. Also, as the cold water sits on the table, it will absorb heat from its surroundings and become warmer than it was at the beginning of the lab activity.

4. Answers will vary depending on the objects measured.

GOING FURTHER: ENRICHMENT

Part I

Have students count the number of centimeters in a meter. The answer should be 100 because we counted. There are exactly 100 cm in 1 m. When we measure, however, we always have to estimate to the nearest half or whole unit on the scale. Therefore, measurements can be "accurate" or even "precise," but they are seldom exact.

Part 2

Have each group select a new set of objects to be measured for one of the work stations. After replacing these items for those presently at the work stations, have students repeat the investigation procedures.

is not exactly equal to the smallest unit of measure on the scale.)

• **Describe some tools that scientists might use to get more accurate measurements.** (Responses might include digital scales or thermometers calibrated to thousandths of a gram or hundredths of a degree, respectively.)

OBSERVATIONS

Check that students have accurately recorded work station data on the class data table.

ANALYSIS AND CONCLUSIONS

1. It is unlikely that class data for each station will be exactly the same. Students should note that the data entries vary within a given station.

2. Answers will vary. In most cases, stations 2, 3, and 4 will have the closest data because the objects measured were relatively exact.

3. In most cases, measurements at stations 1, 5, and 6 will be the most dissimilar. In particular, station 6, in which stu-

Chapter Review

Chapter Review

ALTERNATIVE ASSESSMENT

The Prentice Hall Science program includes a variety of testing components and methodologies. Aside from the Chapter Review questions, you may opt to use the Chapter Test or the Computer Test Bank Test in your *Test Book* for assessment of important facts and concepts. In addition, Performance-Based Tests are included in your *Test Book*. These Performance-Based Tests are designed to test science process skills, rather than factual content recall. Since they are not content dependent, Performance-Based Tests can be distributed after students complete a chapter or after they complete the entire textbook.

CONTENT REVIEW

Multiple Choice
1. b
2. c
3. c
4. c
5. c
6. b
7. d
8. c

True or False
1. F, one thousand
2. T
3. T
4. F, mass
5. F, temperature
6. F, mass, volume
7. T
8. F, volume

Concept Mapping
Row 1: Weight
Row 2: Length, Density
Row 3: Milliliter, Cubic Centimeter
Row 4: Kilogram, Gram
Row 5: Light-year

CONCEPT MASTERY

1. Without a standard system of measurement, scientists all over the world cannot be sure they are comparing their data accurately. They cannot transmit data and be sure the data are being interpreted correctly.

2. Mass is the measure of the amount of matter in an object. The mass of an object does not change unless the amount of matter changes. Weight is a measure of the force of attraction between objects due to gravity. Because the force of attraction between an object and the Earth is greater, for example, than the force of attraction between that same object and the moon, the weight of the object is different on the Earth and on the moon.

3. A millimeter—one thousandth of a meter—might be used to measure the thickness of lead in your pencil. A centi-meter—one hundredth of a meter—might be used to measure the width of your fingernail. A meter—the standard unit of metric length—might be used to measure the length of your classroom. A kilometer—one thousand meters—might be used to measure the distance you travel on a vacation.

4. Density is defined as the mass per unit volume of a substance. Density is an important component in a scientist's effort to define, name, and classify various substances.

Content Review

Multiple Choice

Choose the letter of the answer that best completes each statement.

1. The basic unit of length in the metric system is the
   a. kilometer.
   b. meter.
   c. liter.
   d. light-year.

2. A cubic centimeter is equal in volume to a
   a. kilogram.
   b. graduated cylinder.
   c. milliliter.
   d. millimeter.

3. The amount of matter in an object is called its
   a. density.   c. mass.
   b. volume.   d. weight.

4. Pure water freezes at
   a. 100°C.   c. 0°C.
   b. 32°C.   d. 10°C.

5. A graduated cylinder is divided into
   a. grams.
   b. degrees Celsius.
   c. milliliters.
   d. grams per milliliter.

6. To measure the mass of a solid, you should use a
   a. graduated cylinder.
   b. triple-beam balance.
   c. meterstick.
   d. bathroom scale.

7. Each side of a cube is 4 cm. Its volume is
   a. 16 cc.   c. 16 mL.
   b. 128 cc.   d. 64 cc.

8. In dimensional analysis, the conversion factor must be equal to
   a. the numerator.   c. 1.
   b. the denominator. d. 10.

True or False

If the statement is true, write "true." If it is false, change the underlined word or words to make the statement true.

1. The prefix *kilo-* means <u>one-thousandth</u>.
2. The <u>liter</u> is the basic unit of volume in the metric system.
3. The force of attraction between objects is called <u>gravity</u>.
4. Your <u>weight</u> on the moon would be the same as it is on the Earth.
5. Degrees Celsius are used to measure <u>volume</u>.
6. Density is <u>volume</u> per unit <u>mass</u>.
7. The boiling point of water is <u>100°C</u>.
8. The amount of space an object takes up is called its <u>mass</u>.

Concept Mapping

Complete the following concept map for Section 2–1. Refer to pages A6–A7 to construct a concept map for the entire chapter.

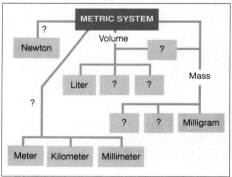

Concept Mastery

Discuss each of the following in a brief paragraph.

1. Describe the importance of a standard system of measurement.
2. Explain why mass is constant whereas weight can change.
3. Discuss the different metric units of length and explain when you might use each one.
4. Describe density in terms of mass and volume. Why is density such an important quantity?

5. Your friend wants you to convert kilograms to meters. Explain why that is not possible.
6. The Earth is about 5 billion years old. Yet some of the light that reaches Earth from distant stars began its journey before the Earth was formed. What does that tell you about the distance to those stars? Explain your answer.

Critical Thinking and Problem Solving

Use the skills you have developed in this chapter to answer each of the following.

1. **Applying concepts** What tool or tools would you use to make the following measurements? What units would you use to express your answers?
   a. Volume of a glass of water
   b. Length of a sheet of paper
   c. Mass of a liter of milk
   d. Length of a soccer field
   e. Volume of an irregular object
   f. Mass of a hockey puck
   g. Ocean temperature
2. **Making calculations** Use dimensional analysis to convert each of the following.
   a. A blue whale is about 33 meters in length. How many centimeters is this?
   b. The Statue of Liberty is about 45 meters tall. How tall is the statue in millimeters?
   c. Mount Everest is about 8.8 kilometers high. How high is it in meters?
   d. A Ping-Pong ball has a mass of about 2.5 grams. What is its mass in milligrams?
   e. An elephant is about 6300 kilograms in mass. What is its mass in grams?
3. **Relating concepts** Explain why every substance has a characteristic density, but no substance has a characteristic mass.

4. **Designing an experiment** A prospector is trying to sell you the deed to a gold mine. She gives you a sample from the mine and tells you it is pure gold. Design an experiment to determine if the sample is pure gold or "fools" gold. *Hint:* You will want to use the concept of density in your experiment.

5. **Using the writing process** Although the metric system is used throughout the world, it has not been officially adopted by the United States. Write a letter to the editor of your local newspaper in which you explain why the United States should or should not convert to the metric system.

---

matter in the object. Cut the object in half, and the mass is also cut in half. Density, however, is a characteristic of a particular material. Each substance has a particular density, and doubling or changing the size of the substance will not change the density of that substance.

4. Experiments might include obtaining a triple-beam balance and a graduated cylinder. Use these tools to find the mass and volume of the substance. Using the density formula $D = M/V$, calculate the density of the substance. The density of gold is 19.32 g/cm^3, and if the density of the substance does not equal 19.32 g/cm^3, that substance is not pure gold.

5. Letters will vary but should include a clearly defined position relative to whether the United States should or should not convert to the metric system. This position should be explained and supported.

KEEPING A PORTFOLIO

You might want to assign some of the Concept Mastery and Critical Thinking and Problem Solving questions as homework and have students include their responses to unassigned questions in their portfolio. Students should be encouraged to include both the question and the answer in their portfolio.

ISSUES IN SCIENCE

The following issues can be used as springboards for discussion or given as writing assignments.

1. Some scientists believe that making many "accurate" measurements and averaging them still gives an "accurate not precise" measure. Other scientists believe that taking many "accurate" measurements and averaging them gives a "precise" measure. What is your opinion and why?

2. Considerable effort has been made in recent years to use the metric system in all aspects of everyday life. Some people object to this, saying that it is an unnecessary nuisance. Other people claim that it is important to standardize world measurements. What is your opinion? Why?

---

5. No conversion factor equaling 1 exists for the conversion of kilograms to meters.
6. The distance to the stars must be equal to or greater than 5 billion light-years. Explanations will vary.

CRITICAL THINKING AND PROBLEM SOLVING

1a. Graduated cylinder or measuring cup; liter or milliliter.
b. Meterstick; centimeter.
c. Triple-beam balance; kilogram.

d. Meterstick; meter.
e. Graduated cylinder; milliliter or cubic centimeter.
f. Triple-beam balance; gram.
g. Celsius thermometer; degree Celsius.
2a. 33 m × 100 cm = 3300 cm.
b. 45 m × 1000 mm = 45,000 mm.
c. 8.8 km × 1000 m = 8800 m.
d. 2.5 g × 1000 mg = 2500 mg.
e. 6300 kg × 1000 g = 6,300,000 g.
3. This statement says that the mass of an object is determined by the amount of

Chapter 3 TOOLS AND THE SCIENCES

SECTION	HANDS-ON ACTIVITIES
3–1 Exploring the Microscopic World pages A62–A71 Multicultural Opportunity 3–1, p. A62 ESL Strategy 3–1, p. A62	**Student Edition** ACTIVITY (Discovering): Abracadabra, It's Gone, p. A65 ACTIVITY BANK: Life In a Drop of Water, p. A108 **Activity Book** CHAPTER DISCOVERY: Exploring Magnification, p. A77 ACTIVITY: Experimental Controls and Variables, p. A81 ACTIVITY BANK: A Sunsational Experiment, p. A135 **Laboratory Manual** The Microscope: A Tool of the Scientist, p. A33 Using the Microscope, p. A39 **Teacher Edition** Seeing With and Without Light, p. A62d
3–2 Exploring the Universe pages A72–A78 Multicultural Opportunity 3–2, p. A72 ESL Strategy 3–2, p. A72	**Student Edition** LABORATORY INVESTIGATION: Constructing a Telescope, p. A86 **Product Testing Activity** Testing Pens
3–3 Exploring the Earth pages A78–A85 Multicultural Opportunity 3–3, p. A78 ESL Strategy 3–3, p. A78	**Student Edition** ACTIVITY (Discovering): Food From the Ocean, p. A79 **Activity Book** ACTIVITY: Building a Seismograph, p. A89 **Teacher Edition** Recording Air Temperature, p. A62d **Laboratory Manual** Tools of the Scientist: The Bunsen Burner and a Filtering Apparatus, p. A45
Chapter Review pages A86–A89	

OUTSIDE TEACHER RESOURCES

Books

Baker, David. *Starwatch*, Rourke Enterprises.

Bleifeld, Maurice. *Experimenting With a Microscope*, Franklin Watts.

Cornell, James, and John Carr. *Infinite Vistas: New Tools for Astronomy*, Charles Scribner.

Limburg, Peter R., and James B. Sweeney. *Vessels for Underwater Exploration*, Crown

Publishers.

National Geographic Society. *Hidden Worlds*.

Taylor, Ron. *Through the Microscope*, Facts on File.

OTHER ACTIVITIES	MEDIA AND TECHNOLOGY
Student Edition ACTIVITY (Reading): Dutchman's Dilemma, p. A64 **Activity Book** ACTIVITY: Microscopic Proportions, p. A81 **Review and Reinforcement Guide** Section 3–1, p. A21	**English/Spanish Audiotapes** Section 3–1
Student Edition ACTIVITY (Writing): A New Comet, p. A76 **Activity Book** ACTIVITY: Measuring Tools, p. A83 **Review and Reinforcement Guide** Section 3–2, p. A23	**Video** Planets (Supplemental) Neptune's Cold Fury (Supplemental) **English/Spanish Audiotapes** Section 3–2
Student Edition ACTIVITY (Reading): Dangerous Depths, p. A80 ACTIVITY (Calculating): Earthquake Waves, p. A81 ACTIVITY (Calculating): A Water Barometer, p. A84 **Activity Book** ACTIVITY: A Water Barometer, p. A85 **Review and Reinforcement Guide** Section 3–3, p. A25	**Video** Buoyancy (Supplemental) **English/Spanish Audiotapes** Section 3–3
Test Book Chapter Test, p. A57 Performance-Based Tests, p. A75	**Test Book** Computer Test Bank Test, p. A63

*All materials in the Chapter Planning Guide Grid are available as part of the Prentice Hall Science Learning System.

Audiovisuals

Imagining a Hidden World: The Light Microscope, film or video, Coronet
Journey Into Microscope: A Photographic

Odyssey, sound filmstrip with cassette, Ward
The Microscope: Light Field Illumination, film loop, PH Media

Chapter 3 TOOLS AND THE SCIENCES

CHAPTER OVERVIEW

The tools scientists use have enabled them to explore the world of microorganisms and the vastness of the universe as well as the Earth. Since van Leeuwenhoek first discovered "animalcules" using his simple microscope, microscopes have been used to view and understand microscopic particles. Compound light microscopes can magnify a specimen 1000 times its actual size, and electron microscopes can magnify a specimen a million times its actual size. X-rays, CT scans, and MRIs have made it possible to look through barriers to the internal structures of living organisms.

Telescopes have opened the universe to scientific study. Optical telescopes use visible light to focus images on the lens of a refracting telescope or on the mirrors of a reflecting telescope. Other telescopes use different light from the electromagnetic spectrum to focus images. These include the radio telescope, the infrared telescope, the ultraviolet telescope, and the X-ray telescope. Amazing discoveries of the universe have been made possible by these specialized telescopes that can focus images millions of light-years away.

Tools for studying the Earth have enabled scientists to explore the ocean, the Earth's crust, and the atmosphere. Submersibles such as the bathysphere and the bathyscaph have enabled scientists to explore the depths of the ocean, where they discovered life forms that live without sunlight for energy. The seismograph has enabled scientists to record and measure earthquakes. Barometers measure air pressure and enable scientists to predict the weather. The vast variety of tools scientists use have increased our understanding of our Earth, our universe, and the nature of matter.

3-1 EXPLORING THE MICROSCOPIC WORLD
THEMATIC FOCUS

The purpose of this section is to introduce students to the visual-aid tools that have enabled scientists to view the microscopic world. Students will identify the advantages and disadvantages of the optical light microscopes and the electron microscopes. They also learn about the tools that have enabled scientists to study the interior of specimens—X-rays, computed tomography, and magnetic-resonance imaging. The main thrust of the section, however, is to help students understand that scientific knowledge of the microscopic world has been enhanced by the technology and tools that are available for scientific study. The themes that can be focused on in this section are scale and structure and unity and diversity.

*Scale and structure: Emphasize that the microscope, through magnification, has made it possible for scientists to study very small specimens and to identify the structure of these specimens. Compound light microscopes can magnify up to 1000 times, and electron microscopes can magnify more than a million times. To dramatize the effect of magnification, refer students to Figure 3–7 on page A69.

*Unity and diversity: Through the use of the microscope, scientists can confirm that all matter in all forms is made up of atoms. From human beings to the smallest protozoa and from air to the largest mountain, all matter has atomic structure.

PERFORMANCE OBJECTIVES 3–1

1. Compare compound light microscopes to electron microscopes.
2. Cite advantages and disadvantages of the compound light microscope and the electron microscope.
3. Identify scientific tools that can provide images of the interior of living organisms.

SCIENCE TERMS 3–1

lens p. A65
compound light microscope p. A66
electron microscope p. 67

3-2 EXPLORING THE UNIVERSE
THEMATIC FOCUS

The purpose of this section is to introduce the tools scientists use to study the universe beyond Earth. Students are introduced to the two types of optical telescopes—the refracting and reflecting telescopes. The structure and limitations of each type of telescope are detailed. The text identifies telescopes that use light other than visible light to focus images. The radio, infrared, ultraviolet, and X-ray telescopes are described. The text points out that infrared, ultraviolet, and X-ray telescopes are all carried into space because the infrared and ultraviolet rays and X-rays do not pass easily through Earth's atmosphere.

The themes that can be focused on in this section are energy, patterns of change, systems and interactions, and unity and diversity.

Energy: As you discuss telescopes that use different light waves to focus images, explain that the electromagnetic spectrum is divided into visible light, ultraviolet light, infrared light, X-rays, and radio waves. Each form of light is characterized by a different amount of energy carried by the light wave.

Patterns of change: The universe is constantly changing as stars go through their life cycles, as planets revolve around the sun, and as galaxies are in motion. Our view of these changes is made possible as we observe the universe through visible light, radio waves, X-rays, ultraviolet light, and infrared light. Our understanding of the universe also changes as the telescopes provide more and more information about the universe.

*Systems and interactions: Ultraviolet light, infrared light, and X-rays do not pass easily through our atmosphere, which either absorbs these forms of light or reflects them back into space. As a result, telescopes are launched into space in order to observe these forms of light emitted by distant objects.

Unity and diversity: All objects in space are unified in that they all are made up of matter and have energy. Yet the amount and type of energy emitted by these objects varies from object to object.

PERFORMANCE OBJECTIVES

1. Compare reflecting telescopes and refracting telescopes.
2. Describe the specialized telescopes that can focus images with forms of light from the electromagnetic spectrum other than visible light.

SCIENCE TERMS

refracting telescope p. A73
reflecting telescope p. A73
electromagnetic spectrum p. A75
radio telescope p. A75
infrared telescope p. A76
untraviolet telescope p. A76
X-ray telescope p. A77

3–3 EXPLORING THE EARTH

THEMATIC FOCUS

The purpose of this section is to introduce students to some of the tools scientists use to study the Earth. Point out that different tools are used to study the Earth's ocean, crust, and atmosphere. Emphasize that our understanding of the ocean has increased tremendously in the past few decades because of new tools such as the bathysphere and the bathyscaph that have made deep-sea exploration possible. Among the tools used by scientists to understand the Earth is the seismograph, which has enabled scientists to record and measure earthquakes. An important tool for studying the atmosphere is the barometer, which measures atmospheric pressure.

The themes that can be focused on in this section are energy, patterns of change, and systems and interactions.

Energy: As you discuss the seismograph, explain that by recording the seismic waves, the seismograph has a record of the tremendous energy of an earthquake. Point out that the primary waves, secondary waves, and surface waves of an earthquake are all forms of energy.

Patterns of change: Explain that both the seismograph and the barometer can be used to record changes. The seismograph records changes caused by earthquakes. The barometer can be used to record changes in atmospheric pressure. Emphasize for students that air pressure varies from location to location and can vary in the same place from hour to hour. Explain that temperature, elevation, and water vapor can all affect changes in air pressure.

Systems and interactions: The barometer is one of the tools scientists use to study weather and weather systems. Air pressure is the result of the interaction of elevation, temperature, and water vapor on the air.

PERFORMANCE OBJECTIVES

1. Identify submersibles that have made ocean exploration possible.
2. Describe a seismograph and its function.
3. Explain the purpose of barometers.

SCIENCE TERMS

bathysphere p. A79
bathyscaph p. A79
seismograph p. A81
barometer p. A83

Discovery *Learning*

TEACHER DEMONSTRATIONS MODELING

Seeing With and Without Light

Place an eye chart on a bulletin board. Darken the classroom as much as possible. Stand about 10 meters from the chart and try to read as many rows on the chart as possible. Have a student volunteer record what you are able to read and have the class determine your accuracy. Turn on the lights in the room and repeat the activity. Once again, repeat the activity, but this time use a pair of binoculars. After each repetition, have students assess your accuracy based on the volunteer's record.

• **Why do you think I was unable to read the chart very well when the lights were out?** (Because it was too dark.)
• **Why was I more accurate when the lights were turned on?** (The lights made it possible to see better.)
• **How did the binoculars help me read better?** (They magnified the images.)

Recording Air Temperature

Place a thermometer near the ceiling and another near the floor. Use a space heater to generate heat. Do not place the heater very close to the thermometers. At five-minute intervals, read the temperatures recorded by both thermometers and list them on the chalkboard.

• **Are the temperature readings the same for both thermometers?** (Students should note that the readings from the thermometer near the ceiling should be slightly higher.)
• **Why would I expect the readings from the thermometer on the ceiling to be higher?** (Warm air is forced up by cooler, denser air.)
• **Where do you think the air pressure is greater, near the ceiling or close to the floor? Why?** (Air pressure is greater near the floor because cooler air is more dense. As a result, it exerts more pressure.)

CHAPTER 1
Tools and the Sciences

INTEGRATING SCIENCE

This science chapter provides you with numerous opportunities to integrate many areas of science, as well as other disciplines, into your curriculum. Blue numbered annotations on the student page and integration notes on the teacher wraparound pages alert you to areas of possible integration.

In this chapter you can integrate social studies (pp. 64, 80), language arts (pp. 65, 76, 80), physical science and physics (p. 67), physical science and light (pp. 70, 75), life science and evolution (p. 71), physical science and optics (p. 73), physical science and heat energy (p. 76), life science and zoology (p. 79), mathematics (pp. 81, 84), earth science and geology (p. 82), and earth science and meteorology (p. 83).

SCIENCE, TECHNOLOGY, AND SOCIETY/COOPERATIVE LEARNING

What can explore nuclear reactors for cracks or biopsy a suspicious lump in the body but is smaller than a snowflake and tinier than a grain of sand? Micromachines. Micromachines are about the size of a baby's fingernail and can sit on a silicon chip 1 centimeter on each side. Like the microscopes and telescopes that opened scientific frontiers in the past, micromachines will allow us access to new scientific frontiers.

The applications for micromachines are limitless—insect-sized robots with special sensors could "pick up" toxic pollutants in water wells or tiny pieces of precious metals from low-grade ore; pumps flowing through the bloodstream could filter out HIV-infected cells or release insulin for diabetics; a micromotor could power minirockets to the far reaches of the solar system. Although these applications sound like science fiction, they are close to science reality.

Silicon micromachines are produced by shining X-rays or light through a stencil to leave a miniature pattern. Plastic layers alternating with the silicon layers on a silicon chip are dissolved when the chip is immersed in an acid bath. The parts of the micromachine are then free

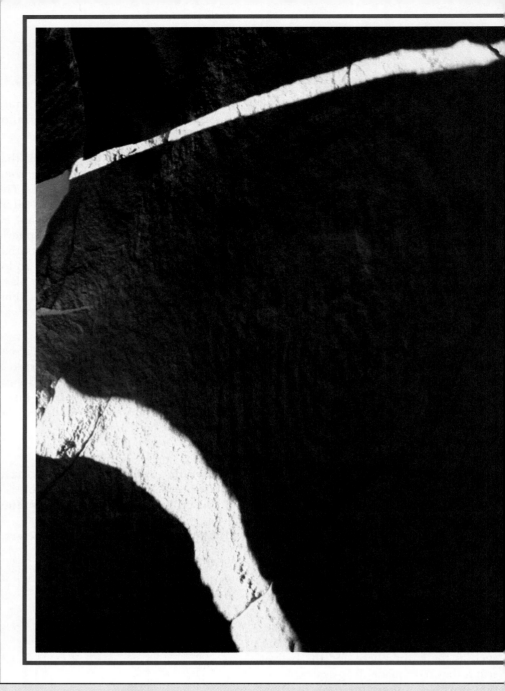

INTRODUCING CHAPTER 3

DISCOVERY LEARNING

▶ *Activity Book*

Begin your teaching of the chapter by using the Chapter 3 Discovery Activity from your *Activity Book*. Using this activity, students will discover the differences in a substance's appearance when viewing it with the aid of a magnifying glass and a microscope.

USING THE TEXTBOOK

Have students examine the photograph on page A62 carefully.

• **What do you see in the picture on this page?** (Two shafts of light on a stone that has swirls.)

• **How do you think the swirls got on the stone?** (Students might suggest that they were carved in the stone.)

Ask students to read the chapter-opening text. You may wish to display a map of the United States and ask a volunteer

Tools and the *Sciences*

Guide for Reading

After you read the following sections, you will be able to

3–1 Exploring the Microscopic World
- Compare compound light microscopes and electron microscopes.

3–2 Exploring the Universe
- Compare refracting and reflecting telescopes.
- Relate the different types of telescopes to the electromagnetic spectrum.

3–3 Exploring the Earth
- Describe the tools used to study the Earth's oceans, crust, and atmosphere.

In the desert of northwestern New Mexico lies an interesting riddle. Two mysterious spirals are carved on a cliff wall behind three slanting stones. At noon on the first day of summer, a single ray of sunlight passes between two of the stones and strikes the larger of the two spirals through its center. At noon on the first day of spring and the first day of autumn, two rays of sunlight pass between the three stones and strike both spirals. At noon on the first day of winter, two rays of sunlight pass between the three stones and strike the large spiral on both sides. What do these spirals mean—and who carved them?

The mysterious spirals and slanting rocks are believed to be part of an astronomical observatory—a place where events in the sky were studied. Scientists think that the people who built the observatory were Anasazi Indians, who lived in the area long before Columbus discovered America.

Modern astronomers have built far more complex observatories. But although the tools of today are more advanced, the basic ways in which scientists try to solve the mysteries of nature may not be very different from those used by the Anasazi Indians. In this chapter you will learn about some of the tools used to explore the world.

Journal *Activity*

You and Your World What would it be like to live in the Southwest before the time of Columbus? Imagine you are a member of the Anasazi Indian tribe. In your journal, describe a typical day in your life.

First winter sunlight at the Anasazi observatory.

---

to point out the northwestern corner of New Mexico.

- **According to scientists, who probably carved the spirals? Why?** (The Anasazi. To record events in the sky, especially the position of the sun at the beginning of the seasons.)
- **What season do you think is shown in the photograph? Why?** (Winter. Shafts of light touch the large spiral on both sides.)
- **Could the Anasazi stones and spirals** **be considered a tool? Why?** (Accept all answers, but lead students to understand that the spirals and stones served as an ancient observatory and as such could be considered a tool.)
- **How is the Anasazi observatory like those of today? How is it different?** (Students should suggest that both have the same purpose, that is, to understand celestial events. Today's observatories have more sophisticated and powerful equipment that provide more detailed information.)

---

to rotate and move. Thousands of micromachines can be produced at one time at an extremely low cost. Recently, the first metal micromachines were produced from nickel. Because metal is more durable and practical than silicon, micromachines may become even more economical to produce. Their micromotors use static electricity as fuel. Some scientists think that micromotors that run on human glucose can be produced for medical applications.

Microtechnology is here; can nanotechnology be far behind? Many scientists feel that micromachines take them one step closer to manipulating matter at the atomic level and producing a whole new generation of technology—nanotechnology.

Cooperative learning: Have preassigned or randomly selected groups complete one of the following assignments.
- Brainstorm a list of possible applications for micromachines and how those applications might change our knowledge of our world and affect our society.
- The governments of some countries, such as Japan, are supporting the research and development of micromachines in an effort to become the world leader in microtechnology. What role do you think the United States should play in the race for microtechnology superiority?

A. Encourage private industry to provide financial support for research and development.

B. Designate large amounts of taxpayer money for research and development.

In chart or grid format, consider the economic, social, and political consequences for each role before reporting your recommendation to the class. Discuss the consequences of each alternative.

See Cooperative Learning in the *Teacher's Desk Reference*.

JOURNAL ACTIVITY

Before students write in their journals, you may wish to have the class discuss what life would have been like in the Southwest between AD 900–1300. Later, encourage students to share excerpts from their journals with the class. They should be instructed to keep their Journal Activity in their portfolio.

3-1 Exploring the Microscopic World

ACTIVITY
READING

Dutchman's Dilemma

If you enjoyed the story of Anton van Leeuwenhoek, you may find the humorous poem *The Microscope* by Maxine Kumin a pleasant reading adventure.

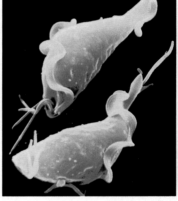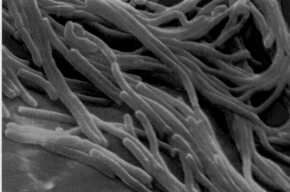

Figure 3-1 *Some of the inhabitants of the microscopic world include bacteria (right) and protists (left).*

3-1 Exploring the Microscopic World

In 1676, a letter was sent to the Royal Society in London (the leading scientific group of that time) that would change forever the way we look at our world. The letter was sent by Anton van Leeuwenhoek, a Dutch drapery-maker who was also an amateur scientist. In his letter, van Leeuwenhoek described his observations of a drop of water. What made his observations so astounding was his announcement that he had seen "living creatures in rain water." Van Leeuwenhoek called these creatures "animalcules."

What van Leeuwenhoek had seen were microscopic organisms, or organisms too small to be seen with the eye alone. Van Leeuwenhoek opened the door to that hidden world by using a simple microscope. Today, over three hundred years later, modern microscopes that van Leeuwenhoek could not even have dreamed would exist have been built. And our exploration of the microscopic world has come well beyond "animalcules." But one thing remains the same: The door to the microscopic world is still open and there is still much to be discovered. Perhaps one day it will be a letter from you that astounds the scientific world. Remember, van Leeuwenhoek was not a professional scientist, just an

ample, a carpenter would use the hammer, a cook would use the pot, and a scientist would use the microscope.

small lenses that could magnify objects more than 200 times. He used a simple, single-lens microscope to discover his "animalcules." Today we know the "animalcules" as protozoa and bacteria. In time, the use of finely ground lenses in compound microscopes opened up the world of the very tiny to scientists.

● ● ● ● **Integration** ● ● ● ●

Use the historical information about van Leeuwenhoek to integrate social studies into your science lesson.

ordinary person with curiosity. Sound like anyone you know?

Microscopes have played an important role in scientific research ever since van Leeuwenhoek's discovery in 1676. **Microscopes are instruments that produce larger-than-life (magnified) images, pictures, or even videotapes.** Most microscopes use light rays to produce a magnified image of an object. Such microscopes are called optical microscopes (optical refers to light).

Optical Microscopes

Have you ever looked at an insect or other object under a magnifying glass? If so, then you have used a type of microscope known as a simple microscope. A magnifying glass is a simple microscope because it has only one lens. A lens is a curved piece of glass. As light rays pass through the glass, they bend. In some kinds of lenses, this bending of light rays increases the size of an object's image.

Scientific lenses are usually made of glass. However, any clear, transparent curved object can act as a lens. Take a look at a leaf that has dew or raindrops on it. If you look carefully through a drop, you will notice that the portion of the leaf under the drop is magnified. Why? The top of a drop of water is curved, much like a lens. Can you think of other examples of lenses that occur naturally? *Hint:* You ① are using two of them right now.

Figure 3-2 *Notice how these drops of water act as lenses, magnifying parts of the leaf.*

A ■ 65

ACTIVITY
DISCOVERING

Abracadabra, It's Gone

Do you think you can make an object disappear before your very eyes? Well, you can—and you will find out how in this activity. The secret lies in understanding refraction—the bending of light as it travels from one medium to another.

1. Gather together the following materials: an empty jar with a lid (preferably a short jar such as a peanut-butter jar), a postage stamp, water.

2. Place the stamp on a tabletop.

3. Place the jar right side up over the stamp. What do you see?

4. Now fill the jar with water and place the lid on it.

5. Look at the stamp. What do you see?

■ Can you explain your observations?

②

ACTIVITY
READING
DUTCHMAN'S DILEMMA

Skill: Reading comprehension

Have students take turns reading the poem aloud. Discuss the idea of using a microscope as the subject for a poem. Encourage students to try writing poems about other scientific instruments.

Integration: Use this Activity to integrate language arts skills into your science lesson.

ACTIVITY
DISCOVERING
ABRACADABRA, IT'S GONE

Discovery Learning

Skills: Making observations, inferring

Materials: jar, stamp

In this activity, students will use their observational skills to explore the effects of refraction. In step 3, students will clearly see the stamp. However, in step 5 the lid prevents students from looking straight down, which would enable them to see the stamp. Due to refraction, when students look through the jar from the side, they will be unable to see the stamp. It will seem to have disappeared.

GUIDED PRACTICE
▶ *Laboratory Manual*

Skills Development

Skills: Identifying functions, making calculations, handling equipment

Have students complete the Chapter 3 Laboratory Investigation, The Microscope: A Tool of the Scientist, in the *Laboratory Manual*. In this investigation students will become familiar with the parts of a microscope and their functions.

FACTS AND FIGURES
MAGNIFICATION

Magnification is normally expressed in linear terms. In other words, an image of a cell magnified 1000 times has a diameter 1000 times greater than the cell itself.

BACKGROUND INFORMATION
MICROSCOPES AND NEW TECHNOLOGY

Several new technologies have expanded the utility of the light microscope. Electronic enhancement of video images, pioneered by Shinye Inoue at the Marine Biological Laboratory, uses high-resolution, low-light video cameras to produce images of living cells. Sophisticated electronic processing of those images dramatically improves their resolution and contrast. The scanning optical microscope, a new device being developed by Aaron Lewis and Michael Isaacson at Cornell University, breaks the "resolution barrier" of light microscopes by eliminating the lenses and apertures that cause light diffraction and scattering. An image is created by scanning back and forth over the specimen with a fine-tipped light-sensitive needle. Theoretically, researchers should be able to see individual molecules within living cells.

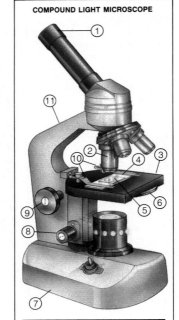

COMPOUND LIGHT MICROSCOPE

1. Ocular lens (eyepiece)
2. Objective lens   3. Stage
4. Glass slide   5. Coverslip
6. Diaphragm (regulates light intensity)
7. Base   8. Fine adjustment knob
9. Coarse adjustment knob
10. Stage clips   11. Arm

Figure 3–3 *This diagram is of a typical compound light microscope. What is another word for the eyepiece?* ❶

Activity Bank

Life in a Drop of Water, p.108

The microscope that you will become most familiar with in your science courses is the **compound light microscope.** A compound light microscope has more than one lens. Like a magnifying glass, a compound microscope uses light to make objects appear larger. A magnifying glass can produce an image a few times larger than the actual object. But by using two lenses, a compound microscope can produce an image up to 1000 times the size of the actual object.

To use a compound microscope, the object to be viewed is first placed between a transparent glass slide and a thin coverslip. Then the slide with coverslip is mounted on the stage of the microscope. See Figure 3–3. Light, usually from a small light bulb at the base of the microscope, passes through the object and then through both lenses. The lens at the bottom of the microscope tube, or the lens closest to the object being observed, is called the objective lens. The lens at the top of the microscope tube, which is the lens through which you look, is called the eyepiece lens, or ocular lens. The magnification of the microscope is equal to the product (multiplication) of both lenses. For example, if the objective lens has a magnification power of 40 and the eyepiece lens has a magnification power of 10, then the object you observe will be magnified 400 times (40 times 10).

Appendix D at the back of this textbook provides detailed instructions on the use of a compound light microscope. Review this appendix carefully before you use a microscope.

Compound light microscopes are extremely useful to life scientists because they allow for the observation of living microscopic organisms. That is, an organism does not have to be killed to be viewed under a compound light microscope. Other microscopes do not have this advantage.

When compound light microscopes were first developed, people assumed that magnification power could be increased by making better and better lenses. It turns out that even the best compound microscopes can magnify no more than about 1000 times. After that, the image begins to get fuzzy and lose detail. Are there ways to magnify objects more than 1000 times? The answer is yes, but such magnification does not involve the use of light.

3–1 (continued)

GUIDED PRACTICE

▶ *Laboratory Manual*

Skills Development

Skills: Preparing slides, making observations

At this point you may want students to complete the Chapter 3 Laboratory Investigation, Using the Microscope, in the *Laboratory Manual.* In this investigation students practice operating a compound light microscope, prepare slides, and make observations about the appearance of a specimen.

CONTENT DEVELOPMENT

Explain that some compound light microscopes are capable of magnifying objects 2000 times larger than they actually are. At this magnification, however, the image is not always clear. Standard light microscopes are seldom used at powers higher than 1000 times because of the clarity problems.

Point out that scientists often stain specimens to make them easier to see under the microscope. Some stains color every part of the specimen, and others color only one part.

REINFORCEMENT/RETEACHING

▶ *Activity Book*

Students who need additional help in understanding the structure of the compound light microscope and in determining total magnification power should complete the chapter activity called Microscopic Proportions. In the activity students label a diagram of the microscope and calculate total magnification.

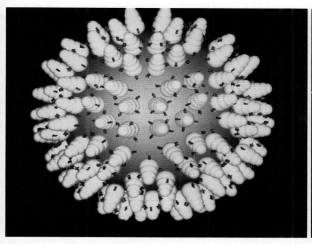

Electron Microscopes

Light microscopes are certainly very useful. But because of the limitation on their magnification power, they cannot be used to observe extremely small objects: living things such as viruses or individual atoms and molecules that make up matter. These objects have been revealed, however. So the question is how?

Today a great deal of scientific research is done using the **electron microscope.** An electron microscope uses a beam of tiny particles called electrons instead of light rays. (Electrons are among the particles that make up an atom.) The beam of electrons is not focused through a lens, as light rays in a light microscope are, but rather by magnets. Objects viewed with an electron microscope can be magnified up to 1 million times. Using electron microscopes, scientists can observe the smallest organisms as well as individual atoms and molecules. In most cases, the magnified image of an object is viewed on a television screen.

There are several types of electron microscopes. You will now read about two of the most common.

TRANSMISSION ELECTRON MICROSCOPE One type of electron microscope is called the transmission electron microscope (TEM). In a TEM, electrons are

Figure 3–4 *Keep in mind that microscopes are but one tool scientists use. Modern science and technology now includes the use of lasers in eye surgery (right) and computer-generated images of disease-causing viruses (left).*

Figure 3–5 *Using a TEM, scientists can study the internal structure of organisms like this single-celled diatom.*

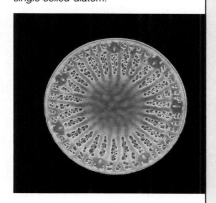

HISTORICAL NOTE
FROM MAGNIFYING LENS TO MICROSCOPE

It was about 95 years from the time that Leonardo da Vinci suggested the use of magnifying lenses to observe tiny objects until the first compound microscopes were actually made. It was over 50 more years before reports of this new invention were published.

BACKGROUND INFORMATION
LASERS

The word *laser* is an acronym for Light Amplification by Stimulated Emission of Radiation. A laser, which produces a powerful highly directional monochromatic beam of light, makes use of the internal energy of atoms and molecules. Lasers have been constructed from ruby crystals, mixtures of inert gases, and cubes of gallium arsenide. Lasers are used in eye surgery, holography, metal cutting, printing, and communications.

GUIDED PRACTICE
Skills Development
Skill: Making observations

Divide the class into groups of three to four students. Give each group a compound light microscope and give each individual a prepared slide. Make sure the slides are labeled so that students know what they are viewing under the microscopes. Have the students in a group view all the slides. They should note the features they see in each slide and report their observations to the class.

ENRICHMENT

Interested students may want to view all the slides. Ask them to write a report or to draw illustrations of their observations.

CONTENT DEVELOPMENT

Help students compare and contrast compound light microscopes and electron microscopes.

• **Which microscope uses lenses to focus light rays?** (Compound light microscope.)

• **Which microscope can magnify objects up to a million times?** (Electron microscope.)

• **Which microscope can view living objects?** (Compound light microscope.)

• **Which microscope are you most likely to find in a school laboratory? Why?** (Compound light microscope. Accept all logical reasons. Students may suggest magnifying needs, cost, or size.)

● ● ● ● **Integration** ● ● ● ●

Use the text information about the electron microscope to integrate the physical science concepts of atomic structure into your lesson.

Light microscopes allow scientists to observe living cells, but they cannot make the tiniest details visible. TEMs reveal details of the cell interior, but only after the cell has been killed, sectioned, and stained. SEMs allow scientists to study the surfaces of objects in three-dimensional detail. All types of microscopes provide scientists with different glimpses of what living cells are. No one microscope is better than the rest. Each is a tool to be used, when appropriate, by a working scientist.

BACKGROUND INFORMATION
ION MICROSCOPE

In addition to the optical and electron microscopes, there is a third type, the ion or field-ion microscope. This powerful instrument can magnify up to 2 million times! It is used principally to study metals. The tip of an extremely thin needle of a metal, many hundreds of times thinner than a pin, is enlarged on a screen. The ion microscope uses the electrical attraction and repulsion of the positively charged needle and the negatively charged screen to create the image of the needle's tip.

3–1 (continued)

FOCUS/MOTIVATION

Direct students' attention to the photographs in Figure 3–7.
- **What do you see in the top photograph?** (Most students will identify the photograph as a flower.)

Allow students enough time to discuss their observations. Explain that they should focus on the stamen, which is made up of the stalklike filament that supports the anther, which produces the flower's pollen. The pollen grains can be seen on the anther. Point out that the center photograph shows the same pollen as seen in the top photograph but that the pollen has been magnified 60 times.

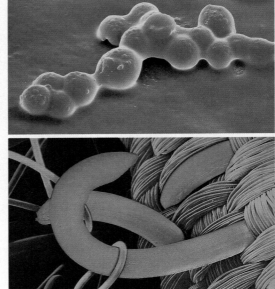
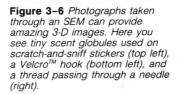
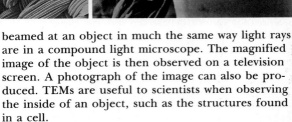

Figure 3–6 *Photographs taken through an SEM can provide amazing 3-D images. Here you see tiny scent globules used on scratch-and-sniff stickers (top left), a Velcro™ hook (bottom left), and a thread passing through a needle (right).*

beamed at an object in much the same way light rays are in a compound light microscope. The magnified image of the object is then observed on a television screen. A photograph of the image can also be produced. TEMs are useful to scientists when observing the inside of an object, such as the structures found in a cell.

SCANNING ELECTRON MICROSCOPE Another type of electron microscope is called the scanning electron microscope (SEM). In an SEM, electrons are beamed at an object and reflected (bounced back) from the object. The reflected electrons produce a three-dimensional photograph of the object. SEMs are useful for observing the outer structure of an object, such as the arrangement of atoms in a solid.

Both TEMs and SEMs do present one problem. The object to be viewed must be sliced into very thin layers and placed in a vacuum (a space from which all air has been removed). As you might expect, such a procedure means that the object cannot be alive. So TEMs and SEMs cannot be used to view living things.

- **How do these appear different from the pollen grains in the top photograph?** (Accept all logical answers. Students may suggest differences in shape and color.)

Explain that the same pollen grains are shown in the bottom photograph but that they are magnified 378 times their normal size.
- **How do these appear different from the pollen grains in the other two photographs?** (Accept all logical answers.

Students may again suggest differences in shape and color. They might also focus on the detail shown for each pollen grain.)

CONTENT DEVELOPMENT

Explain that the tool used by a scientist to view objects would depend on what was to be studied and why. Provide students with a list of specimens to be studied. Explain that they should indicate which tool they would use to make their

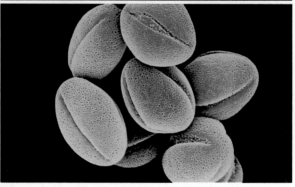

Figure 3-7 *Notice the unmagnified pollen grains visible on the flower (top). Then look at pollen grains that have been magnified 60 times (center). This three-dimensional image of pollen grains (bottom) has been magnified 378 times. What kind of microscope took the photograph at the bottom?* ①

ANNOTATION KEY

Answers
① Scanning electron microscope. (Drawing conclusions)

FACTS AND FIGURES
ABOUT LENSES

Not all lenses form enlarged images. The lens of the eye and the lens of a camera form reduced images.

INTEGRATION
SPACE SCIENCE

Point out to students that many of the tools specifically designed for the space program have been modified and used in medical research and surgery. Interested students may want to research this topic. Suggest that as one resource they write to the National Aeronautics and Space Administration (NASA) at 600 Independence Avenue SW, Washington, DC 20546.

observations and why they would use the specific tools. Tell them that they can use their eyes unaided by a microscope, a compound light microscope, a scanning electron microscope, or a transmission electron microscope. For example, ask these questions.

• **What tool would you use to observe the feeding habits of a unicellular protozoa?** (Compound light microscope because the protozoa are small, and in order to view their feeding habits, they would have to be living.)

• **What tool would you use to view the surface of a red blood cell?** (Scanning electron microscope because of its size and the need to view its surface in detail.)

• **What tool would you use to view the feeding habits of the family dog?** (Special equipment is not needed; students can observe the feeding habits by using their eyes only.)

• **What tool would you use to study the internal structure of a bacterial cell?** (Transmission electron microscope because of the cell's size and the need for detail of internal structure.)

Emphasize that the microscope used by the scientist depends on the specimen being observed and the purpose of the investigation. The most powerful equipment is not always needed to make acceptable and productive observations.

ENRICHMENT

Have one or more students research through library study or interviews the intricate preparation of specimens for viewing under an electron microscope. Ask students to use appropriate visual aids or mock demonstrations to present their findings to the class.

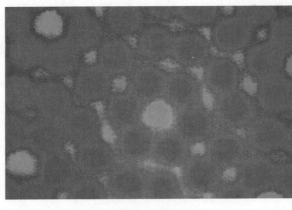

BACKGROUND INFORMATION

MEET THE STM

A type of electron microscope called the scanning tunneling microscope (STM) can be used to magnify objects up to 300 million times. In an SEM, a concentrated beam of electrons is used instead of light to produce an image. Structures smaller than those seen through a light microscope are revealed because the wavelengths of electrons are much shorter than those of light.

In the STM, a tiny probe produces a beam of electrons the thickness of a single atom, which scans an object's surface. (A typical atom is about 3 angstroms, or 12 billionths of an inch, in diameter.) The scanning probe moves up and down, following the contours of the atoms. When the probe finishes one scan, it moves slightly to the side; then it begins another scan parallel to the original path. This process is repeated until the entire object has been scanned. The movement is recorded and processed by a computer, which produces a three-dimensional view of the object's surface.

3–1 (continued)

CONTENT DEVELOPMENT

Explain that as well as being used for scientific inquiry, X-rays, CT scans, and MRIs are also valuable diagnostic tools used by medical personnel. Because it uses X-rays, the CT scan exposes patients to radiation. The MRI uses a magnetic force and radio waves to produce images, and as a result, a patient is not exposed to radiation. Patients with heart pacemakers and artificial metal implants cannot be exposed to the MRI. Its magnetic force would interfere with the operation of the devices. Point out that both the CT scan and the MRI use computers to generate images for study.

● ● ● ●   **Integration**   ● ● ● ●

Use the discussion of X-rays in the text to integrate the physical science concepts of light waves into your lesson.

Use the photographs and caption for Figure 3–10 to integrate the life science concepts of evolution into your lesson.

Figure 3–9 *MRI images help scientists study the inside of the body. What important organ can be studied from this MRI?* 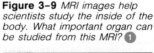 ❶

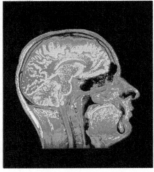

Looking Through Barriers

So far we have been discussing the use of microscopes to produce magnified images of an object. Sometimes, however, scientists do not need to magnify an object but rather to look inside the object. Today there are several tools available that allow scientists to "look through barriers."

X-RAYS Do you know someone who has had a broken bone? Perhaps you have had one yourself. A doctor could cut you open to examine the break, but that would not be a very pleasant experience. As you probably know, there is a better way to do it.

For almost one hundred years, scientists have been using a type of radiation known as X-rays to see through objects. X-rays are similar to light rays, but they are invisible to the eye. Unlike light, however, X-rays pass easily through soft objects such as skin and muscle. But X-rays are blocked by dense objects such as bone. As a result, X-rays can be used to take pictures of bones inside an organism.

CT SCANS Computed Tomography, or CT scan, is a new technique that produces cross-sectional pictures of an object. An X-ray machine in a CT-scanner is used to take up to 720 different exposures of an object. Each picture shows a "slice" of the object. A computer analyzes and combines the exposures to construct a picture. Among its many uses, a CT scan can provide detailed pictures of body parts such as the human brain.

70 ■ A

REINFORCEMENT/RETEACHING

Scientists use tools to enhance their scientific inquiries and findings. Equally as important as the tools are the methods of inquiry. In their scientific studies, scientists often use comparisons based on controls and variables.

▶ *Activity Book*

Students who need practice in identifying controls and variables should complete the chapter activity called Experimental Controls and Variables. In the activity students perform simple experiments and note the control and variable factors.

GUIDED PRACTICE

Skills Development

Skills: Drawing conclusions, applying concepts

Tell students that you have been trying to determine if your goldfish prefers one type of food. Every day at the same time, you feed the fish a different type of food,

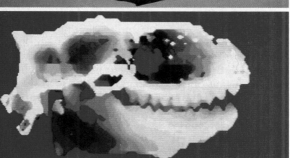

Figure 3–10 *Because this 30-million-year-old skull of a small mammal (top) was a rare find, scientists did not want to break it open. By using a CT scanner, scientists were able to get a three-dimensional view of the inside of the skull (bottom).*

MRI Magnetic resonance imaging, or MRI, is another tool that helps scientists see inside objects. MRI uses magnetism and radio waves to produce images. Scientists can use MRI to study the structure of body cells without harming the living tissue.

3–1 Section Review

1. What is a microscope?
2. Explain the basic difference between a compound light microscope and an electron microscope.
3. Of the three types of microscopes discussed, what kind of research can be performed only by using a compound light microscope?

Connection—*Science and Technology*
4. It has been said that many great discoveries await the tools needed to make them. What does this statement mean to you?

BACKGROUND INFORMATION
MRI

For use in diagnosing a patient's internal disorders, magnetic resonance imaging, or MRI, has several major advantages: It can see through bones and organs, it does not involve surgery, and it does not use radiation.

The patient lies inside a huge tube-shaped magnet, which produces a magnetic field. The magnetic field causes the nuclei in certain atoms to line up. Devices transmit radio waves. When the frequency of the radio waves matches the frequency of the atoms, a *resonance condition* is produced, and the nuclei can absorb the energy of the radio waves. When the magnetic field is shut down, the nuclei return to their original state and send the absorbed energy as radio signals. The devices receive the signals, and a computer translates them into images of the tissues in the patient's body.

---

always making sure to give it the same amount of food. You have found that your fish eats more of type A than of types B and C.

• **What are the controls and variables in the test?** (Controls: time, amount of food; variables: type of food.)

• **What would you conclude about the fish's food preference? Why?** (The fish preferred type A food because it ate more of that food than of the others.)

INDEPENDENT PRACTICE
Section Review 3–1
1. A microscope is an instrument that produces magnified images.
2. A compound light microscope uses light to magnify images. An electron microscope uses a beam of electrons to magnify images. Magnification is greater with an electron microscope.
3. Only a compound light microscope can be used to study living material.
4. Many students may agree with the statement, noting that tools were needed to make many discoveries possible.

REINFORCEMENT/RETEACHING
Monitor students' responses to the Section Review questions. If students appear to have difficulty with any of the concepts, review the appropriate material with them.

CLOSURE
▶ *Review and Reinforcement Guide*
At this point have students complete Section 3–1 in their *Review and Reinforcement Guide.*

3-2 Exploring the Universe

MULTICULTURAL OPPORTUNITY 3-2

Much natural astronomy can be done at home with a pair of binoculars. The moon is one of the easiest celestial bodies to study. Have students invite their families to a private star-gazing party and involve everyone in the homework assignment.

You may wish to tell students about the Mayan civilization, which reached its greatest period about AD 250 and flourished for more than 600 years. The Mayas made outstanding advancements in astronomy and mathematics by observing the positions of the sun, moon, and stars; they made tables predicting eclipses and the orbit of the planet Venus. Interested students may want to research how the Mayas obtained astronomical information and developed their calendar without the tools that modern scientists depend on. You may also want to assign research on the Indian scientist and mathematician Aryabhata and his contributions to astronomy some 1500 years ago in India.

ESL STRATEGY 3-2

Ask students to explain the difference between (1) a microscope and a telescope and (2) a refracting telescope and a reflecting telescope.

Have students take notes and work with an English-speaking "tutor" as they prepare their explanations.

Figure 3–11 *The invention of the telescope opened the door to the incredible vastness of outer space and showed that our sun is but the tiniest drop in an ocean of stars.*

72 ■ A

3–2 Exploring the Universe

As you just learned, the invention of the microscope opened up a previously unknown world. It was not quite the same case with the world beyond planet Earth. People's understanding that the Earth is part of a vast universe did not require any special tools. Even the earliest known records indicate that people wondered about the twinkling lights they observed in the night sky. But knowledge of the universe was quite limited. It was not until the invention of the telescope that people truly began to explore the universe. The moons of Jupiter and the rings of Saturn, for example, did not become visible until the telescope was invented.

The telescope is an instrument used to view and magnify distant objects in space. **Scientists use a variety of telescopes to study the Universe: optical telescopes, radio telescopes, infrared telescopes, ultraviolet telescopes, and X-ray telescopes.** You will now read about these different types of telescopes and discover what kinds of information they provide.

TEACHING STRATEGY 3-2

FOCUS/MOTIVATION

Collect and display various photographs taken with microscopes and telescopes. Discuss with students the need for scientists to see objects that are much farther away and much smaller than can be seen with the unaided eye.

● **Can you think of some situations in which a scientist might need to see very** small objects with the aid of a microscope? (Possible answers include testing water samples for pollutants, examining various soil types, examining cellular structure.)

● **When does a scientist need to use a telescope to see objects that are very far away?** (When studying the stars, planets, and other objects in space.)

CONTENT DEVELOPMENT

An optical telescope can make faraway objects visible because of its ability to gather light. When the human eye looks at an object, the pupil gathers light, and the light is focused into the image within the eye. When an object is very distant, not enough light reaches the eye for the object to be visible.

In a refracting telescope, the lens gathers light, and the light is focused into the image within the telescope. Because the lens of the telescope is much larger than the pupil of the human eye, it can gather much more light. As a result, faraway ob-

Optical Telescopes

The first telescopes used by early astronomers were optical telescopes. (Remember that the term optical refers to light.) An optical telescope collects and focuses visible light from distant objects such as stars and galaxies. Using a series of mirrors, lenses, or a combination of the two, the telescope magnifies ❶ the image formed by the light. The two types of optical telescopes are refracting telescopes and reflecting telescopes.

REFRACTING TELESCOPES In a **refracting telescope,** a series of lenses is used to focus light. (You should recall that an optical microscope uses a series of lenses to magnify microscopic objects.) In general, the larger the lens, the greater the light-gathering power of a telescope. The size of a telescope is given as the diameter of its largest lens. The world's largest refracting telescope is the "40-inch" telescope at Yerkes Observatory in Wisconsin. This telescope has a light-gathering power about 40,000 times greater than the human eye!

REFLECTING TELESCOPES In a **reflecting telescope,** a series of mirrors is used to collect and focus light from distant objects. For technical reasons, the mirrors in a reflecting telescope can be built much larger than the lenses in a refracting telescope. One of the world's largest reflecting telescopes is the "200-inch" Hale telescope at Mount Palomar in California. Telescopes like the Hale telescope can observe objects billions of light-years from Earth. They literally open the door to the very edge of the universe.

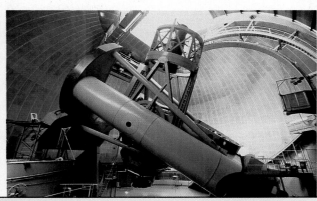

Figure 3–12 *The Hale Telescope at Mount Palomar in California uses one large mirror. What type of telescope is it?* ❶

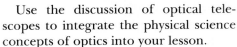
A ■ 73

jects become bright enough to be seen in a telescope.

As might be expected, the larger the lens, the more light a telescope can gather and the more powerful the telescope is. The world's largest refracting telescope has a light-gathering power that is more than 40,000 times greater than that of the human eye.

● ● ● ● **Integration** ● ● ● ●

Use the discussion of optical telescopes to integrate the physical science concepts of optics into your lesson.

REINFORCEMENT/RETEACHING

Reinforce the concept of tools in science by pointing out that microscopes and telescopes are tools used by scientists for different purposes. Ask students to identify various uses of these scientific tools. Tell students that according to the dictionary, a tool is an instrument used or worked by hand. Have students search the classroom to see how many tools they can find based on this definition. As students identify such tools as scissors, pencils, and erasers, ask them to identify the purpose of the tools.

INDEPENDENT ACTIVITY

▶ *Product Testing Activity*

Have students perform the product test on pens from the Product Testing Activity worksheets. Through this activity students will discover that different designs can lead to different uses of tools, even in a common instrument like a pen.

Point out that students are probably used to hearing the word *pollution* used to describe many situations. But they may not be familiar with the term *light pollution*. Light pollution refers to the many lights in cities and other areas that are so bright that they interfere with our ability to see the stars and other objects in the night sky. Light pollution is one reason why most observatories are located in remote places. Ask students to think of other reasons why observatories are located in deserts, on tops of mountains, and away from cities and industrial areas.

FACTS AND FIGURES
WHICH IS THE LARGEST?

The world's largest reflecting telescope is at the Special Astrophysical Observatory in Zelenchukskaya in the Soviet Union. Its mirror is 600 centimeters in diameter. The world's largest refracting telescope is at the Yerkes Observatory in Williams Bay, Wisconsin. Its lens is 102 centimeters in diameter. The world's largest radio telescope is located at the Arecibo Observatory in Arecibo, Puerto Rico. Its reflector is 305 meters in diameter.

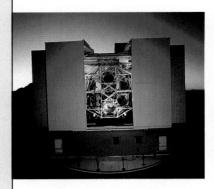

Figure 3–13 *The Multiple Mirror Telescope atop Mount Hopkins in Arizona uses six mirrors.*

MULTIPLE MIRROR TELESCOPES Large reflecting telescopes are extremely difficult and expensive to build. The mirrors in such telescopes must be perfectly constructed and flawless. For many years scientists believed that a 5-meter mirror (approximately 200 inches) was about the largest mirror they could construct. To get around that problem, the Multiple Mirror Telescope was constructed. Sitting high atop Mount Hopkins in Arizona, the Multiple Mirror Telescope contains six "72-inch" mirrors. The six mirrors work together to collect light from distant stars and provide even greater power than the single large mirror in the Hale telescope.

NEW ADVANCES IN OPTICAL TELESCOPES Many new types of optical telescopes are being designed and tested throughout the world. How many will go from the drawing board to actual construction remains to be seen. Each of these new types of telescopes uses a different design to enlarge the size of the mirror it houses. One of the most recently developed telescopes is the Keck telescope in Mauna Kea, Hawaii. The Keck telescope has a "400-inch" mirror. How have scientists solved the problem of building such a large mirror? In a sense, they haven't. For the Keck telescope actually contains 36 individual mirror segments joined together in what looks like a beehive. The 36 mirror segments make the Keck telescope the most powerful optical telescope on Earth—at least until an even newer and larger telescope is built.

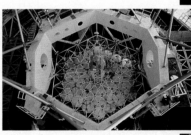

Figure 3–14 *The Keck telescope in Hawaii houses a "400-inch" mirror made up of 36 segments (inset).*

74 ■ A

3–2 (continued)

REINFORCEMENT/RETEACHING

Review with students the basic difference between a refracting and a reflecting telescope. Make sure they understand that refracting telescopes use a series of lenses, whereas reflecting telescopes use a series of mirrors.

• **What type of optical microscope is the Keck telescope in Mauna Kea, Hawaii?** (A reflecting telescope.)

• **What type of telescope is the telescope at Yerkes Observatory in Wisconsin?** (A refracting telescope.)

GUIDED PRACTICE

Skills Development

Skills: Manipulative, applying concepts, making calculations, making observations

At this point have students complete the in-text Chapter 3 Laboratory Investigation: Constructing a Telescope. In this investigation students will build their own telescopes, which they can use to observe objects at a distance.

ENRICHMENT

Have students investigate the impact of light pollution on the effectiveness of telescopes in observatories. Ask students to consider methods of reducing light pollution in communities that have observatories. Students might present the findings in a panel discussion. Sources of information may include library resources or interviews.

Radio Telescopes

No doubt when you think of stars you think of visible light. After all, that's what you see when you look up at the night sky. Visible light, however, is only one part of the **electromagnetic spectrum.** In addition to visible light, the electromagnetic spectrum includes forms of "light" we cannot detect with our eyes. These forms of invisible light include X-rays, ultraviolet rays and infrared rays, and radio waves. And as it turns out, many stars give off both visible and invisible light. Is there a way to view distant stars using invisible light? Yes, but obviously not with an optical telescope.

In Chapter 1, you learned about the discovery of radio astronomy by Karl Jansky and Grote Reber. At that time we said that radio telescopes opened up a new view of the universe—and oh what a view! Because many stars give off mainly radio waves (not visible light), the invention of the radio telescope provided scientists with an opportunity to study the universe in a new and exciting way. It was almost as if a huge part of the universe had been hidden from us, waiting for the discovery of the radio telescope to reveal itself.

An optical telescope can be thought of as a bucket for collecting light waves from space. A **radio telescope** can be thought of as a bucket for collecting radio waves from space. In most radio telescopes, a curved metal dish gathers and focuses radio waves onto an antenna. The signal picked up

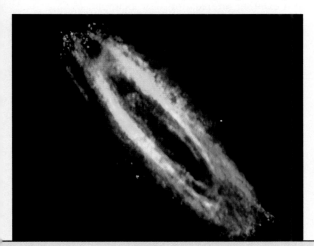

Figure 3–15 *Radio telescopes have produced this image of the Andromeda galaxy, one of our nearest neighbors in space.*

A ■ 75

BACKGROUND INFORMATION
RADIO TELESCOPES

The National Radio Astronomy Observatory (NRAO) operates the Very Large Array near Socorro, New Mexico, which is currently the world's most powerful radio telescope. The NRAO, however, is constructing a system of ten reflectors stretching from Hawaii to the Virgin Islands. The Very Long Baseline Array, or VLBA, controlled from Socorro, will act as a single telescope to produce very detailed pictures of objects in space.

CONTENT DEVELOPMENT

A radio telescope is an instrument that is used to pick up and analyze the radio-frequency electromagnetic radiations of extraterrestrial sources. The two main types of radio telescopes are parabolic reflectors and radio interferometers. Parabolic reflectors are movable instruments that can be pointed at any part of the sky. They reflect incoming radiation onto a small aerial at the focus of the paraboloid. Radio interferometers are instruments that are fixed in one position. They have greater position-finding accuracy than the parabolic reflectors have, and they also have a greater ability to distinguish a small source against an intense background.

● ● ● ● **Integration** ● ● ● ●
Use the text references to the electromagnetic spectrum to integrate the physical science concepts of light into your lesson.

ENRICHMENT

A source of radio-frequency electromagnetic radiation outside the solar system is called a radio source. Radio sources exist both within our galaxy and outside it. A few radio sources have been identified with stars that are visible with an optical telescope. Other radio sources are supernova explosions and remnants, colliding galaxies and gas clouds, quasars, and pulsars.

Figure 3–16 *The Very Large Array in New Mexico is made up of 27 radio telescopes.*

by the antenna is fed into computers, which then produce an image of the object giving off the radio waves. Radio telescopes are usually mounted on movable supports so they can be directed toward any point in the sky. These telescopes have been able to collect radio waves from objects as far away as 14 billion light-years!

In the desert of New Mexico stands a group of 27 radio telescopes known as the Very Large Array, or VLA. The VLA is extremely useful because it combines the radio-wave detecting power of 27 individual radio telescopes. With the VLA, scientists can get a clearer picture of many objects in space than they can with a single radio telescope.

Infrared and Ultraviolet Telescopes

In general, stars are the only objects in space that give off visible light. And some stars are so dim they do not give off enough visible light to be easily observed. But all objects, even dark, cold objects such as planets, give off infrared rays. Recall that infrared is part of the electromagnetic spectrum. Another term for infrared is heat energy. Unfortunately, infrared rays from distant objects in space are not easily detected once they enter Earth's atmosphere. So telescopes that operate using infrared rays are carried out of the atmosphere.

In January, 1983, the Infrared Astronomy Satellite, or *IRAS*, was launched. *IRAS*, the first **infrared telescope** in space, soon provided scientists with new and exciting information. For example, *IRAS* detected heat waves from newborn stars in clouds of gas and dust 155,000 light-years from Earth. *IRAS* also collected information that suggests that the distant star Vega is surrounded by a giant cloud of matter. This cloud may be an early stage in the development of planets. If so, *IRAS* has given us the first view of planets beyond our solar system.

Like infrared, ultraviolet light is an invisible form of light in the electromagnetic spectrum. In order to detect ultraviolet light given off by objects, scientists have constructed **ultraviolet telescopes.** Ultraviolet rays from space do not pass easily through Earth's atmosphere. So ultraviolet telescopes, like infrared telescopes, are usually carried out of the Earth's

ACTIVITY
WRITING

A New Comet

2 One of the first achievements of IRAS was finding a new comet in our solar system. Using library and other reference sources, find out the name of that comet — and the mystery of its triple name. Report your findings in a brief essay.

76 ■ A

3–2 (continued)

CONTENT DEVELOPMENT

Have students compare and contrast the infrared and ultraviolet telescopes with the X-ray telescopes.

• **What do infrared and ultraviolet telescopes have in common with the X-ray telescopes?** (All three use "invisible light" from the electromagnetic spectrum; all three are launched into space because the infrared, ultraviolet, and radio rays do not pass easily through Earth's atmosphere.)

• **How are the telescopes different?** (Students should indicate that each telescope uses different rays of the electromagnetic spectrum to provide images.)

● ● ● ● **Integration** ● ● ● ●

Use the textbook copy to integrate a discussion of the physical science concept of heat energy into your lesson.

ENRICHMENT

Challenge students to find out about the life cycle of a star. Also challenge them to find out how the X-ray telescope has aided scientists in learning about the life and death of stars.

GUIDED PRACTICE

Skills Development

Skill: Constructing charts

Have students develop a chart that lists the different kinds of telescopes and the uses of each kind. Students may want to include any particular discoveries made by each type of telescope that could not have been made by the other types.

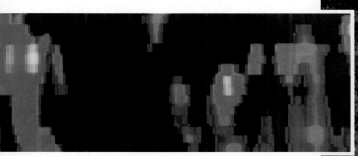

atmosphere. Some of the most dramatic photographs taken with ultraviolet telescopes are of our own sun, which gives off huge amounts of ultraviolet light daily. One of the primary tasks of the *Hubble Space Telescope*, which you will read about shortly, is to detect ultraviolet rays from space using an on-board ultraviolet telescope.

X-ray Telescopes

X-rays are another form of electromagnetic radiation given off by stars. In fact, almost all stars give off X-rays. By now you should not be surprised to learn that **X-ray telescopes** have been constructed to detect the invisible X-rays from space. Of all the forms of light in the electromagnetic spectrum, X-rays are the least able to pass through Earth's atmosphere. (A good thing because if they did, no life as we know it could survive on Earth.) So X-rays from space can only be detected by X-ray telescopes sent into orbit above the Earth.

In 1970, the first X-ray telescope, called *Uhuru*, was launched. *Uhuru* gave scientists their first clear view of X-ray sources in the sky. *Uhuru* and other orbiting X-ray telescopes have provided a wealth of information about the life cycle of stars, particularly what happens to very massive stars as they begin to age and die.

Space Telescope

In Chapter 2, you learned about a flaw in the 2.4-meter mirror of the *Hubble Space Telescope*. What you did not learn at that time was that the *Hubble Space Telescope* also houses several other kinds of

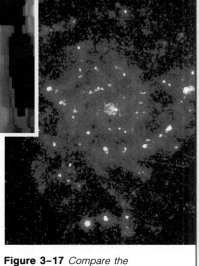

Figure 3–17 *Compare the infrared image of the Dorados nebula (left) with the ultraviolet image of a spiral galaxy (right).*

Figure 3–18 *This X-ray image shows the remains of a star that exploded in what is called a supernova.*

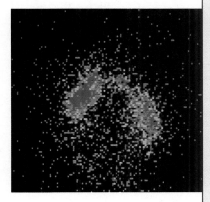

A ■ 77

HISTORICAL NOTE
STONEHENGE

Stonehenge is a group of huge stones set in a pattern of circles and horseshoes. It was built on Salisbury Plain in Wiltshire, England, between about 2800 and 1500 BC. Its original purpose may have been religious, but it is also an astronomical observatory. Sightings made along its stones from different positions can be used to predict summer solstice, sunrise, moonrise, and even eclipses with accuracy. This information must have been important to Stonehenge's builders; it took them hundreds of years to cut, move, and set up the huge stones using the tools of their age: rollers, ropes, and levers.

FACTS AND FIGURES
HUBBLE SPACE TELESCOPE

The *Hubble Space Telescope* is named for American astronomer Edwin Powell Hubble (1889–1953). He was the first astronomer to prove that the universe has other star systems besides the Milky Way. He also determined that the universe is expanding by showing that other galaxies are moving away from Earth.

REINFORCEMENT/RETEACHING

▶ *Activity Book*

Students can use the chapter activity called Measuring Tools to reinforce their understandings of the double pan balance and the graduated cylinder. Through the activity students review measuring tools used by scientists and can extend their understanding of scientific tools to measuring devices as well as visual aids.

CONTENT DEVELOPMENT

The *Hubble Space Telescope* was designed to take the sharpest possible pictures of the universe. This telescope (which cost $1.5 billion), however, has a major flaw. Its main mirror was ground to the wrong curvature, and so it cannot focus properly.

• **Do you think the telescope was worth the expense despite its flaw?** (Accept all opinions. Help students understand that despite its flaw, the telescope is providing valuable information.)

• **A test of the mirror could have identified the flaw before the telescope was launched. Do you think the mirror should have been tested before launching?** (Students are likely to think the mirror should have been tested and may conclude that not testing the mirror was a regrettable oversight.)

3-3 Exploring the Earth

MULTICULTURAL OPPORTUNITY 3-3

How does a "child" influence the weather worldwide? We can read about the effect of *El Niño* on the weather. In Spanish, *el niño* means "child"; when capitalized, it means "the Christ Child." *El Niño* refers to the unusually warm ocean current that appears off the coast of South America every few years. Originally named in the nineteenth century because of its frequent appearance around Christmas, *El Niño* may have been responsible for seasonal flooding, changes in the fishing industry—even the conquest of the Incan Empire! Encourage students to investigate *El Niño*, paying particular attention to the effect of the climatic changes on the people of South America.

ESL STRATEGY 3-3

Enrich students' understanding of the appropriateness of the name *seismograph* by explaining that it comes from the Greek words *seismos,* meaning "earthquake," and *graphos,* meaning "to draw or write." Ask students to use an encyclopedia to discover other scientific uses of the seismograph. What other words do they know with the root *seism* or *graph*? Have them make a list and provide brief definitions of these words.

Also, when discussing the two types of barometers, point out that one uses mercury; hence, the appropriateness of its name. The other's name is appropriate as well; the term *aneroid* is of Greek origin and means "without liquid."

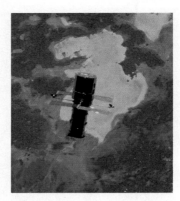

Figure 3–19 *Here you see the* Hubble Space Telescope *floating in orbit above the Earth, as photographed from the Space Shuttle.*

telescopes. So you can think of the *Hubble Space Telescope* as a combination of telescopes—each of which provides a different picture of the universe. In fact, one of the first important discoveries of the *Hubble Space Telescope* was made by its ultraviolet telescope. In 1991, the ultraviolet telescope revealed what could be the beginning of a new solar system forming around a star called Beta Pictoris.

Scientists have nicknamed the *Hubble Space Telescope* the "eye in the sky." With it, they can obtain a detailed view of many objects long hidden from earthbound telescopes. Although the primary mirror is not working perfectly, it still enables the *Hubble Space Telescope* to provide excellent photographs of many distant objects. Combined with the other telescopes on board, the *Hubble Space Telescope* promises to expand our knowledge of the universe in as dramatic a fashion as van Leeuwenhoek's microscope opened up the microscopic world.

3–2 Section Review

1. Compare refracting and reflecting telescopes.
2. Name and describe three types of telescopes that detect invisible light.

Connection—*You and Your World*
3. Doctors use X-rays to take pictures of broken bones and other body parts. Why can the doctor's X-rays pass through the atmosphere but X-rays from space cannot?

Guide for Reading

Focus on this question as you read.
▶ *What tools are used by scientists to study the Earth's oceans, crust, and atmosphere?*

78 ■ A

3-3 Exploring the Earth

We have learned about a few of the tools scientists use to study the microscopic world and the world of outer space. Now you will spend some time learning about the ways in which scientists explore the planet Earth. **In simple terms, we can think of the Earth as being divided into three main parts—water, land, and air.**

3-2 (continued)

INDEPENDENT PRACTICE

Section Review 3-2
1. Lenses are used to focus images in refracting telescopes. Mirrors are used in reflecting telescopes.
2. Infrared telescopes use infrared rays, or heat energy, to focus images. Ultraviolet telescopes use ultraviolet light to focus images, and X-ray telescopes focus images through X-rays.

Because all three types of rays do not pass easily through the atmosphere, they are carried out of Earth's atmosphere. Radio telescopes use radio waves to focus images.
3. X-rays used by doctors can pass through the atmosphere because they do not have to pass through the upper layers of the atmosphere that absorb X-rays. X-rays from space would have to pass through the upper layers in order to reach Earth, but they cannot.

REINFORCEMENT/RETEACHING

Monitor students' responses to the Section Review questions. If students appear to have difficulty understanding any of the concepts, review the material with them.

CLOSURE

▶ *Review and Reinforcement Guide*
At this point have students complete Section 3–2 of their *Review and Reinforcement Guide.*

Exploring Earth's Oceans

More than 70 percent of the Earth is covered by water, and most of that water is found in the oceans. It's no wonder, then, that Earth is often referred to as the water planet.

Scientists use research vessels called submersibles to explore the oceans. Some submersibles carry only scientific instruments; others carry people as well. One kind of submersible is called a **bathysphere** (BATH-ih-sfeer). A bathysphere is a small, sphere-shaped diving vessel. It is lowered into the water from a ship by a steel cable. Because it remains attached to the ship, the bathysphere has limited movement.

A **bathyscaph** (BATH-ih-skaf) is a more useful submersible. It is a self-propelled submarine observatory that can move about in the ocean. Bathyscaphs have reached depths of more than 10,000 meters while exploring some of the deepest parts of the ocean.

The bathyscaph *Alvin* has made thousands of dives into the ocean depths. Some of *Alvin's* discoveries have helped scientists learn more about life on the ocean floor. During one dive, scientists aboard

Food From the Ocean

Visit a supermarket or fish market. List the different seafoods available.

■ Develop a classification system to distinguish the types of seafood sold in your local market.

Figure 3–20 *Among the many unusual organisms discovered by the submersible* Alvin *was a new form of life called tube worms.*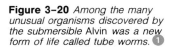

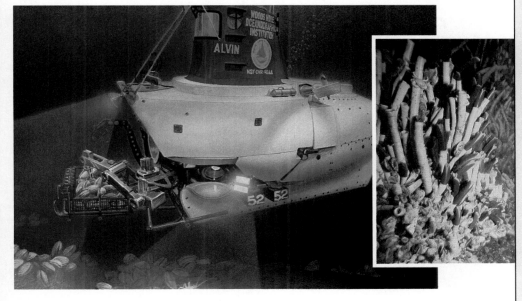

A ■ 79

Integration
❶Life Science: Zoology

ACTIVITY
DISCOVERING
FOOD FROM THE OCEAN

Discovery Learning
Skills: Making charts, observing, comparing, relating

This field activity will enable students to do field research and then organize their data. Suggest that they consider presenting their classification system in a chart, web, or other visual format. Encourage students to share their projects with the class by displaying their visual aid and explaining their system.

Classification systems will vary, depending on the types of seafood and the type of organization students use.

CONTENT DEVELOPMENT

Explain that the ocean is the world's largest ecosystem. Like terrestrial ecosystems, the ocean can remain productive if it is managed properly. The study of the ocean is known as oceanography. Modern oceanographers use many tools to gather information about the ocean and the many organisms that live in this habitat. Tools such as satellites are used to map the ocean, to track the movement of animals such as sea turtles and whales, to record the daily ebb and rise of the tides, and to watch currents and waves.

● ● ● ● **Integration** ● ● ● ●

Use the caption and photograph to integrate life science concepts into your lesson by focusing on the wide variety of life forms in the ocean.

TEACHING STRATEGY 3–3

FOCUS/MOTIVATION

Display a world map.
• **What do you see on the map?** (Answers may include continents, oceans, cities, mountains, etc.)
• **What is Earth made of?** (Land and water.)
• **Is there any part of Earth that is not seen on the map?** (Answers will vary. Guide students to consider the atmo-

sphere as an important part of the Earth.)
• **Is there more land or more water on Earth?** (More water.)

Direct students' attention to the heading at the top of page A79. Ask students how scientists are able to explore the ocean.
• **Can you name tools scientists use to explore the ocean?** (Answers may include ships, sonar, scuba equipment.)

Skill: Reading comprehension

You may want to have students give a brief synopsis of the book. Have volunteers read their favorite parts aloud. Or read aloud and discuss the description of the submersible vessel the *Nautilus*.

Integration: Use this Activity to integrate language arts skills into your science lesson.

HISTORICAL NOTE
BATHYSCAPH TRIUMPH

The bathyscaph was designed by Swiss physicist Auguste Piccard in the 1940s. It was first tested in 1948. In 1960, Piccard's son, Jacques, and Lieutenant Don Walsh of the United States Navy took the bathyscaph *Trieste* into the Mariana Trench. This valley near Guam on the Pacific Ocean floor is one of the lowest places on Earth. The *Trieste* reached a depth of 10,910 meters, only 120 meters from the bottom of the trench.

3-3 (continued)

GUIDED PRACTICE

Skills Development

Skill: Comparing and contrasting

Help students compare and contrast the advantages of each type of submersible. Help them determine why the bathyscaph has more utility than the bathysphere.

• **What advantage does the bathyscaph have over the bathysphere?** (The bathyscaph has greater mobility, which allows it to maneuver better under the ocean.)

ENRICHMENT

The *Alvin* discovered that sea animals live at depths receiving no sunlight. What is the source of energy for these sea animals? Have students conduct library research to answer this question. They may then report their findings to the class through a group presentation.

CONTENT DEVELOPMENT

The *Titanic* was billed as unsinkable by its owners, who spent $8 million building this luxury oceanliner. On its very first voyage from Great Britain to the United States, the *Titanic* hit an iceberg and sank. The lives of 1493 passengers and crew members were lost in the frigid North Atlantic Ocean on the night of

Dangerous Depths

Do you love an action-packed adventure story? If so, you will want to read *Twenty Thousand Leagues Under the Sea*, by Jules Verne.

Alvin found several communities of unusual ocean life near vents, or natural chimneys, in the ocean floor. The vents discharge poisonous hydrogen sulfide into the water. Water temperatures near the vents reach 350°C. The combination of high temperatures and deadly hydrogen sulfide should make the existence of life forms near the vents impossible. But as the scientists discovered, giant tube worms, clams, mussels, and other strange life forms make their homes near the vents. These life forms exist without any sunlight. Some scientists suggest that conditions near the vents may be similar to conditions on distant planets. So the discoveries made by *Alvin* may help astronomers study the possibility of life on other worlds.

In September 1985, another submersible made a remarkable discovery. This submersible is a robot craft that can be guided along the ocean floor from a ship on the surface. The robot craft discovered the remains of the famous steamship *Titanic*. The ship was lying on the ocean floor in very deep water off the coast of Newfoundland, Canada. In 1912, on its maiden voyage, the *Titanic* struck an iceberg and quickly sank.

Figure 3–21 *Notice the robot craft as it is about to explore the wreck of the* Titanic.

80 ■ A

April 15, 1912. A rescue ship sailed into New York harbor with 700 survivors of the fatal disaster on April 18. Although capable of carrying 3500 passengers and crew, the *Titanic* was equipped with only enough lifeboats for 950 people.

● ● ● ● **Integration** ● ● ● ●

Use the textbook historical information about the *Titanic* to integrate social studies into your lesson.

Figure 3-22 *This collapsed California highway is evidence of the tremendous energy unleashed during an earthquake.*

Exploring Earth's Crust

We often tend to take the land we walk on for granted. "Solid as the Earth," is a common phrase. And most of the time, it makes sense. But in the 1980s, residents of Mexico, Armenia, and California (to name just a few places) felt the Earth move beneath their feet. What they felt, in case you haven't guessed, was an earthquake.

Detecting and measuring the strength of earthquakes is an important task for scientists who explore the Earth's crust. One day their studies may enable them to predict earthquakes so that people in the affected area can be warned before the earthquake strikes. Today, unfortunately, our ability to predict earthquakes is limited. But we are well able to detect and measure them using a tool called the **seismograph** (SIGHZ-muh-grahf).

A seismograph is a fairly simple instrument. It consists of a weight attached to a spring or wire. Because the weight is not attached directly to the Earth, it will remain nearly still even when the Earth moves. A pen is attached to the weight. Beside the pen is a rotating drum wrapped with paper.

ACTIVITY

CALCULATING

Earthquake Waves

Earthquake waves, or seismic waves, travel at a speed 24 times the speed of sound. The speed of sound is 1250 km/hr. How fast do seismic waves travel?

③

A ■ 81

epicenter is somewhere on the perimeter of the circle. To precisely locate the epicenter, they must draw circles using distance information from three different locations. The point at which the three circles intersect pinpoints the epicenter of the earthquake.

Earthquakes produce different types of seismic waves. The first waves to be recorded by a seismograph are P waves because these waves travel the fastest. Next to be recorded are S waves. The last waves to be recorded are L waves, which travel the slowest. The L waves cause the most damage because they travel closest to the Earth's surface and cause the ground to rise and fall like an ocean wave. Because P and S waves travel deep in the Earth, these waves have been the most useful to scientists in determining the structure of the Earth's interior.

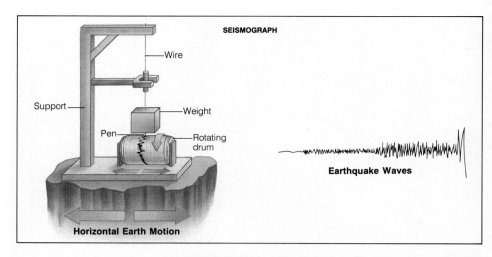

Figure 3–23 *A seismograph (left) detects and records earthquake waves, or seismic waves. A typical pattern of seismic waves is shown (right).*

Because the pen is attached to the weight, it also remains nearly still when the Earth moves. But not so for the drum, which is attached to the Earth and moves with the Earth. When the Earth is still, the pen records an almost straight line on the rotating drum. However, when an earthquake occurs, the pen records a wavy line as the drum moves with the Earth. What kind of line would be recorded during a violent earthquake? ❶

Scientists can determine the strength of an earthquake by studying the height of the wavy lines recorded on the drum. The higher the wavy lines, the stronger the earthquake. Using the seismograph, scientists can detect an earthquake at almost the instant it occurs—anywhere on Earth!

Exploring Earth's Atmosphere

Scientists use many tools to study the Earth's atmosphere. Weather balloons and satellites transmit data to weather tracking stations around the world, enabling scientists to predict the weather far better than they could in the past. Wind vanes measure the speed and direction of the wind, an important thing to know if you are trying to determine if a nearby

---

CONTENT DEVELOPMENT

Point out that primary waves can travel through solids, liquids, and gases and are the fastest of the seismic waves. The primary waves push rock particles into the particles ahead of them, compressing them. After the primary waves pass, the compressed particles bounce back into place. Secondary waves follow the primary waves and can only travel through solids. The primary waves move in a S-type motion, causing rocks to shake at right angles to the wave path. Both primary and secondary waves start at the earthquake's focus, or point of origin. Together, the primary and secondary waves cause surface waves.

● ● ● ●　**Integration**　● ● ● ●

Use the discussion of the seismograph to integrate earth science concepts of geology into your lesson.

FOCUS/MOTIVATION

Have students watch the weather report on a local TV news broadcast. As they watch the report, students should list the information the weather reporter gives. Ask them to identify the tools they think the reporter uses to acquire the in-

formation reported. For example, thermometers are used to record temperatures, and satellite photographs are used to track weather systems.

CONTENT DEVELOPMENT

Write this on the chalkboard: Density = Mass/Volume. Use the definition of density to help students understand how the density of air changes according to temperature, water vapor, and elevation.

Explain that less dense air exerts less

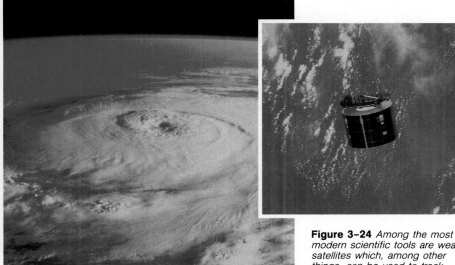

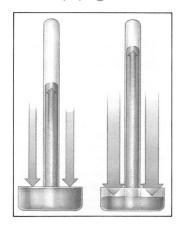

Figure 3–24 *Among the most modern scientific tools are weather satellites which, among other things, can be used to track potentially dangerous hurricanes.*

storm is coming your way. Other instruments measure the humidity (amount of moisture in the atmosphere) and air temperature. The list of instruments to study the atmosphere goes on and on. In this section, we will learn about one instrument you may already be familiar with—the **barometer.**

A barometer is a device that measures air pressure. Although you probably don't often think about it, air is a form of matter and therefore has mass. And as you learned in Chapter 1, the Earth's gravity pulls matter toward the Earth. In simple terms, air pressure is a measure of the force of the atmosphere pushing down on every point on the Earth due to gravity.

There are two different types of barometers. One type is a mercury barometer. A mercury barometer consists of a glass tube closed at one end and filled with mercury (a silvery liquid). The open end of the glass tube is placed in a container of mercury. At sea level, air pushing down on the mercury in the container supports the column of mercury in the glass tube at a certain height. As the air pressure decreases, the column of mercury drops. What will happen if the air pressure increases? ⑶

Figure 3–25 *When air pressure increases, the column of mercury rises in the barometer tube (right). What happens when air pressure decreases (left)?* ⑵

A ■ 83

air pressure. Air expands or spreads out as it is heated. Thus, a given mass of warm air will occupy a larger volume than a given mass of cold air. As a result, the density of the warm air is less, and the pressure it exerts is less. Because water vapor has less mass than other gases in the air, the more water vapor in the air, the less air pressure it exerts. Air at higher elevations gets thinner, is less dense, and as a result exerts less air pressure.

• **Where would you expect to find greater air pressure, on a mountain or at the beach?** (At the beach.)
• **Would you expect the air pressure to be higher on a winter day than on a summer day? Why?** (On a winter day. Cold air is more dense than warm air.)

● ● ● ●   **Integration**   ● ● ● ●

Use the information about the barometer as a tool for measuring air pressure to integrate the earth science concepts of meteorology into your lesson.

Figure 3–26 *An aneroid barometer (inset) is used to measure air pressure anywhere from your hometown to the foggy banks off Kruzof Island in Alaska.*

A more common type of barometer is called an aneroid (AN-er-oid) barometer. See Figure 3–26. An aneroid barometer consists of an airtight metal box from which most of the air has been removed. A change in air pressure causes a needle to move and indicate the new air pressure. Perhaps you have an aneroid barometer at home or in your school. If so, see if you can discover for yourself the relationship between rising and falling air pressure and the weather in your area.

ACTIVITY
CALCULATING

A Water Barometer

❶ Mercury has a density of 13.5 g/cm³. Water has a density of 1.0 g/cm³. If standard air pressure supports a column of mercury 76 cm high, how high would a column of water be supported at this pressure?

3–3 Section Review

1. What are some of the tools used to explore the Earth's oceans, crust, and atmosphere?
2. Can a seismograph be used to predict earthquakes? Explain your answer.

Critical Thinking—*Applying Concepts*

3. Using the term density, explain why air pressure is related to altitude (distance above sea level).

CONNECTIONS

Modern Medicine— Ancient Cure ❷

While preparing bone specimens for microscopic study, a young college student in Detroit made a fascinating discovery. She found that shining ultraviolet light on the bones made them glow yellow-green. The yellow-green color was characteristic of a *modern medicine* called tetracycline used to combat disease. But the bone specimen was over 1600 years old and was part of a skeleton found in the Nubian desert in Africa. How could ancient bones contain a modern medicine?

The answer to the puzzling question lies with a bacterium called streptomyces, which produces tetracycline naturally. Streptomyces also makes up about 60 percent of the bacteria living in Nubian soil. Scientists believe that the streptomyces flourished at the bottom of mud bins used to store grain.

Normally, tetracycline leaves a bitter taste in food. So it is unlikely the people of that time ate the contaminated grain at the bottom of the bin—if they could avoid it. However, every few years that region suffered through serious famines and food became very scarce. At such times we would normally expect disease to rise as people's strength was sapped by the lack of food. But it was during such famines that people were willing to eat the contaminated grain. After all, bitter food is better than no food at all. The ancient people in the Nubian desert could not know how fortunate they were. For just when they needed it most, they ate the grain with the life-saving medicine—without ever realizing how a bacterium was protecting them from disease!

A ■ 85

CONNECTIONS
MODERN MEDICINE— ANCIENT CURE

You may want to discuss the scientific concepts in the article carefully to ensure that all students understand how tetracycline was found in 1600-year-old bones and why the discovery was important. Explain that tetracycline is a family of antibiotics used to treat a wide range of infections caused by bacteria and other microorganisms. Tetracycline interferes with the microorganisms' ability to produce proteins. This family of antibiotics first became available in 1948. Stress the concept of a connection being discovered between a modern medicine and an ancient civilization. Point out that it provided a mystery for scientists to solve.

If you are teaching thematically, you may want to use the Connections feature to reinforce the themes of systems and interactions and scale and structure.

Integration: Use the Connections feature to integrate social studies concepts into your lesson.

Through the investigation students become familiar with the functions and operations of two common scientific tools that they will be using throughout their study of science.

INDEPENDENT PRACTICE

Section Review 3–3
1. Ocean: bathyspheres, bathyscaphs; Earth's crust: seismographs; atmosphere: barometers.
2. Accept all logical answers. Students may think that some seismic activity may precede an earthquake and the seismograph would record the activity, providing an opportunity for short-range predictions.
3. Air is thinner and less dense at high elevations. The reduced density of the air results in lower air pressure at high altitudes.

REINFORCEMENT/RETEACHING

Monitor students' responses to the Section Review questions. If students appear to have difficulty with any of the questions, review the appropriate material with them.

CLOSURE

▶ *Review and Reinforcement Guide*

At this point have students complete Section 3–3 of their *Review and Reinforcement Guide*.

Laboratory Investigation

CONSTRUCTING A TELESCOPE

BEFORE THE LAB

1. At least one day prior to the activity, gather enough materials for the class, assuming six students per group.

2. Check the condition of the lenses to make sure they are clean and not scratched.

3. Determine ahead of time the light source that each group will use. Keep in mind that if the day is cloudy, students will need to use an electric light source.

PRE-LAB DISCUSSION

Discuss with students the basic structure of a telescope. Point out that the eyepiece is the lens closest to the eye, whereas the objective is the lens closest to the object being viewed. The eyepiece has the shorter focal length.

Draw on the chalkboard a simple diagram to illustrate focal length. Show that the focal length is the distance between the center of the lens and the image that is produced.

• **In this activity, where will the image be produced?** (On the screen.)

• **If this is the case, how will you measure the focal length of each lens?** (It will be the distance from the center of the lens to the screen.)

Discuss with students the meaning of the term *refraction*. Explain that light is bent as it passes from one medium to another. This bending is called refraction. In a telescope, light is bent as it passes from the air through each lens.

Laboratory Investigation

Constructing a Telescope

Problem

How does a refracting telescope work?

Materials *(per group)*

> meterstick
> 2 lens holders
> 2 convex lenses or magnifying glasses of different sizes
> unlined index card (to be used as a screen)
> card holder

Procedure 🧪

1. Put the two lenses in the lens holders and place them on the meterstick. Put the index card in its holder and place it between the two lenses.

2. Aim one end of the meterstick at a window or an electric light about 3 to 10 meters away. Light given off or reflected by an object will pass through the lens and form an image of the object on the screen (index card). Carefully slide the lens nearer to the light source back and forth until a clear, sharp image of the light source forms on the screen.

3. The distance between the center of the lens and the sharp image is called the focal length of the lens. Measure this distance to obtain the focal length of that lens. Record your measurement.

4. Turn the other end of the meterstick toward the light source. Without disturbing the screen or the first lens, determine the focal length of the second lens.

5. Point the end of the meterstick that has the lens with the longer focal length toward a distant object. Without changing the positions of the lenses, take the

screen out of its holder and look at the distant object through both lenses. You may have to adjust the lenses slightly to focus the image. You have now constructed a refracting telescope.

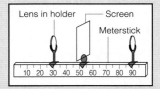

Observations

1. What was the focal length of the first lens? The second lens?

2. How does the image seen through the lens with the shorter focal length differ from the image seen through the lens with the longer focal length?

3. How does the image of an object seen through the lens with the longer focal length appear different from the object itself?

Analysis and Conclusions

1. In a telescope, the lens with the shorter focal length is called the eyepiece. The lens with the longer focal length is called the objective. You can calculate the magnifying power of your telescope by using the following formula:

$$\text{Magnifying power} = \frac{\text{Focal length of objective}}{\text{Focal length of eyepiece}}$$

Using the formula, calculate the magnifying power of your telescope.

2. On Your Own What is the relationship between the telescope's magnifying power and the ratio between the focal lengths of the lenses?

SAFETY TIPS

Caution students not to look directly at any light source.

TEACHING STRATEGY

1. Remind students that the lens nearest the light source is the lens whose focal length is being measured.

2. Have students use the meterstick in the diagram as a guide for the initial placement of the lenses and screen.

DISCOVERY STRATEGIES

Discuss how the investigation relates to the chapter ideas by asking open questions similar to the following.

• **What do the lenses in a refracting telescope do?** (They magnify the image formed by light by gathering and focusing the light.)

• **Why is a refracting telescope better than the human eye?** (It can gather and focus light from much greater distances than the eye can. Therefore, it can see things that the eye cannot.)

• **Why is a telescope a useful tool for scientists?** (It can be used to see distant objects such as stars and galaxies.)

Study Guide

Summarizing Key Concepts

3–1 Exploring the Microscopic World

▲ A microscope is an instrument that produces larger-than-life images of an object.

▲ A magnifying glass is a simple optical microscope with a single lens.

▲ Compound light microscopes contain an eyepiece lens and an objective lens. The magnifying power of the microscope is determined by multiplying the magnifying powers of the lenses.

▲ In order to magnify an object greater than 1000 times, an electron microscope is used. Electron microscopes use a beam of electrons, rather than light, to magnify an object.

▲ The two main types of electron microscopes are the transmission electron microscope (TEM) and the scanning electron microscope (SEM).

▲ X-rays, CT scans, and MRI scans are some of the tools scientists use to look "inside" an object.

3–2 Exploring the Universe

▲ A telescope is an instrument used to view and magnify distant objects.

▲ The two types of optical telescopes are the refracting telescope, which uses a series of lenses, and the reflecting telescope, which uses a series of mirrors to magnify an object.

▲ The electromagnetic spectrum includes visible light as well as infrared, ultraviolet, X-rays, and radio waves.

▲ Many objects in space give off radio waves, which can be observed through the use of a radio telescope.

▲ Infrared, ultraviolet, and X-ray telescopes each provide a different view of the universe.

3–3 Exploring the Earth

▲ In general terms, the Earth can be divided into water, land, and atmosphere.

▲ Scientists use submersibles such as the bathysphere and the bathyscaph to explore ocean depths.

▲ The seismograph is an instrument that detects and measures earthquakes.

▲ One of the most important tools used to study the atmosphere is the barometer, which measures air pressure.

Reviewing Key Terms

Define each term in a complete sentence.

3–1 Exploring the Microscopic World
lens
compound light microscope
electron microscope

infrared telescope
ultraviolet telescope
X-ray telescope

3–2 Exploring the Universe
refracting telescope
reflecting telescope
electromagnetic spectrum
radio telescope

3–3 Exploring the Earth
bathysphere
bathyscaph
seismograph
barometer

A ■ 87

OBSERVATIONS

1. Answers will vary depending on the lenses used. Focal length will likely be about 10 to 15 centimeters.
2. The image seen through the lens with the shorter focal length is larger than the image seen through the lens with the longer focal length.
3. The image of the object is magnified when observed through the lens.

ANALYSIS AND CONCLUSIONS

1. Answers will vary depending on the focal lengths of the lenses used. In general, magnification increases when the objective has a greater focal length than the eyepiece has.
2. The magnifying power increases as either the focal length of the objective increases or the focal length of the eyepiece decreases.

Chapter Review

ALTERNATIVE ASSESSMENT

The Prentice Hall Science program includes a variety of testing components and methodologies. Aside from the Chapter Review questions, you may opt to use the Chapter Test or the computer Test Bank Test in your *Test Book* for assessment of important facts and concepts. In addition, Performance-Based Tests are included in your *Test Book*. These Performance-Based Tests are designed to test science process skills, rather than factual content recall. Since they are not content dependent, Performance-Based Tests can be distributed after students complete a chapter or after they complete the entire textbook.

CONTENT REVIEW

Multiple Choice
1. c
2. c
3. b
4. c
5. d
6. b
7. a
8. c

True or False
1. T
2. F, multiplying
3. F, electron microscope
4. F, electromagnetic
5. F, bathysphere

Concept Mapping
Row 1: electron
Row 2: magnifying glass, SEM
Row 3: series of lenses, interior of objects

Content Review

Multiple Choice

Choose the letter of the answer that best completes each statement.

1. A telescope that uses a series of mirrors to collect and magnify light from distant objects is called a
   a. compound light telescope.
   b. refracting telescope.
   c. reflecting telescope.
   d. none of these
2. A magnifying glass uses
   a. two lenses.   c. a single lens.
   b. a single mirror.   d. two mirrors.
3. The highest magnifying power of a compound light microscope is
   a. 100.   c. 10,000.
   b. 1000.   d. 100,000.
4. To observe the outer structure of a virus, you would use a(an)
   a. TEM.
   b. compound light microscope.
   c. SEM.
   d. MRI.

5. Which telescope would be best placed in outer space?
   a. X-ray telescope
   b. infrared telescope
   c. ultraviolet telescope
   d. all of these
6. Optical telescopes detect
   a. X-rays.   c. infrared energy.
   b. visible light.   d. radio waves.
7. The strength of an earthquake is measured by a(an)
   a. seismograph.   c. MRI.
   b. bathyscaph.   d. series of lenses.
8. A barometer measures
   a. weather conditions.
   b. temperature.
   c. air pressure.
   d. precipitation.

True or False

If the statement is true, write "true." If it is false, change the underlined word or words to make the statement true.

1. In a compound light microscope, the lens closest to the object being observed is called the <u>objective lens</u>.
2. The magnifying power of a microscope is found by <u>dividing</u> the power of the objective lens by the power of the eyepiece lens.
3. One type of <u>compound light microscope</u> is the TEM.
4. The <u>magnetoelectric</u> spectrum includes both visible and invisible light.
5. A submersible that is attached directly to a ship on the ocean's surface is called a <u>bathyscaph</u>.

Concept Mapping

Complete the following concept map for Section 3–1. Refer to pages A6–A7 to construct a concept map for the entire chapter.

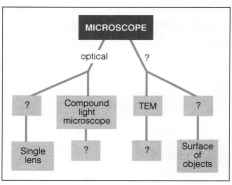

CONCEPT MASTERY

1. A compound light microscope allows scientists to observe living microscopic organisms, but it cannot magnify more than 1000 times. An SEM is useful for observing the outside of an object whereas a TEM is useful for observing the inside of an object, but neither can be used to view living things; the specimen must be sliced and placed in a vacuum.

2. Before van Leeuwenhoek's experiment, people didn't know that microscopic organisms existed because they had never been seen. But of course, they had always been there.

3. Although we can dream, suppose, and postulate about what is out in space, we can observe and study only what we can see and gather information about, and for that, we are dependent on the abilities of the tools that we create and use.

4. The only light that we can see—that literally "meets the eye"—is visible light. But visible light is only one part of the electromagnetic spectrum, which includes many forms of invisible light.

Concept Mastery

Discuss each of the following in a brief paragraph.

1. Discuss the uses and limitations of a compound light microscope, an SEM, and a TEM.
2. Van Leeuwenhoek's experiments with a drop of water have been compared to suddenly discovering that an entire family has been living in your house without your knowledge. Explain the meaning of this comparison.
3. How has our understanding of objects in space been limited by the tools we can use?
4. Explain the meaning of the statement, "There is more to light than meets the eye."
5. Describe the relationship between air pressure and density.

Critical Thinking and Problem Solving

Use the skills you have developed in this chapter to answer each of the following.

1. **Making charts** Construct a chart that shows the different types of telescopes and the kinds of energy each type can detect.
2. **Expressing an opinion** A great deal of money is spent each year on space exploration. Many people feel that this money could be better spent improving conditions on Earth. Other people feel that knowledge gained from space exploration will ultimately bring great benefits to human society. Still others suggest that scientific knowledge is valuable for its own sake and should not be thought of in terms of dollars and cents. What is your opinion? Explain your answer.
3. **Designing an experiment** Ocean water, unlike fresh water, contains salt. The amount of salt in ocean water is called salinity. Design an experiment to determine if the salinity of ocean water changes as the depth of the ocean changes.
4. **Drawing conclusions** At the beginning of this chapter we stated that the way the Anasazi Indians tried to solve the mysteries of nature may not be very different from those used by modern scientists. Now that you have completed the chapter, explain whether you agree or disagree with that statement.
5. **Using the writing process** If telescopes could talk, what stories would they tell? Write a telescope story. *Hint:* First decide what type of telescope you are.
6. **Using the writing process** You have been given the opportunity to travel back to the age of dinosaurs. Which of the tools discussed in this chapter would be most useful in your travels? Explain your answer.

their stories with the class. Then have students add the stories to their portfolio.
6. Students' answers will vary. Name each of the tools from the chapter and have students explain why they chose that tool to take with them. Compile the reasons in chart form on the chalkboard to see which tool is thought to be the most useful.

KEEPING A PORTFOLIO

You might want to assign some of the Concept Mastery and Critical Thinking and Problem Solving questions as homework and have students include their responses to unassigned questions in their portfolio. Students should be encouraged to include both the question and the answer in their portfolio.

ISSUES IN SCIENCE

The following issues can be used as springboards for discussion or given as writing assignments:
1. Small animals such as rats or mice are frequently used in laboratories to test ideas, medicines, or procedures that eventually lead to discoveries that improve human life. Some people think this is justifiable as long as the animals are treated humanely. Other people think that all research using animals should be stopped. What is your opinion? Describe and defend your point of view.
2. Think about all the tools described in this chapter and what they are able to do. Then think of a problem and design a tool to handle it. Use your imagination. After all, visualizing an answer, however strange and unlikely, is often the first step to solving a problem. Prepare a sketch or diagram of your tool to accompany your explanation of its function.

5. Air pressure varies according to the density of the air. Denser air exerts greater pressure than less dense air.

CRITICAL THINKING AND PROBLEM SOLVING

1. Charts will vary but should include optical, radio, infrared, ultraviolet, and X-ray as well as the appropriate part of the electromagnetic spectrum.
2. Opinions will vary, but students should provide reasons for their answers.
3. Experiments will vary but should include some method for collecting samples, measuring salinity, and recording data in a way that establishes a relationship between salinity and depth.
4. Students' answers will vary. Whether they agree or disagree, they should consider the question of the Anasazis' use of basic scientific methods, such as observation and experimentation, as compared to those of modern scientists.
5. Students' stories should be scientifically consistent with the chapter material on telescopes. Ask volunteers to share

STEPHEN HAWKING: CHANGING
OUR VIEW OF THE UNIVERSE

Background Information

With the Newtonian theory of gravity and Einstein's theory of general relativity, it is possible to reliably predict both the location and speed of an object in space. In the world of subatomic particles, however, things are not so easy. The quantum theory, which describes the behavior of particles that make up the atom, includes what is called an "uncertainty principle." This principle states that at a given moment, one cannot predict both the speed and location of a particle inside an atom (thus the need for an "electron cloud" to describe the location of electrons around a nucleus). Dr. Hawking, who is using the quantum theory to study black holes, says that the uncertainty is especially bad there; it is impossible to predict either the speed or the location of a particle emitted from a black hole.

One of the factors that spurs Hawking on is that connecting links between the quantum theory and every known physical field of force except gravity have been proven. Thus Hawking feels that consistency dictates a link between the quantum theory and the force of gravity.

SCIENCE GAZETTE

Scientists have long struggled to find the connection between two branches of physics. One of these branches deals with the forces that rule the world of atoms and subatomic particles. The other branch deals with gravity and its role in the universe of stars and galaxies. Physicist Stephen Hawking has set himself the task of discovering the connection. Leading theoretical physicists agree that if anyone can discover a unifying principle, it will certainly be this extraordinary scientist.

Dr. Hawking's goal, as he describes it, is simple. "It is complete understanding of the universe, why it is as it is and why it exists at all." In order to achieve such an understanding, Dr. Hawking seeks to "quantize gravity." Quantizing gravity means combining the laws of gravity and the laws of quantum mechanics into a single universal law.

STEPHEN HAWKING: Changing Our View of the Universe

TEACHING STRATEGY: ADVENTURE

FOCUS/MOTIVATION

Begin by asking students the following questions.
• **What is the smallest thing you can think of?** (Answers may vary. The smallest thing in the universe is actually a subatomic particle.)
• **What is the largest thing you can think of?** (Answers may vary. Probably the largest imaginable thing is the entire universe.)

Point out that two branches of physics deal with these extremes: (1) the world of the atom and subatomic particles and (2) the world of the stars and galaxies.

CONTENT DEVELOPMENT

Have students read the article about Stephen Hawking.
• **In what way is Dr. Hawking involved in the two branches of physics that we**

Stephen Hawking is a Lucasian professor of mathematics at Cambridge University— a position once held by Isaac Newton. Hawking has received numerous prizes for his work.

Dr. Hawking and other theoretical physicists believe that with such a law, the behavior of all matter in the universe, and the origin of the universe as well, could be explained.

Dr. Hawking's search for a unifying theory has led him to study one of science's greatest mysteries: black holes. A black hole is an incredibly dense region in space whose gravitational pull attracts all nearby objects, virtually "swallowing them up." A black hole is formed when a star uses up most of the nuclear fuel that has kept it burning. During most of its life as an ordinary star, its nuclear explosions exert enough outward force to balance the powerful inward force of gravity. But when the star's fuel is used up, the outward force ceases to exist. Gravity takes over and the star collapses into a tiny core of extremely dense material, possibly no bigger than the period at the end of this sentence.

Hawking has already proved that a black hole can emit a stream of electrons. Prior to this discovery, scientists believed that noth-ing, not even light, could escape from a black hole. So scientists have hailed Hawking's discovery as "one of the most beautiful in the history of physics."

Probing the mysteries of the universe is no ordinary feat. And Stephen Hawking is no ordinary man. Respected as one of the most brilliant physicists in the world, Hawking is considered one of the most remarkable. For Dr. Hawking suffers from a serious disease of the nervous system that has confined him to a wheelchair, and he is barely able to move or speak. Although Dr. Hawking gives numerous presentations and publishes countless articles and papers, his addresses must be translated and his essays written down by other hands.

Hawking became ill during his first years at Cambridge University in England. The disease progressed quickly and left the young scholar quite despondent. He even considered giving up his research, as he thought he would not live long enough to receive his Ph.D. But in 1965, Hawking's life changed. He married Jane Wilde, a fellow student and language scholar. Suddenly life took on new meaning. "That was the turning point," he says. "It made me determined to live, and it was about that time that I began making professional progress." Hawking's health and spirits improved. His studies continued and reached new heights of brilliance. Today, Dr. Hawking is a professor of mathematics at Cambridge University who leads a full and active life.

Dr. Hawking believes that his illness has benefited his work. It has given him more time to think about physics. So although his body is failing him, his mind is free to soar. Considered to be one of the most brilliant physicists of all times, Dr. Hawking has taken some of the small steps that lead science to discovery and understanding. With time to ponder the questions of the universe, it is quite likely that Stephen Hawking will be successful in uniting the world of the tiniest particles with the world of stars and galaxies.

GAZETTE ■ 91

Additional Questions and Topic Suggestions

1. What do theoretical physicists believe would be possible if a single universal law could be discovered? (They believe it would be possible to explain the behavior of all matter in the universe and the origin of the universe as well.)

2. What did Dr. Hawking prove about a black hole? How did his discovery change previous ideas about black holes? (He proved that a black hole can emit a stream of electrons. Prior to this, scientists believed that nothing, not even light, could escape from a black hole.)

3. Many handicapped persons have been extremely successful in their fields. Go to the library and research the story of such a person. Explain how his or her story compares with Dr. Hawking's story.

Critical Thinking Questions

1. Why might the study of black holes be relevant to the unifying principle Dr. Hawking is looking for? (A black hole is a phenomenon that occurs in the universe when a star dies. It is caused by the force of gravity. Yet black holes also emit electrons, which are subatomic particles. These particles would obey the laws of quantum mechanics.)

2. What do you think about the idea that the behavior of the very smallest and very largest things in the universe must somehow obey the same law? Discuss your ideas in a brief paragraph.

just discussed? (He is attempting to discover a unifying principle that combines the laws of gravity with the laws of quantum mechanics.)

Stress to students the inspiring story of Dr. Hawking's success as a scientist despite his illness and physical handicaps. Point out that Dr. Hawking feels that his illness has actually enhanced his career because it has given him more time to think about physics.

INDEPENDENT PRACTICE

▶ *Activity Book*

After students have read the Science Gazette article, you may want to hand out the reading skills worksheet based on the article in your *Activity Book.*

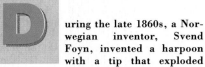

ISSUES IN SCIENCE

ARE WE DESTROYING
THE GREATEST CREATURES
OF THE SEA?

Background Information

The vote of the International Whaling Commission (IWC) to ban all commercial whaling as of 1986 was an important victory for conservationists. The decision also reflects the convincing arguments of IWC's Scientific Committee, which maintains that there is a clear scientific basis for cessation of all commercial whaling. The vote has brought tremendous opposition, however, for member nations with profitable whaling industries. Among these are Japan, Norway, the Soviet Union, Iceland, Brazil, Peru, and South Korea. Each of these nations voted against the resolution, and each is determined to overturn it or circumvent it if possible.

The nations that oppose the resolution have several options. First, they can formally object. Such action would release the objecting nation from the mandate of the resolution and extend the time allowed for other nations to file objections. Most countries are reluctant to take this course of action, probably because they fear possible economic sanctions by the United States and other conservationist countries.

A second option for objecting nations is to pressure other members of the IWC to reverse the resolution. For example, Japan has already threatened Jamaica with loss of its coffee trade if Jamaica continues to favor whale conservation.

Perhaps the most drastic protest option is for a nation to withdraw from the IWC entirely and become a "pirate" whaler. If this happened, other IWC nations would be forced to retaliate. For example, the United States would be required by law to impose economic sanctions on Japan if Japan should choose to become a pirate whaler.

Are We Destroying the Greatest Creatures of the Sea?

During the late 1860s, a Norwegian inventor, Svend Foyn, invented a harpoon with a tip that exploded when it hit its target: a whale. This new weapon enabled whalers to kill their prey much faster and easier than ever before. Foyn's harpoon led to the development of modern whaling and the slaughter of the world's whales.

Since the beginning of this century, more than three million whales have been killed. Several species are now endangered. The number of blue whales, the largest living creatures, has dropped from 100,000 to less than 1,000. There are only small numbers of right whales and bowheads left. Many other species also are declining in number.

Most countries that once carried on commercial whaling, including the United States, have long since stopped. But a few, such as Japan and Norway, continue to hunt whales for profit. Whaling nations contend that they do not hunt endangered species, only those species that are still common. Conservationists argue that even whales of common species are dropping too rapidly in number. These people believe that, for several years at least, no whales of any species should be hunted.

STOPPING THE SLAUGHTER

In response to conservationists, the International Whaling Commission voted in 1982 to ban commercial whaling starting in 1986. Set up to regulate whaling, the commission has members from more than two dozen nations, the United States and whaling countries among them. But the ban does not guarantee that the killing will stop. For one thing, a country can withdraw from the commission at any time and kill all the whales it wants to.

Moreover, within 90 days after the ban was voted upon, Norway, Japan, and other whaling nations filed protests against it with the commission. Under commission rules, this exempts them from the ban.

Even so, however, the nations that protested may choose not to take advantage of their exemption. If they did take advantage of their exemption, their actions could

◄ One job of The International Whaling Commission is to control the killing of whales, such as these sperm whales.

TEACHING STRATEGY: ISSUE

FOCUS/MOTIVATION

Collect and display pictures of various types of whales.
• **Have any of you ever seen a whale?** (Answers may vary.)
• **What are some characteristics of whales?** (Accept all reasonable answers. Students should recognize that whales are mammals, that they are the largest mammals, that they live in the ocean, and that there are many different species of whales.)
• **Do you think whales are important to ocean life? Why or why not?** (Accept all answers.)

CONTENT DEVELOPMENT

Discuss with students the concern of conservationists about the dwindling numbers of whales.
• **Why do you think the population of**

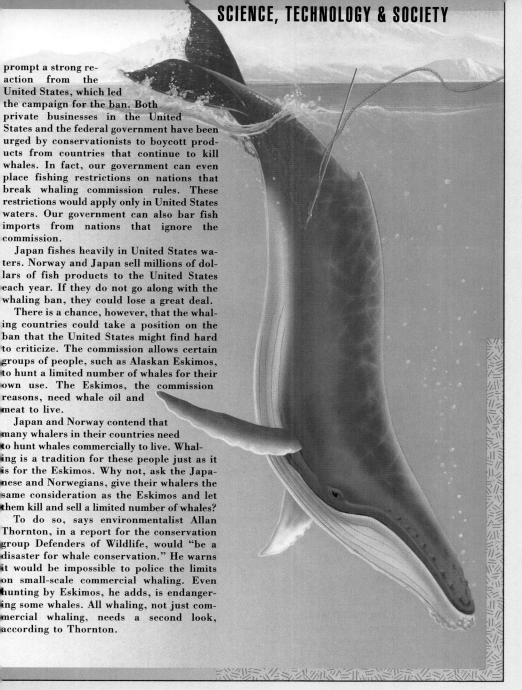

prompt a strong re-action from the United States, which led the campaign for the ban. Both private businesses in the United States and the federal government have been urged by conservationists to boycott products from countries that continue to kill whales. In fact, our government can even place fishing restrictions on nations that break whaling commission rules. These restrictions would apply only in United States waters. Our government can also bar fish imports from nations that ignore the commission.

Japan fishes heavily in United States waters. Norway and Japan sell millions of dollars of fish products to the United States each year. If they do not go along with the whaling ban, they could lose a great deal.

There is a chance, however, that the whaling countries could take a position on the ban that the United States might find hard to criticize. The commission allows certain groups of people, such as Alaskan Eskimos, to hunt a limited number of whales for their own use. The Eskimos, the commission reasons, need whale oil and meat to live.

Japan and Norway contend that many whalers in their countries need to hunt whales commercially to live. Whaling is a tradition for these people just as it is for the Eskimos. Why not, ask the Japanese and Norwegians, give their whalers the same consideration as the Eskimos and let them kill and sell a limited number of whales?

To do so, says environmentalist Allan Thornton, in a report for the conservation group Defenders of Wildlife, would "be a disaster for whale conservation." He warns it would be impossible to police the limits on small-scale commercial whaling. Even hunting by Eskimos, he adds, is endangering some whales. All whaling, not just commercial whaling, needs a second look, according to Thornton.

Additional Questions and Topic Suggestions

1. As a class, discuss some further information about this issue that you might like to have. Then compose a letter asking for this information and send it to the Whale Protection Fund, Center for Environmental Education, 624 Ninth Street, NW; Washington, DC 20001.

2. Go to the library and read about the importance of whaling in the nineteenth-century United States, particularly in New England. Report your findings to the class.

3. Another ocean species that is endangered is the Alaskan king crab. Find out what Alaska has done about this problem and how it has affected Alaska's fishing industry.

---

whales is decreasing? (Answers may vary; the most obvious answer is that the whale population is decreasing as a result of human activities, particularly commercial whaling.)

• **Which nations are particularly involved in commercial whaling?** (Japan and Norway.)

• **What are some products that can be obtained from whales?** (Oil, meat, ivorylike material from the teeth, and whalebone.)

Point out that at one time, the United States had a significant whaling industry. However, the products produced by this industry—especially whale oil—are no longer in common use. As a result, the United States gave up whaling some time ago. Only the Eskimos in Alaska still depend on whale oil and whale meat.

• **What products are still being used by nations that have continued whaling?** (Primarily whale meat.)

• **Do you think it is necessary for people to have whale meat? Could they not eat some other kind of meat from an animal that is not in danger of extinction?** (Accept all answers. A possible consideration is that for some groups of people, such as the Eskimos, few alternative food sources may be available.)

Critical Thinking Questions

1. Use your imagination to create a story about what could have happened to dinosaurs if humans had been on Earth shortly before dinosaurs became extinct. Might some of the same arguments have been used to save these creatures as are now being used to save the whales? (Accept all answers.)

2. How might a concerned citizen take action to protest if a nation such as Japan or Norway refuses to obey the IWC's resolution to ban commercial whaling? (Answers may vary. Possible answers include refusing to buy products, especially fish, from all these countries; writing to our nation's representatives on the IWC; and pressuring supermarkets and import companies to refuse to buy or stock products from the offending nations.)

3. How is the Eskimos' need for whales different from Japan's or Norway's needs for whales? (The Eskimos primarily need products from the whales—specifically meat and oil—in order to live. Japan and Norway need primarily the income from the whaling industry, not the products themselves.)

Class Debate

Challenge students to simulate a meeting of the IWC. Each student or pair of students should choose a different nation to represent, then find out what this nation's position is with regard to the resolution to ban commercial whaling.

ISSUE (continued)

GUIDED PRACTICE

Skills Development

Skill: Relating cause and effect

Direct students' attention to the photograph of the humpback whale on page A94. Emphasize the importance of conservation as it applies to the preservation of nature's food chains.

• **What happens when an animal near the bottom of a food chain becomes extinct?** (Animals higher up in the chain lose their food source and become endangered.)

• **What happens when an animal in the middle of a food chain becomes ex-**

▲ The huge humpback whale is at the top of an important food chain. If whales vanished, the balance of life in the sea might be forever changed.

AN AGE THAT HAS PASSED

Whaling was once a worldwide business, and brave men in sailing vessels roamed the globe to hunt the huge creatures. Oil from whales was burned in lamps. Whalebone was used in making women's undergarments. The teeth of some whales were used to make piano keys. Today, however, many whale products can be or have been replaced by other materials. But whale meat still has a market, most notably in Japan. So whaling can still be profitable, even if not as profitable as in the past.

Even in Japan, however, whale meat accounts for less than 1 percent of the protein eaten by the Japanese. Echoing conservationists, United States Representative Don Bonker noted in Congress, "There is no reason to continue commercial whaling at any level."

Conservationists view whales as a symbol. If people cannot preserve the largest animals on Earth, they say, there is little hope for any other part of nature.

Whales, moreover, play an important part in keeping the ocean environment balanced.

The largest whales, such as the blue whale, feed on tiny shrimplike creatures and other small organisms, collectively known as krill. The whales obtain the krill by straining it from the water with huge sievelike structures in their mouths called baleen, or whalebone.

The baleen whales are at the top of an important food chain. They eat krill, which feed on microscopic plants, which in turn convert the sun's energy and sea salts into food. The waste excreted by whales provides nutrients for microscopic plants and other organisms in the water. All in all, the relationship between the whale and the other organisms in the food chain is a neatly balanced natural cycle that constantly renews the food resources of the sea.

If the baleen whales disappear, the cycle will be broken. What will happen then? Scientists are not sure. But there is no doubt that the fragile balance of nature in the ocean would tip—and not in our favor.

▼ If the hunting of whales is not stopped, scenes such as this humpback whale in Alaska may not be seen in the future.

---

tinct? (Animals higher in the chain tend to lose their food source, whereas animals lower in the chain tend to increase in population.)

• **What happens when an animal at the top of a food chain becomes extinct?** (Animals lower in the chain that are normally eaten by the extinct animal tend to increase in population. This may endanger the species that is next lower in the chain because there would be many more predators seeking to eat them.)

ENRICHMENT

Interested students may enjoy going to the library and learning about a medieval legend that claimed magical healing powers for a substance derived from the tooth of a narwhal, a small Arctic whale. The substance was sold in medieval apothecaries as "unicorn horn."

INDEPENDENT PRACTICE

▶ *Activity Book*

After students have read the Science Gazette article, you may want to hand out

WANTED!

Space Pioneers

Background Information

NASA is currently involved in research on the use of the Space Shuttle to build and supply orbiting manufacturing centers. These centers would use materials mined in space as well as materials brought from Earth.

NASA has recently undertaken a major sales effort to interest private companies in space mining and manufacturing. Among the companies that have decided to move ahead with experiments aboard the Space Shuttle is McDonnell Douglas.

One of the most promising aspects of space mining is the ease of materials processing due to weightlessness. The molecules of certain materials that are difficult or impossible to separate on Earth can be easily separated in the zero-gravity environment of space. Because some of the substances in this category are used to make pharmaceuticals, this industry stands to gain a great deal from the new technology.

Despite the appeal of space mining, however, private industry on the whole has not been quick to make commitments. As a *New York Times* writer explained, the rewards of space ventures may be dozens of years away, and most companies work on a three- to five-year plan. Everyone is waiting for someone else to prove and perfect the technology.

Space mining would probably become more attractive to industry if an inexpensive and reliable method of space travel could be developed. At the present time, the Space Shuttle is just too expensive to make space manufacturing centers economically practical. As an official at NASA's Johnson Space Center pointed out, a Space Shuttle, "like the first train west out of Saint Louis a century ago," must come first if space mining and manufacturing are to become a reality.

Kansas City Star: January 12, 2021

WANTED:

Miners and Engineers to provide new space [colony] with building materials. We're looking for [people] who can turn moon rocks and lunar topsoil [into u]sable metals such as aluminum, magnesium, [and ti]tanium. These metals will be used to make [tools] and to build support structures for the colony. [We al]so want workers who can extract silicon from [the] moon's silicates. Silicon is needed to make [solar] cells and computer chips. Glass that will be [used] for windows in space colony homes also [com]es from lunar silicates. And iron and carbon [mine]d from the moon need to be turned into steel. [In] addition, we're looking for lunar gold miners [to s]earch the moon's surface for deposits of gold, [as w]ell as nickel and platinum. And oxygen, which [will] be used for both life-support systems and [rock]et fuel, needs to be extracted from moon rocks.

Terry had answered the advertisement. Now, in the year 2024, she was hard at work at Moon Mine Alpha.

Terry expertly plunged the heavy shovel of her bulldozer into the soil to pick up another load of valuable material. When she raised the shovel, it was filled with moon rocks and lunar dust. Terry dumped her cargo into her lunar hauler. "My last truckload of the day," she thought, jumping down from the bulldozer. "Now I can go watch the mass driver in action."

Terry swung into the driver's seat of the lunar hauler. Soon she was bumping along the moon highway, a dusty path her hauler and others like it had carved out of the lunar topsoil over the past few months.

GAZETTE ■ 95

---

the reading skills worksheet based on the article in your *Activity Book*.

TEACHING STRATEGY: FUTURE

FOCUS/MOTIVATION

Have students read the "want ad" on the opening page of this article.
• **Does this sound like the typical want ad you would find in a local newspaper?** (Answers may vary. Obviously, the ad describes a job that is located on the moon and one that involves some very futuristic things such as a space colony, moon mines, and homes in outer space.)
• **Where might an ad like this appear?** (Answers may vary. Most likely, this ad would appear in a newspaper or other publication at some time in the future, when moon mining and space colonies are a reality.)
• **How would you feel about answering an ad like this?** (Accept all answers.)

◄ **A typical lunar colony with all the comforts of home!**

Additional Questions and Topic Suggestions

1. The moon contains significant quantities of aluminum, iron, silver, and oxygen. Find out some important uses of these elements and then make a chart to display your findings.

2. How does soil on the moon differ from soil on Earth? (The moon's soil is made of rocks and dust. Unlike soil on Earth, it contains no water or living things. In some ways, the soil resembles that of the most barren deserts on Earth. Because there is no wind and no water, there is no soil erosion on the moon.)

3. What type of education and background do you think a person would need to qualify for the jobs of moon or asteroid miner and engineer? (Accept all logical answers. Students should consider that a person would need education and training similar to that of an astronaut, as well as training in engineering and/or mining.)

FUTURE (continued)

CONTENT DEVELOPMENT

Emphasize to students that the possibility of space mining offers two major advantages. First, space mining would provide more resources for use on Earth—a benefit that is particularly important in light of dwindling supplies of certain elements and minerals. Second, space mining could provide the raw materials needed to support colonies in space. Space colonies may become increasingly important as research in space extends to other planets and as space travel becomes more commonplace. These colonies would not be able to exist if all necessary resources had to be "imported" from Earth.

Fifteen minutes later, she spotted the huge piece of machinery known as the mass driver. She saw the "flying buckets" of the mass driver suspended magnetically above special tracks. The buckets, filled with packages of lunar rocks, soon would be sent speeding along above these tracks by powerful magnetic forces. When the buckets reached high enough speed, they would fling their contents into space at 2.4 kilometers per second. At this speed, an object can escape the moon's gravity. Hundreds or thousands of kilometers away, a mass catcher would be waiting to grab the lunar cargo. The lunar materials would then be turned into fuel or building materials for a new space colony. Surely the mass driver, developed in the 1970s at the Massachusetts Institute of Technology, had proved to be a valuable tool for space colonization.

What will this space colony be like? Stationed nearly 400,000 kilometers from the Earth, a huge sphere more than 1.5 kilometers in diameter will rotate in space. The rotation will create artificial gravity on the inner surface of the sphere. Here 10,000 people or more will live and work inside an earthlike environment powered by the sun. The Space Colony will be constructed of materials mined almost entirely on the moon.

RESOURCES IN SPACE

As many scientists see it, our growing needs for raw materials, energy, and jumping-off places for journeys to the planets and stars make us look into space. Where else is there a free, continuous supply of solar energy, uninterrupted by darkness or weather? Where else does weightlessness, which will aid in the construction of huge structures, exist? Where else is there an untapped source of minerals?

A wealth of energy and materials is available in space. Let's start with the moon, a mere 356,000 kilometers away. This natural satellite could be an important source of aluminum, iron, silicon, and oxygen. A permanent base established on the moon could supply all the resources needed to support space settlement and exploration. Although these resources are abundant on the Earth, bringing millions of tons of materials into space is out of the question!

The moon could become a gigantic "supply station" in the sky. Metals and lunar soil could be mined to build huge structures inside of which comfortable, earthlike homes would be constructed. Since the moon's grav-

CONTENT DEVELOPMENT

Point out that part of the task of mining asteroids may involve "capturing" a nearby asteroid and bringing it closer to Earth. This proposed idea has generated considerable controversy. For one thing, some experts worry about what will happen if scientists "miss" when they try to harness the asteroid—the asteroid could come crashing to Earth with the force of a nuclear explosion. In addition, the capture of an asteroid raises some thorny political questions. For example, who

would own this new satellite? Would it be the sole property of the nation that brought it to Earth? Or would any nation with sufficient technology have the right to land on the asteroid and extract its mineral riches?

GUIDED PRACTICE

Skills Development

Skill: Forming an opinion

Have students work in small groups. Challenge each group to imagine that

▶ **Mining the asteroids yields precious metals, minerals, and water.**

itational force is one sixth the strength of the Earth's, it would be cheaper and easier to build such space factories and colonies on the moon. These buildings could become part of the permanent moon base.

Almost half of the moon is made up of oxygen. This oxygen could be used to make rocket fuel. Liquid hydrogen mixed with liquid oxygen is a basic rocket fuel. Rockets bound for the outer planets could be launched more easily from the moon than from Earth, where the pull of gravity is six times greater.

A NEW FRONTIER

The moon is not the only source of natural materials in near space. Asteroids are also vast treasure houses of minerals. They contain metals such as nickel, iron, cobalt, magnesium, and aluminum. Phosphorus, carbon, and sulfur are also present on asteroids. And they may contain the precious metals gold, silver, and platinum. Asteroids are also important sources of water. One small asteroid can perhaps yield between 1 and 10 billion tons of water.

"Hey, Terry, how's it going?" The voice belonged to Bill, one of the workers who ran the mass driver.

"Oh, I still like being a moon miner," Terry answered, "but a few years from now, I hope to be mining the asteroids instead. It should be a challenge trying to capture a small asteroid or land on a big one."

"I hope you like traveling, Terry," Bill said with a worried look. "The trip could take months or years."

"It would be worth it," said Terry as she waved to Bill and headed to her two-room apartment under the plastic dome of Hadleyville. Turning on her TV set to watch live coverage from Earth of the 2024 Summer Olympics, Terry tuned in the *Moon Miner's Daily Herald*, a TV "newspaper." Suddenly, an advertisement caught her eye.

WANTED:
Asteroid Miners and Engineers to capture small asteroids and collect samples from larger asteroids. Workers must be willing to spend long periods of time far from home. Travel to the asteroid belt, which lies between the orbits of Mars and Jupiter about 160 to 300 million kilometers away, is required.

"Why not?" Terry thought as she began to type out a reply on her computer.

GAZETTE ■ 97

Critical Thinking Questions

1. Observe the photograph on page A96 and read the caption. Do you agree that this typical lunar colony has "all the comforts of home"? Explain your answer. (Accept all answers. Encourage students as they answer the question to imagine what life would be like in a colony such as this one.)

2. What are some advantages of developing human colonies in space? (Answers may vary. Possible advantages include relieving some of the overpopulation on Earth; obtaining valuable resources such as those described in the article; increasing human knowledge about the universe; and providing people with a new and unusual lifestyle.)

3. Why would it be easier and cheaper to construct a large building on the moon than on Earth? (Gravity on the moon is only one sixth that of gravity on Earth. This means that building materials would weigh less. It would take less manpower to move and handle materials, less energy to transport the materials, and less human energy to construct the building. These factors would result in reduced costs.)

---

they are board members of a corporation that is considering building a manufacturing center in space. Have students list the pros and cons of such a venture. Then have each group present to the class a dramatization of a board meeting in which the proposal is debated. Based on the information presented, have the class decide whether they think the corporation should go ahead with the project.

ENRICHMENT

Challenge students to imagine that they are real estate salespeople attempting to sell the latest space colony home or apartment. Have students compose newspaper ads for the futuristic dwelling, using the real estate section of a local newspaper as a model for style. Encourage students to emphasize not only the indoor features of the house or apartment but the advantages of location as well. For example, an ad might read, "just a few blocks away from the nearest Space Shuttle" or "a quick commute to Moon Mine Alpha."

INDEPENDENT PRACTICE

▶ *Activity Book*

After students have read the Science Gazette article, you may want to hand out the reading skills worksheet based on the article in your *Activity Book*.

For Further Reading

If you have been intrigued by the concepts examined in this textbook, you may also be interested in the ways fellow thinkers—novelists, poets, essayists, as well as scientists—have imaginatively explored the same ideas.

Chapter 1: What Is Science?

Adamson, Joy. *Born Free, a Lioness of Two Worlds*. New York: Pantheon.

Ames, Mildred. *Anna to the Infinite Power*. New York: Scribner.

Doyle, Sir Arthur Conan. *Adventures of Sherlock Holmes*. New York: Berkley Pub.

Freeman, Ira, and Mae Freeman. *Your Wonderful World of Science*. New York: Random House.

Chapter 2: Measurement and the Sciences

Clarke, Arthur C. *2001: A Space Odyssey*. New York: New American Library.

Duder, Tessa. *In Lane Three, Alex Archer*. Boston: Houghton-Mifflin.

Kohn, Bernice. *The Scientific Method*. Englewood Cliffs, NJ: Prentice-Hall.

Merrill, Jean. *The Toothpaste Millionaire*. Boston: Houghton-Mifflin.

Chapter 3: Tools and the Sciences

Asimov, Isaac. *Fantastic Voyage*. Boston: Houghton-Mifflin.

Merle, Robert. *The Day of the Dolphin*. New York: Simon & Schuster.

Walsh, Jill Paton. *Toolmaker*. New York: Seabury.

Activity Bank

> Welcome to the Activity Bank! This is an exciting and enjoyable part of your science textbook. By using the Activity Bank you will have the chance to make a variety of interesting and different observations about science. The best thing about the Activity Bank is that you and your classmates will become the detectives, and as with any investigation you will have to sort through information to find the truth. There will be many twists and turns along the way, some surprises and disappointments too. So always remember to keep an open mind, ask lots of questions, and have fun learning about science.

A ■ 99

Activity Bank

COOPERATIVE LEARNING

Hands-on science activities, such as the ones in the Activity Bank, lend themselves well to cooperative learning techniques. The first step in setting up activities for cooperative learning is to divide the class into small groups of about 4 to 6 students. Next, assign roles to each member of the group. Possible roles include Principal Investigator, Materials Manager, Recorder/Reporter, Maintenance Director. The Principal Investigator directs all operations associated with the group activity, including checking the assignment, giving instructions to the group, making sure that the proper procedure is being followed, performing or delegating the steps of the activity, and asking questions of the teacher on behalf of the group. The Materials Manager obtains and dispenses all materials and equipment and is the only member of the group allowed to move around the classroom without special permission during the activity. The Recorder, or Reporter, collects information, certifies and records results, and reports results to the class. The Maintenance Director is responsible for cleanup and has the authority to assign other members of the group to assist. The Maintenance Director is also in charge of group safety.

For more information about specific roles and cooperative learning in general, refer to the article "Cooperative Learning and Science—The Perfect Match" on pages 70–75 in the *Teacher's Desk Reference*.

ESL/LEP STRATEGY

Activities such as the ones in the Activity Bank can be extremely helpful in teaching science concepts to LEP students—the direct observation of scientific phenomena and the deliberate manipulation of variables can transcend language barriers.

Some strategies for helping LEP students as they develop their English-language skills are listed below. Your school's English-to-Speakers-of-Other-Languages (ESOL) teacher will probably be able to make other concrete suggestions to fit the specific needs of the LEP students in your classroom.

• Assign a "buddy" who is proficient in English to each LEP student. The buddy need not be able to speak the LEP student's native language, but such ability can be helpful. (**Note:** *Instruct multilingual buddies to use the native language only when necessary, such as defining difficult terms or concepts. Students learn English, as all other languages, by using it.*) The buddy's job is to provide encouragement and assistance to the LEP student. Select buddies on the basis of personality as well as proficiency in science and English. If possible, match buddies and LEP students so that the LEP students can help their buddies in another academic area, such as math.

• If possible, do not put LEP students of the same nationality in a cooperative learning group.

• Have artistic students draw diagrams of each step of an activity for the LEP students.

You can read more about teaching science to LEP students in the article "Creating a Positive Learning Environment for Students with Limited English Proficiency," which is found on pages 86–87 in the *Teacher's Desk Reference*.

Activity Bank

OBSERVING A FISH

BEFORE THE ACTIVITY

1. At least one day prior to the activity, gather all your materials for your groups, assuming from four to six students per group.

2. A five-gallon aquarium or similarly sized clear plastic container should be adequate. A pet store salesperson can best advise you of the appropriate water plants and fish food for this activity.

PRE-ACTIVITY DISCUSSION

Have students read the activity carefully before beginning the procedure. Focus their attention on the purposes of the activity by asking the following questions.

• **How many of you have pets of your own at home?** (Answers will vary. For those students who do have pets, ask them to describe them in as much detail as possible.)

• **What makes you aware of changes in a pet's behavior?** (Observing an organism's activities over a period of time will identify changes in behavior.)

• **Why are such observations important?** (Careful observations reveal a great deal of information about an organism's condition and help identify the need for changes in its environment.)

• **What is the purpose of keeping records?** (Records are data that are later analyzed in the quest to answer questions and find solutions.)

• **Do you think there is a difference in the water you observe with the unaided eye and the water you will observe under a microscope in a later activity?** (Yes. Water observed under a microscope will probably show the existence of a variety of microscopic life forms.)

SAFETY TIPS

1. Alert students to wash the aquarium carefully so that there will be no breakage. Make sure they use salt and not soap and that they rinse thoroughly to avoid any residue.

2. Caution students that they must situate their aquarium before they fill it with water. Remember, the density of water is

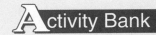
Many people keep fish in an aquarium. To be successful, you have to have a good idea of the kind of conditions a fish needs to survive. In this activity you will observe a fish in an environment you create. This is actually a long-term investigation because you will be responsible for caring for your fish after this activity is over. You and your classmates might want to keep records about the growth of your fish, the amounts and kinds of foods eaten, and any changes in your fish's behavior over time. In a later activity you will examine some of the water in your fish's aquarium under a microscope. Then you will use another tool of the scientist.

Materials

aquarium or large unbreakable clear plastic container	fish food
	hand lens
	brown paper bag (slit along the sides)
gravel	
water plants	plastic bucket
several rocks	pitcher (1L)
small goldfish	

Procedure

1. Wash the aquarium or jar thoroughly. Use table salt on a sponge to clean the glass. Do not use soap. Thoroughly rinse the aquarium or jar when you are finished. Place the aquarium or jar near a window where it will get some light for part of the day. **CAUTION:** *Do not try to move the aquarium or jar when it is filled with water.*

2. Place the gravel in a plastic bucket. Place the bucket in a sink. Let cold water run into the bucket. (You may also do this in the backyard if you have access to a garden hose.) Put your

hand into the bucket and gently move the gravel around. The gravel dust will become suspended in the water and will be carried away as the water runs over the top of the bucket. You can stop rinsing the gravel when clear water runs out. Carefully empty the water out of the bucket.

3. Pour the gravel into the aquarium or jar. Smooth it out.

4. Place the sheet of brown paper over the gravel. Use a pitcher to gently pour water onto the paper in the aquarium or jar. Stop adding water when the aquarium or jar is two-thirds full. Remove the paper.

5. Position the rocks in the gravel. Place the plants in the gravel. Try to make your underwater scene look realistic. Now gently add water almost to the top edge of the aquarium or jar. Do not add fish to the aquarium or jar for a few days. (During this time the water may become cloudy. It will clear up over time.)

1 g/mL — which makes a filled aquarium very heavy!

TEACHING STRATEGY

1. Move among the student groups as they prepare their aquarium, making certain they are cleaning and filling it correctly.

2. Students may show some impatience in waiting 20 minutes while the plastic bag containing the goldfish floats in the aquarium. Remind them that this is being done for the benefit of the goldfish; the temperature of the water in the bag and in the aquarium should be equal. You might use this waiting time to discuss why it is important to the goldfish that the temperatures be equalized.

3. One of the most common mistakes is to feed the goldfish too much food. Demonstrate to your students exactly what is meant by a "small pinch of food." Again, you might want to take this opportunity to discuss why such a small quantity is enough for the goldfish.

6. A salesperson in a pet store will place the fish you select in a plastic bag. Float the plastic bag in the aquarium or jar for 20 minutes to allow the temperature of the water in the bag and in the aquarium or jar to equalize. Open the bag and let your fish swim into its new home. Allow the fish a few minutes of quiet time to explore its new surroundings.

7. Now add a small pinch of food to the surface of the water.

8. Use the hand lens to observe the fish's head.

Observations

1. How did the fish behave in its new home?

2. What fins did the fish use to move itself forward in the water? What fins did it use to remain in the same place?

3. How did the fish behave when you placed a pinch of food in the tank?

4. Describe what you observed when you used the hand lens to examine the fish's head.

5. In what part of the aquarium or jar does the fish spend most of its time?

Analysis and Conclusions

1. In what ways is a fish able to live in water?

2. How does your fish get food?

Going Further

You might like to read more about keeping fish. Your library or pet shop will have a selection of books about how to keep and raise fish. Report to your class on what you learn.

response to various stimuli can be observed only if data are collected over time.

OBSERVATIONS

1. Observations will vary. Fish will swim around the tank, maybe dart about when first placed in.

2. The tail fin propels the fish forward in the water. The pectoral fins (fins located near the gills on each side of the fish) are used by the fish to maintain one position. Sometimes the tail, moving back-and-forth slowly, is also used to maintain position.

3. The fish may move to the top to eat at the surface if the food floats. Some fish will eat food as it falls to the bottom of the tank.

4. Answers will vary. Students might mention the opening and closing of the coverings of the gills, the opening and closing of the mouth, the shape and position of the eyes, scales, and so on.

5. Answers will vary. In clean water, fish generally swim throughout the tank; if the water becomes cloudy—usually as a result of too heavy a hand while feeding—fish will be found near the water's surface where the oxygen level is higher.

ANALYSIS AND CONCLUSIONS

1. Fish have fins that are used for movement; fish have gills that are used to extract oxygen from the water and to give off carbon dioxide to the water. Many fish have scales and secrete a slime layer to protect their bodies and enable them to move through the water with ease. Other answers are possible.

2. A fish gulps in food through its mouth. Food may be eaten at the water's surface or as it falls to the bottom.

DISCOVERY STRATEGIES

Discuss how this activity relates to the chapter content by asking questions such as the following.

• **In what ways are you acting as a scientist?** (Answers will vary, but students should realize they are observing the world around them, asking and answering questions, recording data, and making some type of conclusion.)

• **How can you use the results of this activity in a larger context?** (Students should understand that what they have learned about the behavior of a goldfish can be applied to the behavior of all living things.)

• **To what branch of science does this activity belong?** (Life science.)

• **At what level is the goldfish being studied?** (Macroscopic level.)

• **Why is this activity actually a long-term one?** (The observations of the goldfish's behavior can generate conclusions only if they are made over an extended period of time. Behaviors that are constant can be determined, and behaviors that change in

Activity Bank

WHAT DO SEEDS NEED TO GROW?

BEFORE THE ACTIVITY

1. At least one day prior to the activity, gather the required materials. You might ask students to bring the plastic flowerpots/food containers and the tray/saucers from home.

2. You may wish to do the Laboratory Investigation on page A34 prior to doing this activity. If so, students should be familiar with some of the conditions needed by molds for growth.

3. It is recommended that students work in groups for this activity. Groups of four to six students work best. Within the group, however, each student can grow a different kind of seed, or each person can test a different variable. Bean and radish seeds are recommended because they germinate rapidly. If you wish to use other types of seeds, check the information given on the seed package for germination rate. If you do choose slower-germinating seeds, students should be informed that this will be a long-term activity.

PRE-ACTIVITY DISCUSSION

Students should read the activity thoroughly before they begin. Ask the following questions to help students focus on the purposes of the activity.

• **What is the purpose of having four different pots?** (One pot is the control; the other three pots are each testing a variable.)

• **What variable is being tested in pots B,C, and D?** (B: absence of light; C: absence of water; D: absence of sunlight and warmth.)

• **Is pot A necessary to the activity? Explain.** (Pot A is the control; it receives light, water, and warmth. Without pot A, one would not be able to determine the effects of each variable.)

• **In what ways is this activity an illustration of the scientific method?** (The scientific method usually begins with a question the answer to which is determined by gathering information, forming a hypothesis, experimenting, recording and analyzing data, and repeating the work. Almost all of these steps are contained in

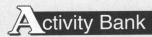
If you completed the investigation on page A34, you are now familiar with some of the conditions molds need in order to grow. In this activity you will learn about conditions that must be present in order for plant seeds to grow. You may wish to do this investigation with several classmates. Each person can grow a different kind of seed, or each person can test a different variable. Share your information with one another and with the rest of the class when the activity is completed.

You Will Need

4 plastic flowerpots or 4 plastic food containers
tray or 4 saucers
potting soil
bean or radish seeds
2 thermometers
masking tape

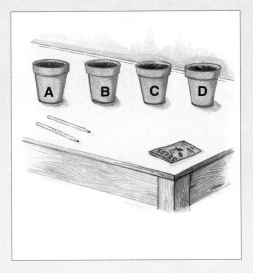

Procedure

1. If you use plastic food containers, make sure they are clean. Have an adult punch some holes in the bottom of the containers. The holes will let excess water drain out of the containers. Use the saucers or tray to collect any water that runs out of the pots when they are watered.

2. Fill the pots or containers almost to the top with potting soil.

3. Place several seeds in each pot. Gently press the seeds into the soil. You may wish to add a thin layer of soil on top of the seeds.

4. Use the masking tape to label the pots A through D.

5. Water pot A and place it on a windowsill. This is your control plant. Water this plant when the soil feels dry to the touch.

6. Water pot B and place it in a dark place. Make sure this pot also receives water when the top of the soil feels dry to the touch.

7. Tape a thermometer to the outside of pot C. Do not water pot C now or for the duration of the activity. Place it on a windowsill next to pot A. The thermometer will provide the temperature for all the pots placed on the windowsill.

8. Tape the other thermometer to pot D. Water pot D and place it in a refrigerator.

9. In a data table similar to the one shown on page 103, record the temperature of each pot as indicated by its attached thermometer. Continue to take the temperature of the pots each day for three weeks. Record these readings.

---

this activity.)

• **What is your hypothesis about what seeds need to grow?** (Answers will vary but will most likely include the necessity of light, water, warmth.)

SAFETY TIPS

Alert students to the need to use care in the handling of the thermometers.

TEACHING STRATEGY

1. Circulate among student groups to be sure that holes have been punched in the

bottoms of the containers if containers are being used instead of flowerpots. Also make sure that the pots (containers) have been placed on a tray or on individual saucers for the watering part of the procedure.

2. If students have difficulty planting their seeds, you may wish to demonstrate the correct procedure.

3. Taping the thermometers to the pots may be difficult for students, so you may want to move about the groups supervising this procedure. You may also want to

DATA TABLE

TEMPERATURE		
Day	Windowsill	Refrigerator
1		
2		
3		
4		
5		
6		
7		
8		
9		
10		
11		
12		
13		
14		
15		
16		
17		
18		
19		
20		
21		

Observations

1. What did you observe in each pot?
2. In which pots did the seeds grow best?
3. Which pots showed the poorest results?
4. Why is pot A considered a control?

Analysis and Conclusions

1. Why did you need a control?
2. What variable were you testing in pot B?
3. What variable were you testing in pot C?
4. What variable were you testing in pot D?
5. On the basis of your observations, what conditions do seeds need to begin to grow well?
6. It might be argued that there were two variables in pot D. What was the other variable? Was it a critical factor in the activity? Why or why not?

observe students as they take their initial temperature readings to be sure they are doing so correctly and accurately. Although exact temperature readings are not vital to the outcome of this activity, it is a good time to stress the need for careful and accurate observations and measurements.

DISCOVERY STRATEGIES

Discuss how this activity relates to the concepts developed in the chapter by asking the following questions.

• **What conditions are necessary for seeds to grow?** (Light, warmth, water, soil.)
• **How did you arrive at your conclusion?** (The growth/nongrowth of seeds in various variable pots indicates the conditions that must be present for germination.)
• **Could you have arrived at your conclusion without pot A? Explain.** (It would not have been possible for students to arrive at a scientifically correct conclusion without pot A because this pot is the control. Without the control, the variables responsible for particular results cannot

be identified with any degree of certainty.)
• **Why do you think bean and radish seeds are the best choice for this activity?** (These two types of seeds germinate very quickly. Results can be observed shortly after beginning the activity.)
• **Why do you think it was unnecessary to provide the seeds with food?** (Accept all logical answers. It is possible that some students will already know that the seed contains stored food, which it uses as it germinates.)

OBSERVATIONS

1. Observations will vary, but the pots placed in a warm place and watered will show seeds sprouting and plant growth within a few days.
2. Pots A and B should show growth.
3. Pots C and D should show the poorest growth or no growth at all.
4. Pot A received water, warm temperatures, and light. These were the variables tested in the other three pots.

ANALYSIS AND CONCLUSIONS

1. All experiments need a control. It is used to compare the results of the plants when growing conditions are varied.
2. The response of the seeds to light.
3. The response of the seeds to a lack of water.
4. The effects of cold temperature on the growth of seeds.
5. Seeds need warmth and water to grow well. Some students might argue that seeds also need light to grow. This is true for the very small seeds of some plant species that are scattered over the soil surface. Seeds that are planted below the soil surface, such as the seeds used in this activity, will not receive light.
6. Some students might observe that there was also an absence of light in pot C, not only cold temperatures. Probably not, since the seeds are covered with soil. Keep in mind, however, that the soil in pot A might have been warmed by the sun, which may also have affected the growth of the seeds.

Activity Bank

CALCULATING DENSITY

BEFORE THE ACTIVITY

1. At least one day prior to the activity, gather the required materials for each group. Assume there are four to six students in each group. The objects listed here are easy to obtain and use. If your students would like to determine the density of other objects, encourage them to bring the objects to class for your review and approval.

2. Have students review the material on the use of the triple-beam balance provided in Appendix E, page A117, before they undertake this activity. If necessary, demonstrate the correct use of the balance.

3. It is very important that students be able to read the water meniscus in the graduated cylinder so that they can obtain accurate data. On page A54, Figure 2-16 provides an excellent photograph of a water meniscus. Have students look at this figure carefully and discuss it in preparation for their own work.

PRE-ACTIVITY DISCUSSION

Have students read the activity carefully before they begin to work. Focus their attention on the purposes of the activity by asking the following questions.

• **What is volume? How is it calculated?** (Volume is the amount of space an object occupies. The volume of a regular solid is determined by multiplying its length times its width times its height. The volume of a liquid or of an irregular solid is determined by reading the liquid level in a graduated cylinder or by the water displacement method, respectively.)

• **Why is density an important measurement?** (Density is a physical property of matter that can often be used to identify a substance and thereby distinguish it from other substances. Density is also important in comparing the behavior of different substances. For example, knowing the density of a substance as compared to that of water, one can determine if that substance will float or sink in water.)

• **What is the formula for calculating density?** (D = M/V)

• **What relationship must exist between**

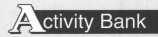

Calculating the density of a regular solid such as a cube is easy. Measure the sides of the object with a metric ruler and calculate the volume. Place the object on a balance to determine its mass. Then use the formula D = M/V to calculate the object's density. But can you determine the density of an object that has an irregular shape and is not easy to measure? A rock, for example. It's easy when you know how. Follow along and you can become the density calculator for your class.

Materials

graduated cylinder
rock
small piece of metal pipe
large nut or bolt
triple-beam balance
metric ruler
string

Procedure and Observations

1. Select one of the objects whose density you wish to calculate. Place the object on a balance and determine its mass. Enter the mass in a data table similar to the one shown on page 105.

2. Place some water in the graduated cylinder. Look at the water in the cylinder from the side. The water's surface will be shaped like a saucer. Notice that the water level dips slightly in the center. Add water carefully until the lowest part of the water's surface (the bottom of the dip) is at one of the main division lines on the side of the graduated cylinder. Enter the water-level reading in your data table.

3. You are going to determine the volume of your irregularly shaped object by

water displacement. To do this, first tie a piece of string around the object you are going to use. Make sure the string is well tied.

4. Hold the end of the string and carefully lower the object into the water in the graduated cylinder. Read the new water level. Enter this reading in your data table. Subtract the first water-level reading from the second to determine the volume of the object. Enter this volume in your data table.

5. Repeat this procedure for each remaining object.

6. Use the formula D = M/V to calculate the density of each object you selected.

the volume of an irregular object and the amount of water it displaces? (They are equal.)

SAFETY TIPS

Make sure students exercise care in the use of the triple-beam balance and glassware.

TEACHING STRATEGY

1. Move among the student groups to be sure that students are using the triple-beam balance correctly. Remind them to

record units of measurement as well as numerical values. Also remind them that they may have to convert units (dimensional analysis) so that they express density in the correct units.

2. Students may have trouble reading the water meniscus. You may wish to demonstrate the correct method to the class or to circulate among the groups offering help when needed.

3. This activity lends itself to cooperative learning strategies. Encourage students to assign roles within their group as they

DATA TABLE

Object	Mass	First Water Level	Second Water Level	Water Displaced (mL)

Analysis and Conclusions

1. What is the volume of an object whose dimensions are 1.0 cm × 6.0 cm × 2.0 cm? Remember to include the proper units.

2. If the mass of this object is 60 g, what is its density?

3. What are the densities of the objects you measured?

4. Which object is made of the densest material?

Think About This

1. If an object with a density of 10 g/cm^3 is cut into two equal pieces, what is the density of each piece? Why?

2. Could the water displacement method be used to determine the volume of a rectangular object as well as an irregularly shaped object?

3. Why is the density of a substance important?

---

ric system to measure length, volume, mass, weight, density, and temperature.)

• **What is density? How is it determined for an irregular solid?** (Density is the mass per unit volume of a substance. D = M/V. The density of an irregular solid is determined using this formula. The volume component, however, must be determined by the water displacement method.)

• **What tools are used in the determination of the density of an irregular solid?** (The measurement tools used are the triple-beam balance for determining mass and the graduated cylinder for determining volume of displaced water.)

• **How would inaccurate measurements affect the results of this activity?** (Inaccuracies in either the mass or volume calculations would yield an incorrect density for the object. If you were using density to identify an unknown substance, you might easily misidentify it.)

ANALYSIS AND CONCLUSIONS

1. 12 cubic centimeters (cm^3)
2. 5 g/cm^3
3. Answers will vary.
4. Answers will vary.

THINK ABOUT THIS

1. 10 g/cm^3. The density of a substance does not change.
2. Yes, it would be easier to measure the object, but you can calculate its density using the water displacement method.
3. Scientists use density to identify substances. Density can also be used to predict how substances will behave in certain situations. For example, a substance with a density greater than the density of water will sink when placed in water.

---

proceed. Then students should switch roles so that everyone gets an opportunity to practice the skills developed in the activity.

DISCOVERY STRATEGIES

Discuss how this activity relates to the concepts developed in this chapter by asking the following questions.

• **Why are measurements important?** (Measurements are often the form in which experimental data are expressed. Measurements become a form of language to

scientists.)

• **Why must measurements be expressed in a universal language?** (Because measurements are a form of scientific language, they must be communicated easily among the scientific community. Thus a universal system, or a system understood by all people, must be used.)

• **What is the universal system of measurement? Describe it.** (The metric system, which is a system based on the number 10 and multiples of 10, is the universal measurement system. Scientists use the met-

Activity Bank

BEFORE THE ACTIVITY

1. Gather all materials at least one day prior to the activity. You should gather enough materials to meet your class needs, assuming four students per group.
2. You can obtain several colors of food coloring if possible, but only one is necessary.
3. Because of the amount of oil required, you may want to limit the part of the activity described in step 1 to one or two groups and let the rest of the class observe the results.

PRE-ACTIVITY DISCUSSION

Ask students to read the complete activity procedure. Then have them predict the outcome of the various steps by asking them questions similar to the following.
• **What do you think will happen when you place an ice cube in a container of oil?** (Answers will vary. Some students will predict that it will float. Others will expect the ice cube to sink.)
• **What do you think will happen when you place an egg or potato in a container that is filled half way with salt water and half way with plain water?** (Answers will vary.)
• **What do you expect to see when you squeeze the warm colored water into the cold plain water?** (Most students will not know what to predict so answers will vary.)

Review the concept of density and buoyancy with students so that they keep it in mind as the carry out the steps of the activity.

TEACHING STRATEGY

1. If you have chosen to limit step 1 due to the amount of oil required, you may wish to begin the activity by preparing step 1 as a class and then leaving it in an accessible location for students to observe occasionally as they complete the rest of the activity.
2. Circulate through the class to assist students having difficulty. You may need to show students how to add the plain water to the salt water by pouring it over a spoon or piece of tissue paper. If stu-

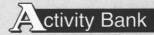

Throw a rock into a pond and it sinks beneath the surface of the water. Throw a rubber ball into a pond and it bobs along on the surface. Why do some things float in water while others sink? The answer has to do with density. An object floats only if it is less dense than the substance it is in. In this activity you will make your own investigation into density.

Materials

2 250-mL beakers
cooking oil (about 125 mL)
ice cube
salt
spoon or small sheet of tissue paper (optional)
hard-boiled egg or small uncooked potato
medicine dropper
dishwasher liquid
food coloring

Procedure

1. Fill a beaker half-full with cooking oil. Very gently place an ice cube on the surface of the oil. What happens to the ice cube? Watch the ice cube for the next 15 to 20 minutes. What happens as the ice cube melts?

2. Use the dishwasher liquid to thoroughly clean the beaker. Fill the beaker half-full with water. Make sure you measure the amount of water you put into the beaker.
3. Add plenty of table salt to the water. Stop adding salt when the water becomes cloudy. The amount of salt you add will vary depending upon the amount of water you use.
4. Add the same amount of water you used in step 2 to another beaker. Do not add salt to the water in this beaker. Slowly and gently pour the unsalted water into the beaker that contains the water you added salt to. You may need to pour the water onto a spoon or piece of tissue paper so that it hits the salt water more gently.
5. Gently place the egg or small potato in the beaker. Describe and draw what you see.
6. Clean the two beakers. Add a small amount of hot tap water, about 10 mL, to one of the beakers. Add a few drops of food coloring to the hot water. Make sure you add enough food coloring so that the color can easily be seen.

dents simply dump the plain water into the salt water, the two will mix together. However, if the plain water is poured gently enough, it will float on the salt water as is necessary.
3. Make sure that students realize that they only need a small amount of colored water in steps 8 and 9. They want to be able to see whether the colored water rises or falls.

DISCOVERY STRATEGIES

Discuss how the activity relates to the chapter ideas by asking questions similar to the following.
• **What was the purpose of adding salt to half of the water in step 3?** (The salt made the solution more dense than water alone.)
• **What do you think would happen if you placed the egg or potato in salt water alone? Plain water alone?** (Students should realize from the activity that the ob-

7. Fill the other beaker with cold tap water.

Food coloring

8. Use the medicine dropper to pick up a few drops of the hot colored water.

9. Place the tip of the medicine dropper in the middle of the cold water in the other beaker. Slowly squeeze a drop of the hot colored water into the cold water. Describe and draw a picture of what you observe.

Analysis and Conclusions

1. Explain what you observed when you watched the ice cube in the oil in step 1.

2. Explain your observations regarding the egg in the beaker of water.

3. What does this investigation tell you about the density of hot water compared to the density of cold water?

4. Predict what will happen if you repeat steps 6 through 9, but this time add a drop or two of cold colored water to a beaker of hot water.

2. The egg or potato remains suspended in the middle of the salt water and plain water. Because the egg is more dense than tap water but less dense than salt water, it sinks only to the middle of the beaker and then floats on the salt water.

3. The hot colored water rises in the cold water. Students should realize from this that hot water is less dense than cold water because the hot water essentially floats in the cold water. The color will spread out as it rises. Sometimes it resembles a genie rising out of a bottle.

4. Students should predict opposite results from step 9 for this experiment. The cold colored water will sink when added to the hot tap water because, as students found previously, cold water is more dense than hot water.

ject would float in salt water alone but sink in plain water alone.)
• **How can you relate your observations with warm water and cold water to the behavior of warm air and cold air?** (Warm air, which is less dense than cold air, rises in cold air and cold air sinks in warm air. Students may consider how a room in their home is heated or cooled.)

ANALYSIS AND CONCLUSIONS

1. Liquid water does not float in oil. But when water freezes, its molecules expand into rigid ice crystals that take up more space than do the liquid molecules. Because the molecules weigh the same but have a greater volume as ice, the ice is less dense than the liquid water. Thus the ice floats in oil. Students can see that the water sinks as soon as it melts out of the ice phase. They will observe huge drops of water sinking from the melting ice cube.

Activity Bank

BEFORE THE ACTIVITY

1. At least one day prior to the activity, gather the materials listed for each group. Groups of four to six students are recommended.

2. Because this activity involves the use of a microscope and the preparation of a microscope slide, it is advisable to review both these procedures prior to doing the actual activity. Have students read the material in Appendix D, pages A114–115. Then have a class discussion and demonstration of the correct and safe handling and use of the microscope and slides.

3. The water for this activity will come from the aquarium set up by each group in the activity titled Observing a Fish, pages A100–101. If you have not done this activity, you will have to obtain pond water.

PRE-ACTIVITY DISCUSSION

Students should read the activity thoroughly before they begin. Focus their attention on the purposes of the activity by asking the following questions.

• **Why is the microscope an important scientific tool?** (The microscope is essential in the study of science because it enables one to see things that are too small to be seen with the unaided eye. It also allows one to look more closely at the fine details of larger objects.)

• **What are the different lenses on a microscope? Describe them.** (One lens, the one closest to the eye, is the ocular. The lenses closest to the slide are the objectives. There are two objectives: the low-power objective and the high-power objective.)

• **How is magnification of a microscope determined?** (Magnification is determined by multiplying the magnification of the ocular by the magnification of the objective.)

• **Why do you think there is a limit to the magnification ability of your microscope?** (Accept all logical answers. What you should hope to elicit from students is the understanding that beyond a certain magnification, the image becomes fuzzy and loses detail.)

Just as good building tools can help a carpenter produce a fine home, so can good scientific tools aid a scientist in a variety of endeavors.

In this activity you will use one of the basic tools of life science: a microscope, a tool that lets scientists study worlds too small to be seen with the unaided eye.

You Will Use

microscope
glass slide
coverslip
water from your aquarium or pond water
medicine dropper

CAUTION: *Before you begin, make sure that you understand how to use a microscope.* Follow your teacher's instructions exactly. Examine the illustration of a microscope in Appendix D. A microscope is an expensive and valuable tool. Exercise care when using it and when using the slide and coverslip as well.

Now You Can Begin

1. Make sure that your microscope is in the correct position before you use it. Have your teacher check your setup before you begin. Use the illustration on page 115 in your textbook to familiarize yourself with the parts of your microscope.

2. There are several lenses on a microscope. The lens nearest the eye is called the ocular. The lenses closest to the slide are called the objectives. Note that each lens has a number etched on it. The number tells you how many times a particular lens magnifies the image that is viewed through it. Note the number on the ocular and the num-

---

LIFE IN A DROP OF WATER

ber on the smallest objective lens. Multiply one number by the other. This will tell the total magnification when these two lenses are used together. Enter the magnification near any drawing you make of what you observe.

3. Pick up a glass slide from your supply table. You will make a slide of a drop of water from your aquarium. (If you do not have an aquarium you can examine pond water that your teacher will supply. **CAUTION:** *Do not try to collect pond water without the help of an adult.*) Place one drop of aquarium water in the center of your slide.

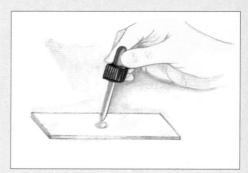

SAFETY TIPS

Correct handling and use of the microscope is absolutely necessary. Spend at least one class period, if not more, on reviewing and reinforcing this idea. Also alert students to the fact that they will be using glass slides and coverslips and must use appropriate care.

TEACHING STRATEGY

1. It might be advisable to have the groups of students bring their microscope to their work station one group at a time so that you can observe the handling of the equipment.

2. Once each group is ready to begin, review the parts of the microscope and the proper use. One of the most important steps to emphasize is the use of the adjustment knobs. Lowering and raising the body tube correctly with the coarse ad-

4. Pick up one of the coverslips and hold it as shown in the illustration. Carefully lower the coverslip onto the drop of water.

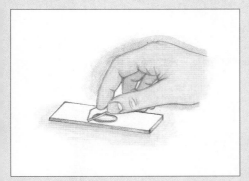

5. Place the slide on the microscope. Make sure the smallest, or low-power, lens is in position. Look through the ocular. Carefully turn the coarse adjustment knob until the image is in focus. Use the fine adjustment knob to get a clear image. Move the slide slowly back and forth. Draw what you observe.

6. Repeat the procedure with a drop of tap water.

7. When you are finished, follow your teacher's instructions for cleaning up.

Observations

1. What kinds of things did you observe in the drop of water from the aquarium?

2. Did these organisms move around or remain in one place?

3. What did you observe in the drop of tap water?

Analysis and Conclusions

1. How has the microscope helped scientists to study the natural world?

2. How can you explain the differences you observed in the aquarium water and the tap water?

Going Further

You can examine some other substances. Make a plan of study and check with your teacher before you proceed.

microscopes that use beams of electrons.)

• **Can the optical microscope be used to observe living and nonliving specimens? Explain.** (Yes. It is not necessary to kill the specimen prior to observing it as must be done with an electron microscope.)

• **Were you surprised by the results of this activity?** (Answers will vary. Hopefully students will see many microscopic organisms in the water sample and thus gain an appreciation for the many life forms they have up until now been unfamiliar with. The great diversity of life as well as the contribution of the microscope to the study of this diversity will become apparent.)

OBSERVATIONS

1. Answers will vary. Students will notice microscopic organisms; some may observe detritus from the bottom of the tank. Perfectly round circles seen under the microscope are probably air bubbles that became trapped under the coverslip when it was placed on the slide.

2. Most microorganisms are able to move, even under the weight of the coverslip. Air bubbles will not move.

3. Students should notice that tap water contains no microorganisms.

ANALYSIS AND CONCLUSIONS

1. The microscope has opened up the world of very small life. This tool has enabled scientists to study life forms unseen before the invention of the microscope.

2. Chlorine and other chemicals are often added to tap water to kill microorganisms.

justment will eliminate the potential for crushing the glass slide.

3. Students may need to be reminded to keep both eyes open when viewing a specimen. Their natural inclination is to shut one eye and view with the other. Discuss the advantages of keeping both eyes open.

DISCOVERY STRATEGIES

Discuss how this activity relates to the concepts in the chapter by asking the following questions.

• **What are the advantages of your microscope? What are its limitations?** (The microscope allows you to see things not visible to the unaided eye. The microscope also enables you to look more closely at the fine details of larger objects. The magnification power of the microscope has a limit beyond which objects become fuzzy and lack detail.)

• **Why is your microscope called an optical microscope?** (An optical microscope uses light rays to produce a magnified image of an object. This is in contrast to

Appendix A

The metric system of measurement is used by scientists throughout the world. It is based on units of ten. Each unit is ten times larger or ten times smaller than the next unit. The most commonly used units of the metric system are given below. After you have finished reading about the metric system, try to put it to use. How tall are you in metrics? What is your mass? What is your normal body temperature in degrees Celsius?

Commonly Used Metric Units

Length The distance from one point to another

meter (m) A meter is slightly longer than a yard.
1 meter = 1000 millimeters (mm)
1 meter = 100 centimeters (cm)
1000 meters = 1 kilometer (km)

Volume The amount of space an object takes up

liter (L) A liter is slightly more than a quart.
1 liter = 1000 milliliters (mL)

Mass The amount of matter in an object

gram (g) A gram has a mass equal to about one paper clip.
1000 grams = 1 kilogram (kg)

Temperature The measure of hotness or coldness

degrees
Celsius (°C)
0°C = freezing point of water
100°C = boiling point of water

Metric–English Equivalents

2.54 centimeters (cm) = 1 inch (in.)
1 meter (m) = 39.37 inches (in.)
1 kilometer (km) = 0.62 miles (mi)
1 liter (L) = 1.06 quarts (qt)
250 milliliters (mL) = 1 cup (c)
1 kilogram (kg) = 2.2 pounds (lb)
28.3 grams (g) = 1 ounce (oz)
°C = 5/9 x (°F – 32)

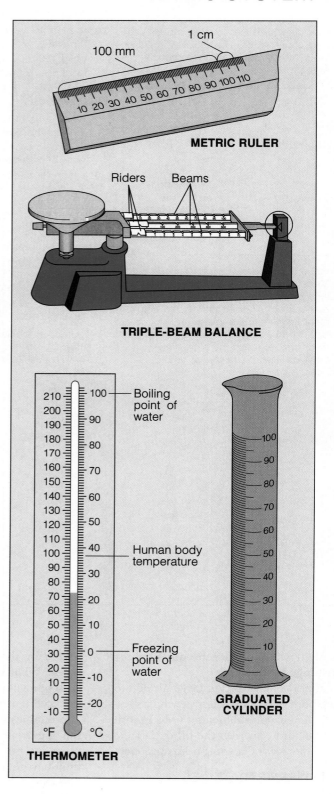

METRIC RULER

Riders Beams

TRIPLE-BEAM BALANCE

Boiling point of water

Human body temperature

Freezing point of water

THERMOMETER

GRADUATED CYLINDER

ppendix B

LABORATORY SAFETY
Rules and Symbols

Glassware Safety

1. Whenever you see this symbol, you will know that you are working with glassware that can easily be broken. Take particular care to handle such glassware safely. And never use broken or chipped glassware.
2. Never heat glassware that is not thoroughly dry. Never pick up any glassware unless you are sure it is not hot. If it is hot, use heat-resistant gloves.
3. Always clean glassware thoroughly before putting it away.

Fire Safety

1. Whenever you see this symbol, you will know that you are working with fire. Never use any source of fire without wearing safety goggles.
2. Never heat anything—particularly chemicals—unless instructed to do so.
3. Never heat anything in a closed container.
4. Never reach across a flame.
5. Always use a clamp, tongs, or heat-resistant gloves to handle hot objects.
6. Always maintain a clean work area, particularly when using a flame.

Heat Safety

Whenever you see this symbol, you will know that you should put on heat-resistant gloves to avoid burning your hands.

Chemical Safety

1. Whenever you see this symbol, you will know that you are working with chemicals that could be hazardous.
2. Never smell any chemical directly from its container. Always use your hand to waft some of the odors from the top of the container toward your nose—and only when instructed to do so.
3. Never mix chemicals unless instructed to do so.
4. Never touch or taste any chemical unless instructed to do so.
5. Keep all lids closed when chemicals are not in use. Dispose of all chemicals as instructed by your teacher.

6. Immediately rinse with water any chemicals, particularly acids, that get on your skin and clothes. Then notify your teacher.

Eye and Face Safety

1. Whenever you see this symbol, you will know that you are performing an experiment in which you must take precautions to protect your eyes and face by wearing safety goggles.
2. When you are heating a test tube or bottle, always point it away from you and others. Chemicals can splash or boil out of a heated test tube.

Sharp Instrument Safety

1. Whenever you see this symbol, you will know that you are working with a sharp instrument.
2. Always use single-edged razors; double-edged razors are too dangerous.
3. Handle any sharp instrument with extreme care. Never cut any material toward you; always cut away from you.
4. Immediately notify your teacher if your skin is cut.

Electrical Safety

1. Whenever you see this symbol, you will know that you are using electricity in the laboratory.
2. Never use long extension cords to plug in any electrical device. Do not plug too many appliances into one socket or you may overload the socket and cause a fire.
3. Never touch an electrical appliance or outlet with wet hands.

Animal Safety

1. Whenever you see this symbol, you will know that you are working with live animals.
2. Do not cause pain, discomfort, or injury to an animal.
3. Follow your teacher's directions when handling animals. Wash your hands thoroughly after handling animals or their cages.

Appendix C

One of the first things a scientist learns is that working in the laboratory can be an exciting experience. But the laboratory can also be quite dangerous if proper safety rules are not followed at all times. To prepare yourself for a safe year in the laboratory, read over the following safety rules. Then read them a second time. Make sure you understand each rule. If you do not, ask your teacher to explain any rules you are unsure of.

Dress Code

1. Many materials in the laboratory can cause eye injury. To protect yourself from possible injury, wear safety goggles whenever you are working with chemicals, burners, or any substance that might get into your eyes. Never wear contact lenses in the laboratory.

2. Wear a laboratory apron or coat whenever you are working with chemicals or heated substances.

3. Tie back long hair to keep it away from any chemicals, burners and candles, or other laboratory equipment.

4. Remove or tie back any article of clothing or jewelry that can hang down and touch chemicals and flames.

General Safety Rules

5. Read all directions for an experiment several times. Follow the directions exactly as they are written. If you are in doubt about any part of the experiment, ask your teacher for assistance.

6. Never perform activities that are not authorized by your teacher. Obtain permission before "experimenting" on your own.

7. Never handle any equipment unless you have specific permission.

8. Take extreme care not to spill any material in the laboratory. If a spill occurs, immediately ask your teacher about the proper cleanup procedure. Never simply pour chemicals or other substances into the sink or trash container.

9. Never eat in the laboratory.

10. Wash your hands before and after each experiment.

First Aid

11. Immediately report all accidents, no matter how minor, to your teacher.

12. Learn what to do in case of specific accidents, such as getting acid in your eyes or on your skin. (Rinse acids from your body with lots of water.)

13. Become aware of the location of the first-aid kit. But your teacher should administer any required first aid due to injury. Or your teacher may send you to the school nurse or call a physician.

14. Know where and how to report an accident or fire. Find out the location of the fire extinguisher, phone, and fire alarm. Keep a list of important phone numbers—such as the fire department and the school nurse—near the phone. Immediately report any fires to your teacher.

Heating and Fire Safety

15. Again, never use a heat source, such as a candle or burner, without wearing safety goggles.

16. Never heat a chemical you are not instructed to heat. A chemical that is harmless when cool may be dangerous when heated.

17. Maintain a clean work area and keep all materials away from flames.

18. Never reach across a flame.

19. Make sure you know how to light a Bunsen burner. (Your teacher will demonstrate the proper procedure for lighting a burner.) If the flame leaps out of a burner toward you, immediately turn off the gas. Do not touch the burner. It may be hot. And never leave a lighted burner unattended!

20. When heating a test tube or bottle, always point it away from you and others. Chemicals can splash or boil out of a heated test tube.

21. Never heat a liquid in a closed container. The expanding gases produced may blow the container apart, injuring you or others.

22. Before picking up a container that has been heated, first hold the back of your hand near it. If you can feel the heat on the back of your hand, the container may be too hot to handle. Use a clamp or tongs when handling hot containers.

Using Chemicals Safely

23. Never mix chemicals for the "fun of it." You might produce a dangerous, possibly explosive substance.

24. Never touch, taste, or smell a chemical unless you are instructed by your teacher to do so. Many chemicals are poisonous. If you are instructed to note the fumes in an experiment, gently wave your hand over the opening of a container and direct the fumes toward your nose. Do not inhale the fumes directly from the container.

25. Use only those chemicals needed in the activity. Keep all lids closed when a chemical is not being used. Notify your teacher whenever chemicals are spilled.

26. Dispose of all chemicals as instructed by your teacher. To avoid contamination, never return chemicals to their original containers.

27. Be extra careful when working with acids or bases. Pour such chemicals over the sink, not over your workbench.

28. When diluting an acid, pour the acid into water. Never pour water into an acid.

29. Immediately rinse with water any acids that get on your skin or clothing. Then notify your teacher of any acid spill.

Using Glassware Safely

30. Never force glass tubing into a rubber stopper. A turning motion and lubricant will be helpful when inserting glass tubing into rubber stoppers or rubber tubing. Your teacher will demonstrate the proper way to insert glass tubing.

31. Never heat glassware that is not thoroughly dry. Use a wire screen to protect glassware from any flame.

32. Keep in mind that hot glassware will not appear hot. Never pick up glassware without first checking to see if it is hot. See #22.

33. If you are instructed to cut glass tubing, fire-polish the ends immediately to remove sharp edges.

34. Never use broken or chipped glassware. If glassware breaks, notify your teacher and dispose of the glassware in the proper trash container.

35. Never eat or drink from laboratory glassware. Thoroughly clean glassware before putting it away.

Using Sharp Instruments

36. Handle scalpels or razor blades with extreme care. Never cut material toward you; cut away from you.

37. Immediately notify your teacher if you cut your skin when working in the laboratory.

Animal Safety

38. No experiments that will cause pain, discomfort, or harm to mammals, birds, reptiles, fishes, and amphibians should be done in the classroom or at home.

39. Animals should be handled only if necessary. If an animal is excited or frightened, pregnant, feeding, or with its young, special handling is required.

40. Your teacher will instruct you as to how to handle each animal species that may be brought into the classroom.

41. Clean your hands thoroughly after handling animals or the cage containing animals.

End-of-Experiment Rules

42. After an experiment has been completed, clean up your work area and return all equipment to its proper place.

43. Wash your hands after every experiment.

44. Turn off all burners before leaving the laboratory. Check that the gas line leading to the burner is off as well.

The microscope is an essential tool in the study of life science. It enables you to see things that are too small to be seen with the unaided eye. It also allows you to look more closely at the fine details of larger things.

The microscope you will use in your science class is probably similar to the one illustrated on the following page. This is a compound microscope. It is called compound because it has more than one lens. A simple microscope would contain only one lens. The lenses of the compound microscope are the parts that magnify the object being viewed.

Typically, a compound microscope has one lens in the eyepiece, the part you look through. The eyepiece lens usually has a magnification power of 10X. That is, if you were to look through the eyepiece alone, the object you were viewing would appear 10 times larger than it is.

The compound microscope may contain one or two other lenses. These two lenses are called the low- and high-power objective lenses. The low-power objective lens usually has a magnification of 10X. The high-power objective lens usually has a magnification of 40X. To figure out what the total magnification of your microscope is when using the eyepiece and an objective lens, multiply the powers of the lenses you are using. For example, eyepiece magnification (10X) multiplied by low-power objective lens magnification (10X) = 100X total magnification. What is the total magnification of your microscope using the eyepiece and the high-power objective lens?

To use the microscope properly, it is important to learn the name of each part, its function, and its location on your microscope. Keep the following procedures in mind when using the microscope:

1. Always carry the microscope with both hands. One hand should grasp the arm, and the other should support the base.

2. Place the microscope on the table with the arm toward you. The stage should be facing a light source.

3. Raise the body tube by turning the coarse adjustment knob.

4. Revolve the nosepiece so that the low-power objective lens (10X) is directly in line with the body tube. Click it into place. The low-power lens should be directly over the opening in the stage.

5. While looking through the eyepiece, adjust the diaphragm and the mirror so that the greatest amount of light is coming through the opening in the stage.

6. Place the slide to be viewed on the stage. Center the specimen to be viewed over the hole in the stage. Use the stage clips to hold the slide in position.

7. Look at the microscope from the side rather than through the eyepiece. In this way, you can watch as you use the coarse adjustment knob to lower the body tube until the low-power objective almost touches the slide. Do this slowly so you do not break the slide or damage the lens.

8. Now, looking through the eyepiece, observe the specimen. Use the coarse adjustment knob to raise the body tube, thus raising the low-power objective away from the slide. Continue to raise the body tube until the specimen comes into focus.

9. When viewing a specimen, be sure to keep both eyes open. Though this may seem strange at first, it is really much easier on your eyes. Keeping one eye closed may create a strain, and you might get a headache. Also, if you keep both eyes open, it is easier to draw diagrams of what you are observing. In this way, you do not have to turn your head away from the microscope as you draw.

10. To switch to the high-power objective lens (40X), look at the microscope from the side. Now, revolve the nosepiece so that the high-power objective lens clicks into place. Make sure the lens does not hit the slide.

11. Looking through the eyepiece, use only the fine adjustment knob to bring the specimen into focus. Why should you not use the coarse adjustment knob with the high-power objective?

12. Clean the microscope stage and lens when you are finished. To clean the lenses, use lens paper only. Other types of paper may scratch the lenses.

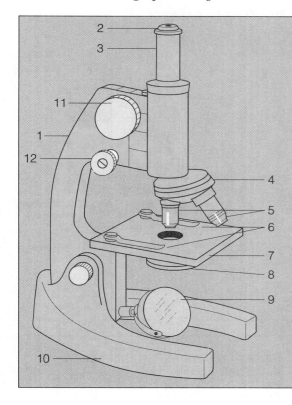

Microscope Parts and Their Functions

1. **Arm** Supports the body tube
2. **Eyepiece** Contains the magnifying lens you look through
3. **Body tube** Maintains the proper distance between the eyepiece and the objective lenses
4. **Nosepiece** Holds the high- and the low-power objective lenses and can be rotated to change magnification
5. **Objective lenses** A low-power lens, which usually provides 10X magnification, and a high-power lens, which usually provides 40X magnification
6. **Stage clips** Hold the slide in place
7. **Stage** Supports the slide being viewed
8. **Diaphragm** Regulates the amount of light let into the body tube
9. **Mirror** Reflects the light upward through the diaphragm, the specimen, and the lenses
10. **Base** Supports the microscope
11. **Coarse adjustment knob** Moves the body tube up and down for focusing
12. **Fine adjustment knob** Moves the body tube slightly to sharpen the image

The laboratory balance is an important tool in scientific investigations. You can use the balance to determine the mass of materials that you study or experiment with in the laboratory.

Different kinds of balances are used in the laboratory. One kind of balance is the double-pan balance. Another kind of balance is the Triple-beam balance. The balance that you may use in your science class is probably similar to one of the balances illustrated in this Appendix. To use the balance properly, you should learn the name, function, and location of each part of the balance you are using. What kind of balance do you have in your science class?

The Double-Pan Balance

The double-pan balance shown in this Appendix has two beams. Some double-pan balances have only one beam. The beams are calibrated, or marked, in grams. The upper beam is divided into ten major units of 1 gram each. Each of these units is further divided into units of 1/10 of a gram. The lower beam is divided into twenty units, and each unit is equal to 10 grams. The lower beam can be used to find the masses of objects up to 200 grams. Each beam has a rider that is moved to the right along the beam. The rider indicates the number of grams needed to balance the object in the left pan. What is the total mass the balance can measure?

Before using the balance, you should be sure that the pans are empty and both riders are pointing to zero. The balance should be on a flat, level surface. The pointer should be at the zero point. If your pointer does not read zero, slowly turn the adjustment knob so that the pointer does read zero.

The following procedure can be used to find the mass of an object with a double-pan balance:

1. Place the object whose mass is to be determined on the left pan.

2. Move the rider on the lower beam to the 10-gram notch.

3. If the pointer moves to the right of the zero point on the scale, the object has a mass less than

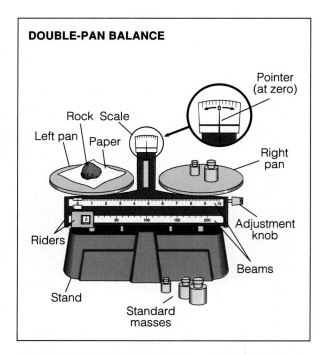

DOUBLE-PAN BALANCE

Pointer (at zero) · Rock · Scale · Left pan · Paper · Right pan · Riders · Adjustment knob · Beams · Stand · Standard masses

Parts of a Double-Pan Balance and Their Functions

Pointer Indicator used to determine when the mass being measured is balanced by the riders or masses of the balance

Scale Series of marks along which the pointer moves

Zero Point Center line of the scale to which the pointer moves when the mass being measured is balanced by the riders or masses of the balance

Adjustment Knob Knob used to set the balance at the zero point when the riders are all on zero and no masses are on either pan

Left Pan Platform on which an object whose mass is to be determined is placed

Right Pan Platform on which standard masses are placed

Beams Horizontal strips of metal on which marks, or graduations, appear that indicate grams or parts of grams

Riders Devices that are moved along the beams and used to balance the object being measured and to determine its mass

Stand Support for the balance

10 grams. Return the rider on the lower beam to zero. Slowly move the rider on the upper beam until the pointer is at zero. The reading on the beam is the mass of the object.

4. If the pointer did not move to the right of the zero, move the rider on the lower beam notch by notch until the pointer does move to the right. Move the rider back one notch. Then move the rider on the upper beam until the pointer is at zero. The sum of the readings on both beams is the mass of the object.

5. If the two riders are moved completely to the right side of the beams and the pointer remains to the left of the zero point, the object has a mass greater than the total mass that the balance can measure.

The total mass that most double-pan balances can measure is 210 grams. If an object has a mass greater than 210 grams, return the riders to the zero point.

The following procedure can be used to find the mass of an object greater than 210 grams:

1. Place the standard masses on the right pan one at a time, starting with the largest, until the pointer remains to the right of the zero point.

2. Remove one of the large standard masses and replace it with a smaller one. Continue replacing the standard masses with smaller ones until the pointer remains to the left of the zero point. When the pointer remains to the left of the zero point, the mass of the object on the left pan is greater than the total mass of the standard masses on the right pan.

3. Move the rider on the lower beam and then the rider on the upper beam until the pointer stops at the zero point on the scale. The mass of the object is equal to the sum of the readings on the beams plus the mass of the standard masses. ance at the zero point when the riders are all on zero and no masses are on either pan

The Triple-Beam Balance

The Triple-beam balance is a single-pan balance with three beams calibrated in grams. The front, or 100-gram, beam is divided into ten units of 10 grams each. The middle, or 500-gram, beam is divided into five units of 100 grams each. The back, or 10-gram is divided into ten major units of 1 gram each. Each of these units is further divided into units of 1/10 of a gram. What is the largest mass you could find with a triple-beam balance?

The following procedure can be used to find the mass of an object with a triple-beam balance:

1. Place the object on the pan.

2. Move the rider on the middle beam notch by notch until the horizontal pointer drops below zero. Move the rider back one notch.

3. Move the rider on the front beam notch by notch until the pointer again drops below zero. Move the rider back one notch.

4. Slowly slide the rider along the back beam until the pointer stops at the zero point.

5. The mass of the object is equal to the sum of the readings on the three beams.

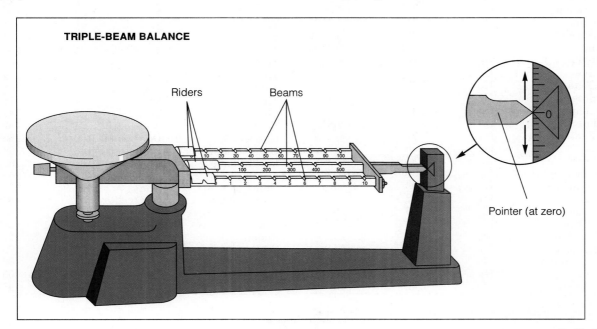

TRIPLE-BEAM BALANCE

Riders   Beams

Pointer (at zero)

NAME	SYMBOL	ATOMIC NUMBER	ATOMIC MASS†	NAME	SYMBOL	ATOMIC NUMBER	ATOMIC MASS†
Actinium	Ac	89	(227)	Neodymium	Nd	60	144.2
Aluminum	Al	13	27.0	Neon	Ne	10	20.2
Americium	Am	95	(243)	Neptunium	Np	93	(237)
Antimony	Sb	51	121.8	Nickel	Ni	28	58.7
Argon	Ar	18	39.9	Niobium	Nb	41	92.9
Arsenic	As	33	74.9	Nitrogen	N	7	14.01
Astatine	At	85	(210)	Nobelium	No	102	(255)
Barium	Ba	56	137.3	Osmium	Os	76	190.2
Berkelium	Bk	97	(247)	Oxygen	O	8	16.00
Beryllium	Be	4	9.01	Palladium	Pd	46	106.4
Bismuth	Bi	83	209.0	Phosphorus	P	15	31.0
Boron	B	5	10.8	Platinum	Pt	78	195.1
Bromine	Br	35	79.9	Plutonium	Pu	94	(244)
Cadmium	Cd	48	112.4	Polonium	Po	84	(210)
Calcium	Ca	20	40.1	Potassium	K	19	39.1
Californium	Cf	98	(251)	Praseodymium	Pr	59	140.9
Carbon	C	6	12.01	Promethium	Pm	61	(145)
Cerium	Ce	58	140.1	Protactinium	Pa	91	(231)
Cesium	Cs	55	132.9	Radium	Ra	88	(226)
Chlorine	Cl	17	35.5	Radon	Rn	86	(222)
Chromium	Cr	24	52.0	Rhenium	Re	75	186.2
Cobalt	Co	27	58.9	Rhodium	Rh	45	102.9
Copper	Cu	29	63.5	Rubidium	Rb	37	85.5
Curium	Cm	96	(247)	Ruthenium	Ru	44	101.1
Dysprosium	Dy	66	162.5	Samarium	Sm	62	150.4
Einsteinium	Es	99	(254)	Scandium	Sc	21	45.0
Erbium	Er	68	167.3	Selenium	Se	34	79.0
Europium	Eu	63	152.0	Silicon	Si	14	28.1
Fermium	Fm	100	(257)	Silver	Ag	47	107.9
Fluorine	F	9	19.0	Sodium	Na	11	23.0
Francium	Fr	87	(223)	Strontium	Sr	38	87.6
Gadolinium	Gd	64	157.2	Sulfur	S	16	32.1
Gallium	Ga	31	69.7	Tantalum	Ta	73	180.9
Germanium	Ge	32	72.6	Technetium	Tc	43	(97)
Gold	Au	79	197.0	Tellurium	Te	52	127.6
Hafnium	Hf	72	178.5	Terbium	Tb	65	158.9
Helium	He	2	4.00	Thallium	Tl	81	204.4
Holmium	Ho	67	164.9	Thorium	Th	90	232.0
Hydrogen	H	1	1.008	Thulium	Tm	69	168.9
Indium	In	49	114.8	Tin	Sn	50	118.7
Iodine	I	53	126.9	Titanium	Ti	22	47.9
Iridium	Ir	77	192.2	Tungsten	W	74	183.9
Iron	Fe	26	55.8	Unnilennium	Une	109	(266?)
Krypton	Kr	36	83.8	Unnilhexium	Unh	106	(263)
Lanthanum	La	57	138.9	Unniloctium	Uno	108	(265)
Lawrencium	Lr	103	(256)	Unnilpentium	Unp	105	(262)
Lead	Pb	82	207.2	Unnilquadium	Unq	104	(261)
Lithium	Li	3	6.94	Unnilseptium	Uns	107	(262)
Lutetium	Lu	71	175.0	Uranium	U	92	238.0
Magnesium	Mg	12	24.3	Vanadium	V	23	50.9
Manganese	Mn	25	54.9	Xenon	Xe	54	131.3
Mendelevium	Md	101	(258)	Ytterbium	Yb	70	173.0
Mercury	Hg	80	200.6	Yttrium	Y	39	88.9
Molybdenum	Mo	42	95.9	Zinc	Zn	30	65.4
				Zirconium	Zr	40	91.2

†Numbers in parentheses give the mass number of the most stable isotope.

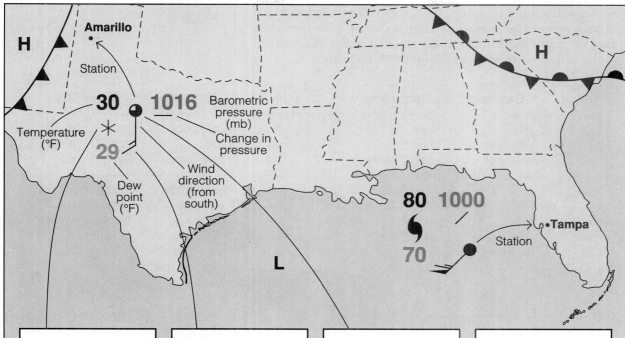

Weather	Symbol
Drizzle	
Fog	
Hail	
Haze	
Rain	
Shower	
Sleet	
Smoke	
Snow	
Thunderstorm	
Hurricane	

Wind Speed (mph)	Symbol
1–4	
5–8	
9–14	
15–20	
21–25	
26–31	
32–37	
38–43	
44–49	
50–54	
55–60	
61–66	
67–71	
72–77	

Cloud Cover (%)	Symbol
0	
10	
20–30	
40	
50	
60	
70–80	
90	
100	

Fronts and Pressure Systems	Symbol
Cold front	
Warm front	
Stationary front	
Occluded front	
High pressure	H
Low pressure	L
Rising	/
Steady	—
Falling	\

Glossary

Pronunciation Key

When difficult names or terms first appear in the text, they are respelled to aid pronunciation. A syllable in SMALL CAPITAL LETTERS receives the most stress. The key below lists the letters used for respelling. It includes examples of words using each sound and shows how the words would be respelled.

Symbol	Example	Respelling
a	hat	(hat)
ay	pay, late	(pay), (layt)
ah	star, hot	(stahr), (haht)
ai	air, dare	(air), (dair)
aw	law, all	(law), (awl)
eh	met	(meht)
ee	bee, eat	(bee), (eet)
er	learn, sir, fur	(lern), (ser), (fer)
ih	fit	(fiht)
igh	mile, sigh	(mighl), (sigh)
oh	no	(noh)
oi	soil, boy	(soil), (boi)
oo	root, rule	(root), (rool)
or	born, door	(born), (dor)
ow	plow, out	(plow), (owt)

Symbol	Example	Respelling
u	put, book	(put), (buk)
uh	fun	(fuhn)
yoo	few, use	(fyoo), (yooz)
ch	chill, reach	(chihl), (reech)
g	go, dig	(goh), (dihg)
j	jet, gently, bridge	(jeht), (JEHNT-lee), (brihj)
k	kite, cup	(kight), (kuhp)
ks	mix	(mihks)
kw	quick	(kwihk)
ng	bring	(brihng)
s	say, cent	(say), (sehnt)
sh	she, crash	(shee), (krash)
th	three	(three)
y	yet, onion	(yeht), (UHN-yuhn)
z	zip, always	(zihp), (AWL-wayz)
zh	treasure	(TREH-zher)

barometer: instrument that measures air pressure

bathyscaph (BATH-ih-skaf): self-propelled submarine observatory

bathysphere (BATH-ih-sfeer): small, sphere-shaped diving vessel used for underwater research

Celsius: temperature scale in which there are 100 degrees between the freezing and boiling points of water

centimeter: one-hundredth of a meter

control: an experiment run without a variable in order to show that any data from the experimental setup was due to the variable being tested

compound light microscope: microscope having more than one lens and that uses a beam of light to magnify objects

conversion factor: fraction that always equals one, which is used for dimensional analysis

cubic centimeter: metric unit used to measure the volume of solids; equal to a milliliter

data: recorded observations and measurements

density: mass per unit volume of a substance

dimensional analysis: method of converting one unit to another

electromagnetic spectrum: arrangement of electromagnetic waves that includes visible light, ultraviolet light, infrared light, X-rays, and radio waves

electron microscope: microscope that uses a beam of electrons to magnify an object

gram: one-thousandth of a kilogram

hypothesis (high-PAHTH-uh-sihs): a proposed solution to a scientific problem

infrared telescope: telescope that gathers infrared light from distant objects in order to produce an image of that object

kilogram: basic unit of mass in the metric system

kilometer: one thousand meters

law: a basic scientific theory that has been tested many times and is generally accepted as true by the scientific community

lens: any transparent material that bends light passing through it

light-year: distance light travels in a year

liter: basic unit of volume in the metric system

meter: basic unit of length in the metric system

metric system: standard system of measurement used by all scientists

milligram: one-thousandth of a gram

milliliter: one-thousandth of a liter

millimeter: one-thousandth of a meter

newton: basic unit of weight in the metric system

radio telescope: telescope that gathers radio waves from distant objects in order to produce an image of that object

reflecting telescope: telescope that uses a series of mirrors to gather and focus visible light from distant objects

refracting telescope: telescope that uses a series of lenses to gather and focus visible light from distant objects

scientific method: a systematic approach to problem solving

seismograph (SIGHZ-muh-grahf): instrument that detects and measures earthquake waves

theory: a logical, time-tested explanation for events that occur in the natural world

ultraviolet telescope: telescope that gathers ultraviolet light from distant objects in order to produce an image of the object

variable: the factor being tested in an experimental setup

weight: measure of the gravitational attraction between objects

X-ray telescope: telescope that gathers X-rays from distant objects in order to produce an image of that object

Index